METHOD AND CATHOLIC
MORAL THEOLOGY

METHOD AND CATHOLIC MORAL THEOLOGY

The Ongoing Reconstruction

TODD A. SALZMAN

CREIGHTON UNIVERSITY PRESS
Omaha, Nebraska
Association of Jesuit University Presses

ISBN 1-881871-30-4 (cloth)
ISBN 1-881871-31-2 (paper)

EDITORIAL
Creighton University Press
2500 California Plaza
Omaha, Nebraska 68178

MARKETING & DISTRIBUTION
Fordham University Press
University Box L
Bronx, New York 10458

Printed in the United States of America

Table of Contents

The Contributors

Lisa Sowle Cahill is J. Donald Monan, S.J., Professor in the Theology Department, Boston College. She has numerous scholarly publications in the areas of bioethics; sex, gender, marriage and family; Scripture and ethics; and natural law tradition. Her most recent book is *Sex, Gender and Christian Ethics*.

Charles E. Curran is Elizabeth Scurlock University Professor of Human Values at Southern Methodist University. He has served as president of the *American Theological Society*, the *Catholic Theological Society of America*, and the *Society of Christian Ethics*. His latest book is *The Origins of Moral Theology in the United States: Three Different Approaches*.

Richard M. Gula, S.S., is Professor of Moral Theology at the Franciscan School of Theology of the Graduate Theological Union in Berkeley, CA. He is the author of *Reason Informed by Faith: Foundations of Catholic Morality*. His most recent works are *Ethics in Pastoral Ministry, Moral Discernment* and *The Good Life: Where Morality and Spirituality Converge*.

Bernard Hoose is a Lecturer in Christian Ethics at Heythrop College, University of London. He is the author of *Proportionalism: The American Debate and Its European Roots* and *Received Wisdom?: Reviewing the Role of Tradition in Christian Ethics*. He also recently edited *Christian Ethics: An Introduction*.

James F. Keenan, S.J., is Associate Professor of Moral Theology at Weston Jesuit School of Theology. Among his books are *Goodness and Rightness in Thomas Aquinas' Summa Theologiae, The Context of Casuistry* which he edited with Thomas Shannon, and *Virtues for Ordinary Christians*. He is chair of the Catholic Theological Coalition on HIV/AIDS Prevention.

Richard A. McCormick, S.J., is John A. O'Brien Professor Emeritus of Christian Ethics at the University of Notre Dame. His publications are numerous and include the series "Notes on Moral Theology" in *Theological Studies* which he published for twenty consecutive years. His most recent book is *Corrective Vision: Explorations in Moral Theology*.

Mark O'Keefe, O.S.B., is President-Rector and Associate Professor of Moral Theology at Saint Meinrad School of Theology. He is the author of *Becoming Good, Becoming Holy: On the Relationship of Christian Ethics and Spirituality* and *What Are They Saying About Social Sin?*, as well as numerous articles and reviews.

Jean Porter is Professor of Christian Ethics/Moral Theology in the Department of Theology, University of Notre Dame. She has authored numerous articles in scholarly journals. Her most recent book is *Moral Action and Christian Ethics*.

Todd A. Salzman is Assistant Professor in Theology at Creighton University. He is the author of *Deontology and Teleology: An Investigation of the Normative Debate in Roman Catholic Moral Theology*.

Joseph A. Selling is Professor and Chair of the department of Moral Theology at the Katholieke Universiteit Leuven (Belgium). He has published numerous scholarly articles and is editor of *Personalist Morals: Essays in Honor of Professor Louis Janssens*, and co-editor of *The Splendor of Accuracy: An Examination of the Assertions Made by Veritatis Splendor*.

Edward Collins Vacek, S.J., is a Professor of Moral Theology at Weston Jesuit School of Theology, Cambridge, MA. He has published numerous articles in scholarly journals and is author of *Love, Human and Divine: The Heart of Christian Ethics*.

James J. Walter is Professor of Christian Ethics at Loyola University Chicago. Currently, he is co-chair of the "Research Seminar on Genetics" in *The Catholic Theological Society of America*. He has published two books and numerous scholarly articles in the areas of fundamental ethics and bioethics.

Introduction

Todd A. Salzman

The purpose of this book is to investigate the ongoing methodical reconstruction of Catholic moral theology. In so doing, it honors the extensive
scholarly work of Norbert Rigali, S.J., who has been such an important
and inspirational contributor to this reconstruction.

RECONSTRUCTING MORAL THEOLOGY

Catholic moral theology has been in a concentrated state of renewal and
transition for some thirty years, since the close of Vatican Council II.
The Council's inauguration of a new era in moral theology marks a decisive break with the traditional manual approach to moral theology in
place since the Council of Trent. Up until Vatican II, the manuals of
moral theology were *the* authoritative source of moral theology within
Catholicism. These manuals originated in response to the Council of
Trent's call for an educated clergy and functioned primarily, if not exclusively, to train seminarians to hear confessions. As a result, they
tended to be practical without a great deal of theoretical reflection,
philosophical analysis, or methodical discussion or development. The
call for the renewal of moral theology, which was already underway
prior to the Council, was officially announced at Vatican II and clearly
challenged the genre of the manual tradition.

Given the historical context out of which the manuals arose and the
purpose for which they were used, it is quite fitting that the call for renewal would be proclaimed in the Vatican II document entitled *Decree
on Priestly Formation* (*Optatam Totius*). The frequently cited quotation
is taken from paragraph sixteen of this document:

> Special attention needs to be given to the development
> of moral theology. Its scientific exposition should be
> more thoroughly nourished by scriptural teaching. It
> should show the nobility of the Christian vocation of the
> faithful, and their obligation to bring forth fruit in char-
> ity for the life of the world.[1]

In this passage, certainly the importance of the renewal of moral theology is articulated. More importantly, however, essential to this renewal
is the incorporation of those dimensions which are specific to Christianity, i.e., Scriptural teaching and the nobility of the Christian vocation
grounded in charity as the essence of Christian ethics. This call fundamentally reoriented moral theology away from the primary, if not exclusive, consideration of a universal natural law morality based on the
commandments to a morality based on specifically Christian sources.
This reorientation was not, however, an 'either/or' proposition, either a
natural law morality or a morality grounded in Christian sources. Rather,
the entreaty reflected a 'both/and' in balance, content and method.

The one-sided balance of the manual natural law approach needed to
be complemented with specifically Christian sources. This task, however, did not involve merely 'inserting' Christian sources into moral
theology where appropriate. Such was the case with the scriptural
'proof-texting' of the manuals. Essentially, the manual approach to
moral theology was nothing more than a "touched up philosophical
ethic."[2] Rather, renewal called for a fundamental deconstruction and reconstruction of moral theology since its manualist foundation was
somewhat *aChristian*. Consequently, the manual approach to moral theology had to be abandoned and in its place moral theologians have been
reconstructing moral theology. This reconstructed moral theology utilizes the 'both/and' of the valid, though historically and culturally bound,
insight of Thomas Aquinas that knowledge of natural law is accessible
to all human beings through the use of right reason while, at the same
time, recognizing and incorporating the specific Christian perspective
and justification for that law. The specific Christian perspective and justification include Scripture, tradition, Christology, soteriology, sacramentality, ecclesiology, spirituality, and the magisterium, to name just a
few dimensions. Thus, the balance between a natural law morality and
the sources for Christian ethics requires an ongoing dialogue which has
been a focus in the reconstruction process.

The content of this 'both/and' of natural law and specific Christian sources for ethics, reflected in normative ethics in particular, attempts to maintain a delicate balance between recognizing the specific contributions of Christian ethics while, at the same time, remaining faithful to Thomas's insight on the knowability of the precepts and principles of natural law. This balance is all the more important in a pluralistic society with a plurality of ethical theories, systems and methods. To emphasize too much the specificity of Christian ethics and its normative content is to run the risk of sectarianism and to endanger dialogue with other ethical systems and religious traditions. To emphasize too much the universality of natural law norms is to sacrifice that which makes Christian ethics Christian and not secular, humanist, Buddhist or Jewish. The 'both/and' of normative content, then, while recognizing the universality of what Aquinas referred to as the first precept of natural law, do good and avoid evil,[3] further recognizes the 'good' is always incarnate and specific historically, culturally, and communally.

One way in which the delicate balance of this 'both/and' is to be reached, and the normative content is to be formulated is exemplified in a previous paragraph of the "Declaration on Priestly Formation." Paragraph 14 asserts that "in the revision of ecclesiastical studies, the first object in view must be a better integration of philosophy and theology" (§14). The following paragraph goes on to explain the importance of the dialogue between philosophy and theology in clarifying and coming to a deeper understanding of the "mysteries of salvation" (§15). Certainly the call for philosophical integration is expanded to moral theology as well. In fact, much of the renewal in moral theology has been to utilize philosophical methods and insights in reconstructing moral theology.

FR. NORBERT RIGALI'S CONTRIBUTIONS TO MORAL THEOLOGY'S RECONSTRUCTION

One truly gifted and internationally recognized moral theologian who has contributed extensively to the reconstruction of Catholic moral theology is Fr. Norbert Rigali, S.J., to whom this collection of essays is dedicated. Spanning some thirty years, his numerous contributions to scholarly journals have been both an inspiration and a challenge to moral theologians who are working towards that reconstruction. The development of a method which utilizes the tools of philosophy for its formulation and expression and yet is authentically Christian has been a predominant theme of his scholarly work.

First, much of Rigali's work utilizes philosophical insights and methodical developments in worldview, anthropology, and epistemology to reconstruct moral theology. The shift in worldview from classicism to historical consciousness most aptly demonstrated in the Vatican II document *The Pastoral Constitution on the Church in the Modern World* (*Gaudium et spes*) represents a profound methodical shift in moral theology and has been at the center of much of Rigali's work. The manuals were grounded in a classicist worldview based on essences. According to this worldview, natural law is static, necessary, fixed and universal. Hence, the normative content of natural law is timeless, universal and immutable. Historical consciousness, based on an existentialist philosophical method, fundamentally challenged this view of reality and, by implication, morality. According to an historically conscious worldview, reality is dynamic, evolving, changing, and particular. The implications for moral theology are that there is no "universal moral law." Rather, there are norms and systems of ethics that are historically, culturally, and communally bound. Perhaps no other moral theologian has been as focused and diligent in an attempt to transform and reconstruct moral theology from a classicist to an historically conscious worldview as has Fr. Rigali.

On numerous occasions Rigali clearly demonstrates the implications of this change in worldview for anthropology and morality. Most recently, he points out that from a classicist worldview, the human person is an essence of rational animality. *Recta ratio* binds human nature allowing human beings access to the one, universal moral law. From an historically conscious worldview, however, the human person is understood as "embodied spiritual self-transcendence" (the universal dimension of anthropology) in relation to society, culture, and history (the particular dimension of anthropology). The implications of the human person's "universality-in-particularity" for morality is that Christian morality is a particular morality rooted in the particular system of moral values, worldview, culture, and story of a particular people.[4] The universality of this morality is reflected not in the adjective, but the noun. Thus, Christian morality is a particularization-of-universality of a universal morality.

Intimately related to the transformation of worldview and anthropology is the further question of epistemology. If our understanding of reality is transformed as well as the nature of the human within this reality, then the human as knower is transformed as well. The naïve real-ism of Aquinas and the Neoscholastics envisioned the human knower primarily as "rational-animal-subject."[5] On the basis of this shared, uni-versal rationality, one can posit a universal, timeless moral law common to all. Historical consciousness, however, posits the human knower only secondarily as rational-animal-subject. Primarily, the human knower is "a person in relation to other persons."[6] It is in and through these rela-tions that a person both discovers the knowledge of a community to which that person belongs, and constructs knowledge on the basis of ongoing interaction and dialogue within the community. From the per-spective of the human knower in relation to other persons moral knowl-edge is an evolving process that is both discovered and created in and through a variety of human relations. An historically conscious moral epistemology, then, does not reflect a timeless, cultureless, universal morality. Rather, it builds upon moral knowledge that is rooted in the past, lived in the present, and is evolving towards the future.

Second, Rigali's work utilizes these philosophical methods in dia-logue with a specifically Christian reality to reconstruct an authentic Christian morality. For Rigali, a morality based on authentic Christianity must take the Incarnation as its point of departure. While many manuals do not even include Jesus, Christ or Lord in their indexes, notes Rigali, a renewed moral theology must "relate Christology to the moral lives of Christians."[7] Basing moral theology on the Incarnation, Jesus becomes the ultimate norm for humanity. The implications for moral theology are profound. No longer is the *actus humanus* of the manuals the primary focus of morality. Rather, the *vita humana*, taken in its totality as a way of being in the world, becomes the primary focus. While Jesus' Incarna-tion transcends history, the moral imperative of Christ is an ongoing in-carnational reality. The task of moral theology, reflecting this shift to Christology, becomes the ongoing reflection and discernment of Chris-tian communities on what it means to imitate Christ given the historical, cultural and communal context in which Christians live.

To facilitate this discernment process, spirituality or ascetic theol-ogy and moral theology must be reunited. With Trent's call for the for-malization of seminary education, moral theology became a distinct sci-ence from dogmatic and ascetic theology. Furthermore, an alliance was formed with canon law so that moral theology and canon law became, in a sense, "sister sciences."[8] This gave moral theology a very legalistic, juridical character. The challenge for moral theology which Rigali has aptly demonstrated and is gaining more attention in theological literature is that moral theology must become a science of Christian perfection. Christian ethics and/or morality are not primarily about laws, acts, rules or obligations. Rather, authentic Christianity, and the ethics and/or morality that are based on that Christianity, forms the core of one's very identity and is about a way of being *in* the world that is Christ *to* the world. Christian spirituality is not a peripheral discipline of Christian ethics and/or morality. Rather, it is in and through spirituality—the ongoing discovery, formation, and development of one's relationship with the living Christ as it is experienced in and through relationships—that moral theology finds its source. Spirituality is at the very heart of moral theology.

A fundamental question that evolves out of the phenomena of the 'both/and'—both a universal natural law and a morality based on specifically Christian sources—and to which Rigali has devoted a great deal of his writings, is the question of a specifically Christian morality. Stated briefly, given the traditionally affirmed assertion and approach of the manuals that knowledge of the natural law is accessible to all human beings through the use of right reason, in what sense, if any, does Christianity add specifically to this morality? Though Rigali has consistently argued that the question itself is a classicist question based on an essentialist anthropology and view of reality and is dissolved from an historically conscious perspective, some moral theologians continue to see it as an important question. The reason for this is that, in working out the methodical structure of a specifically Christian ethic and the moral contents of that ethic, one must also consider whether or not there is a common ground for dialogue with a plurality of other ethical approaches and traditions? That is, even from an historically conscious worldview that necessarily recognizes a plurality of ethical systems, what are the common grounds for dialogue within that plurality? Therefore, an attempt to respond to the question is imperative for dialogue among all ethicists.

CONTENTS OF THIS BOOK

This collection of essays investigates four distinct, though intimately related, questions in the renewal movement which reflect both the methodical contributions of Rigali's work and the practical implications and application of some dimensions of his work. The first group of essays investigates various normative methods, the reality of polarity

within various ethical approaches, and the impact of historical consciousness on natural law and its consideration of acts and persons.

The second group of essays focuses on clarifying those sources
which are specifically Christian, and how those sources impact our understanding of the universal and particular in Catholic moral theology.
The specific Christian dimensions addressed are in the realms of spirituality, theology—God's gifts to humanity—and ecclesiology.

The third group of essays investigates the tension between the
'both/and' of the universal natural law morality of tradition with the
specificity of Christian ethics and/or morality. The discussion which has
been ongoing and to which Rigali has been an invaluable source in his
scholarly contributions, investigates the relationship between the universality of a natural law ethic with the particularity of a specifically Christian ethic and/or morality.

The final group of essays combines both the methodical insights of
philosophy with the traditional Christian sources in their investigation of
biomedical ethical issues to investigate creative approaches to new ethical issues sparked by medical technology. One of the limitations in the
area of biomedical ethics is that technology and its possibilities frequently seem to dictate ethical method and moral decisions rather than
ethics determining what we should or ought to do given technological
capabilities. These two essays investigate the application of traditional
Christian approaches to biomedical ethical situations utilizing contemporary philosophical methods in their exploration.

The contributors to this volume represent various areas of expertise
in Catholic moral theology and levels of personal involvement with the
historical evolution of moral theology in the pre- and post-Vatican II
eras. What unites these moral theologians is a deep commitment to the
Catholic tradition, to the ongoing reconstruction of moral theology, and
to recognizing and celebrating the contributions which Norbert Rigali
has made to moral theology and his influence on their own scholarly
work. We all are indebted to Fr. Rigali and wish him the best in his retirement.[9]

NOTES

1. Walter M. Abbot (ed.), *The Documents of Vatican II* (New York:
America Press, 1966), § 16, 452.

2. Norbert Rigali, S.J., "After the Moral Catechism," *Chicago Studies* 20

(1981), 161.

3.   *S.T.*, I–II, q. 94, a. 2.

4.   Rigali, "Christian Morality and Universal Morality: The One and the Many," *Louvain Studies* 19 (1994), 28–9.

5.   *Id.*, "Human Experience and Moral Meaning," *Chicago Studies* 13 (1974), 93–96.

6.   *Id.*, "New Epistemology and the Moralist," *Chicago Studies* 11 (1972), 238–42.

7.   *Id.*, "Christ and Morality," in Charles E. Curran and Richard A. McCormick, S.J., eds., *Readings in Moral Theology No. 2: The Distinctiveness of Christian Ethics* (New York: Paulist Press, 1980), 113.

8.   Timothy E. O'Connell, *Principles for a Catholic Morality* (New York: HarperSanFrancisco, 1990, rev. ed.), 19.

9.   I would like to thank Chuck McGavren and Dr. Brent Spencer for their technical assistance and editorial comments in preparing this manuscript for publication.

METHOD IN ETHICS

Normative Methods in Ethics:
Surveying the Landscape of Ethical Pluralism

Richard M. Gula, S.S.

Moral issues greet us each morning as we scan the newspaper with our eye-opening cup of coffee, they face us in the workplace, and they bid us good night on the evening news. Trying to deal with questions of justice in our public policies, with the right use of medical technology, or with the morality of business practices can often be very perplexing. What are we supposed to think about these issues? How are we to go about deciding what to do about them?

For Christian believers, ethics is grounded in God's decisive covenant with humanity in Jesus Christ. Our basic response to God's self-giving love in Jesus is faith. Faith, in turn, shows itself in love. The Christian moral life is fundamentally about love flowing from our experience of God's self-giving love in Jesus. To follow the way of Jesus as disciples are to do, then, is to be informed and animated by loving God, neighbor, and self. But how do we determine what love demands? Normative method in ethics tries to answer that.[1]

Since Vatican II, Catholic moral theology has been in the process of revising the highly juridical model of ethics which characterized the manuals in use up to the time of the council. Norbert Rigali has participated in the development of a revised moral theology by addressing and clarifying many of the issues that pertain to method in ethics. He is no stranger to the reality of pluralism in ethics. He has taken seriously the challenge of the shift from classicism to historical consciousness in moral theology and has examined the implications of a relational model for ethics in a personalistic framework.[2]

This chapter will survey some of the prominent methods in ethics today. To do this, I will try to catch the spirit of Norbert Rigali as teacher and moral theologian by assuming the posture of the ethics teacher who says to the class, "I'm less interested in what decision you make than in how you came to that decision." In this way, this chapter will not tell us what to think about any of the pressing moral problems of our day, but it will give us some direction on how to think through whatever moral issue we might have to face.

The methods that I will review are consequentialism, principlism, casuistry, virtue, and feminist ethics.

By reviewing these methods, I hope to demonstrate that there is more than one way to think through a moral issue. I want to challenge any naïve assumption that one method is superior to the others. Each method emphasizes a certain aspect of moral experience, but no one of them expresses the whole of it. I will offer these methods, then, not as alternatives, or rival adversaries. I see them as allies, not enemies, in the process of moral reflection. Thus, the overlap and infiltration of one method into another will be inevitable.

I hope that the reader will benefit from this survey by appreciating these methods as complementary ways to the full flowering of love for which disciples of Jesus ought to strive. Therefore, I want to mine each method for its strengths while recognizing that each must also be supplemented to compensate for its limitations.

To provide a common point of illustration for these methods, and to show how we really mix methods together in practice, I will examine them in light of an example that everyone, I think, will agree is ethical in nature. My example is taken from James Gould Cozzens's novel *By Love Possessed*. The ethical question it raises is "What should a lawyer do when he discovers that one of his partners has embezzled from a fund entrusted to the firm's administration?" If Arthur Winner reports Noah Tuttle's theft, his own law practice will be wrecked and he will be ruined financially. Nevertheless, Winner believes that making the disclosure is what he ought to do, since every citizen is obliged to report a crime that comes to his or her attention. But the third partner, Julius Penrose, has a different view. He argues in favor of a cover up. He wants to protect Tuttle and give him a chance to repay the embezzled funds. Here is an excerpt from their exchange that will serve as the common point of reference to illustrate various methods in ethics:

> "So how long have I known? Well, let's say, twelve years, give or take a month or two."
>
> "And you said nothing? Julius, I think that's indefensible."
>
> "Do you? To be able to know and still say nothing often seems to me the most creditable of human accomplishments.... What purpose but mischief, and what re-

sult but more mischief, could my saying something have? From my standpoint, the business was strictly Noah's.... How, then, could saying something be my business?... My eye was on the certain results, the fruits.... Whether I'm morally obliged to be my brother's keeper always seemed to me moot. However, my bother's ruiner and destroyer, and for no earthly reason, and for no personal necessity or profit—that I *surely* have no moral obligation to be...."

Arthur Winner said: "Julius, what you seem to be suggesting just isn't possible. There's an honest course; and a course that isn't honest. If you take the course that isn't honest, you're in trouble immediately—"

"Affirmed as stated," Julius Penrose said. "Honesty's always the easiest policy. Could that be why men so often call it the best? Weaving tangled webs is really work, very demanding."

"No, Julius. It's no good. I cannot be party to doing what's dishonest."

"But you *could* be party to causing [Noah to be prosecuted?].... I've a fair idea of your current commitments. I imagine you're doing something for your mother. I know you're helping Lawrence.... The expense of maintaining a place at Roylan is well known to me. You have a daughter to educate; you have a wife.... You'd be sorry, I'm sure, to see either without proper provision. Yet, by the time you'd made your partner's stealings good, I don't think there'd be a great deal left."...

Arthur Winner said: "What, exactly, do you propose?"

"Ah, my old friend," Julius Penrose said. "That's better! I propose that we let matters proceed as far as possible as they've been proceeding...I think I am a man of judgment. I know you are. Let us put this judgment to use...."

"I don't think you realize just how great some of the risks are."

"If you mean there are some I don't happen to know about, you may be right. But I'm confident I'll be suffi-

ciently sharp to see them as they appear; and I'm not un-
confident that, as I see them, I'll see what to do about
them...I think we should try for a while telling Noah
nothing...."

"Meanwhile, what we don't and can't escape is a
whole life of lies," Arthur Winner said.[3]

I will use this conversation now to illustrate dimensions of the five
methods that I want to review.

CONSEQUENTIALISM

Consequentialism has broad appeal. All of us, in whatever walk of life,
act with the expectation that certain results will follow. Most professionals, I think, are "bottom-line" thinkers. Since we are so set on producing
results, we feel very much at home with the pragmatic tendencies of this
method.

In the exchange between Julius Penrose and Arthur Winner, Julius is
very much a consequentialist. After assuming the disinterested posture
that Noah Tuttle's business is not his business, Julius shows consequentialist leanings when he says, "My eye was on certain results, the fruits."
Arthur Winner pushes this tendency further when he says to Julius, "I
don't think you realize just how great some of the risks are."

Undoubtedly, there is a certain attraction to the pragmatic realism of
focusing on consequences. After all, we adopt a particular course of action because we expect something good to come of it. In medical ethics,
for example, a form of consequentialism is often present when we talk
about seeking the patient's well-being by weighing benefits and burdens.
We often decide whether to treat or not to treat on the basis of maximizing benefits and minimizing burdens from the patient's perspective.
The advantage of paying attention to consequences is that it forces us to
hold the big picture in view. It makes us ask, "Where is everything going? What are we creating?" Consequentialism sees morality in terms of
promoting welfare, so it takes the future seriously. It affirms that outcomes are integral to the meaning of an action.

But while we must certainly take the outcomes seriously, we know
that we cannot predict the future accurately. So relying on a consequentialist method alone will not be our best guide. Furthermore, to rely only
on expected results for determining what to do easily runs roughshod

over the present. It ignores past commitments as well as the character of the agent doing the action. It too easily overrides individual rights or ignores the means we use to achieve the end. How we produce the consequences is morally significant. The end does not justify any means whatsoever, especially when the means are immoral acts as judged by the standards of common morality, as in the case of some research protocols that deceive or inflict pain on human subjects without their consent. Considering consequences must be kept in tension, then, with features highlighted by other methods.

PRINCIPLISM

Principlism is the method that I have found many people readily associate with ethics. For so many people, morality is no more than a matter of obedience, and moral living is exhausted by a commitment to some guides for action which they regard as standards to which everyone ought to adhere. They call these standards principles, norms, rules, or laws. While these standards can be distinguished on the basis of their specificity of content and scope of application, I am not making a strict distinction of them here.

In the opening scenario, Arthur Winner faces a conflict because his partner, Julius Penrose, does not share his depth of commitment to the principle that citizens ought to report any crime that comes to their attention. Winner accepts as a principle that the law ought to be obeyed, even to one's own disadvantage. But these principles would be violated if he protects Noah Tuttle. On the other hand, Penrose formulates for him other principles which he would violate if he were to denounce Tuttle—principles which Winner also accepts, such as his obligation to his family, and his duty to exercise compassion. These principles conflict in a web of tangled demands. Which is to be given preference in directing action? How do we decide? Such is the challenge of principlism.

Principles have come to us from revelation, such as the ten commandments; and principles have come to us from natural law or accumulated human wisdom, such as "be true to yourself," "one favor deserves another," or, "to each according to his or her due." Principles have been used with great effect to give structure and direction to specialized fields of ethics. Bioethics is a prime example. Four principles, which have become known as the mantra of bioethics, form the structure of the Beauchamp and Childress volume, *Principles of Biomedical Eth-*

ics,[4] generally recognized as the major theoretical statement in the field of bioethics. The four principles are autonomy, beneficence, nonmaleficence, and justice:

> *Autonomy* is what makes a life one's own. It stipulates that patients should be treated as individuals in control of their own affairs. It gives priority to the informed patient's preference to accept or to reject treatment according to his/her life plan.
>
> *Beneficence* expresses the duty to serve the best interests of the patient.
>
> *Nonmaleficence* expresses the fundamental commitment of the Hippocratic tradition: do no harm.
>
> *Justice* is concerned with the fair distribution of burdens and benefits, and with treating in a similar fashion patients who are in similar situations.

Principles are sometimes expressed in the language of "human rights." We even find ourselves interchanging the principle of the "sanctity of life" with the "right to life." In the abortion and euthanasia debates, it has been put in opposition to the "right to choose" derived from the principle of autonomy. In our day, the "right to choose" has been raised to a supreme level and invested with an aura of inviolability so that anything which stands in the way of "free choice" is taken as an assault on personal dignity. The sheer fact that the choice is *my* choice becomes its sole right-making characteristic. In the Catholic tradition, however, autonomy stands in tension with our responsibility to promote the common good. The common good asks us to face the limits of our freedom as individuals and to open ourselves to the demands of justice which are required from us as social persons.

Principles are necessary in ethical reflection. For one thing, they tell us what our duties are, as in the principle of professional ethics which says, "Whoever holds the greater power holds the greater burden of responsibility." Principles also guide us towards what helps or hinders personal well-being by testifying to values that we must take into account, such as respecting life, telling the truth, or keeping a secret. Sometimes principles tell us how to act towards values, as in "do not take the life of an innocent person," "do not bear false witness," or "give back to others what belongs to them." With principles, we do not have to start from scratch every time we make a decision. They take some of the pressure off those hard choices because principles bear the wisdom of past decisions. In this way, principles rely on our experiences of consequences.

To the extent that principles have a common meaning in practice (like murder and stealing), they give us a common vocabulary so that we can talk to one another about our moral gut feelings. Principles that have a common meaning are an identifiable source of shared values. They provide some stability in dealing with one another in an ever-changing world because they put us in touch with a shared morality within a diverse culture. So we should not be surprised to hear the continued call for principles in a world of increasing moral diversity.

But important and necessary as principles are, they also have limitations. They may tell us what is important about being human, but they do not tell us what is *more* important in a given case. With no hierarchical ordering, principles can run up against one another, as autonomy and justice often do in addressing the demands of health care delivery.

Another problem with principlism is to determine what authority to give to a principle. Some principles are *absolute*. They have no exceptions. Some absolute principles are expressed in abstract terms, such as do good and avoid evil, respect life, be just, be truthful, be chaste, be merciful, love God and love your neighbor. These are abstract because they do not tell us which actions are good, evil, or loving, nor do they tell us what being just, merciful, truthful or chaste look like.

Another kind of absolute principle uses "synthetic" terms which describe and evaluate an action at the same time, such as the prohibitions against murder, stealing, lying, cheating, rape, torture, and genocide. To use these principles correctly we have to be sure that we have properly qualified the action which they describe ("killing") so that the true meaning of the action ("murder") fits the evaluation ("unjust").

Other principles are concrete, such as the prohibition against killing, bearing false witness, coveting our neighbor's goods, or the prescription to keep a professional confidence or to seek informed consent from patients before treating them. These principles express a strong presumption to avoid a certain kind of evil or to do some good. They are binding unless some strong countervailing reason exists to justify overruling the principle. Take professional confidentiality as an example. It binds in nearly all cases. But if we know on the basis of confidential information that someone is in clear and present danger of very grave harm, then we have a justifying reason to break the confidence. Confidentiality binds unless it conflicts with another pressing obligation, such as the demands of justice. The binding force of keeping a confidence means that the burden of proof falls on the one who would break the confidence. The proper use of concrete, non-absolute principles puts a great deal of emphasis on the ability to discern subtle differences among otherwise similar circumstances.

In addition to interpreting the authority of a principle is the difficulty of interpreting its meaning. Not everyone shares a common judgment about the meaning and application of all principles. Take justice, for example. The scope of what it obliges is not always obvious. It is generally taken to be concerned with the distribution of benefits and burdens so that everyone gets his or her due. But how is the distribution to be made? According to need? Merit? Individual ability? Social contribution? What is one due? Another example is the principle to respect the sanctity of life. Its scope is broad and its meaning unclear. For example, it can be used to lump together situations of a very different sort—such as to prohibit abortion as well as to demand the use of medically assisting nutrition and hydration for a patient in the permanent vegetative state. "Sanctity of life" can also be used to prohibit killing as well as to support allowing to die.

Moreover, concrete principles are limited expressions of value and of how to promote the value. Since they cannot account for the details of all conceivable circumstances in which they must be applied, they are inevitably open to diverse applications. For example, they do not account for the contextual factors of cases, such as the persons involved and their gender, cultural backgrounds and life stories, the consequences that may result, or the significance of relationships in a person's life. While concrete principles illuminate values and point us in the direction of protecting them in most cases, they are open to exceptions as the details of the situation change. St. Thomas recognized as much.[5]

Furthermore, the assumption that all decisions need to rest on a principle has a certain attractiveness to it, especially for those who need clarity and closure. But principles alone give a false security about the certainty of our moral conclusions. In actual cases, principles can only take us so far. They seldom solve cases. Principles are subject to constant interpretation and so are the situations to which they must be applied. For example, the principle that directs us to honor the wishes of a duly informed, competent patient also requires that we ask whether the patient really understands the information given. Perhaps the patient is so impaired by an illness that parentalistic intervention is justified.

Principlism has suffered in ethics because we have asked principles to do too much.[6] While they are doubtlessly important, they can too easily preempt other aspects of moral judgment. The more we rely on principles alone to solve cases, the further removed we get from the actual circumstances which make the case. It is unlikely that principlism will escape further criticism and revision. The move from principles to cases calls for the exercise of wisdom, discretion, and discernment. That leads us to other methods, such as casuistry and virtue.

CASUISTRY

Casuistry is the most common method used when teaching ethics by the case method. It fell into disrepute in the manualist era of Catholic moral theology when it was reduced to a deductive method of applying principles. But it has since been revived and revised.[7] Modern versions of casuistry are evident in the Jonsen, Siegler, Winslade handbook, *Clinical Ethics*,[8] in the issue-oriented *Journal of Clinical Ethics*, and in the "Case Study" section of *The Hastings Center Report*. While the opening scenario does not demonstrate casuistry at work, it does set up a situation for it. It forces us to ask whether this case of a cover up is justifiable given the age of the senior partner, Noah Tuttle, and the great risk to destroying the law firm and incurring a serious financial loss.

Casuistry at work goes something like this. In its simplest form, the casuistic method tries to resolve a new case by comparing it against one or two similar cases that already enjoy a successful resolution. The successfully resolved case becomes the paradigm against which to measure new cases. Take the famous Karen Quinlan case, for example. There is general agreement that she did not require ventilator support because she was in a permanent vegetative state. From the perspective of principles, she satisfied the conditions that would make the burdens of a ventilator disproportionate to the benefits and thus would not be an obligatory means of life-support. For this reason, the Quinlan case is often used as the paradigm against which to understand the proportionate/disproportionate means standard (formerly known as the ordinary/extraordinary means standard). It is also a reference point for comparing the circumstances of new cases before deciding whether to treat or not.

Casuistry moves by way of analogy from a consensus, paradigm case to a more complex case to unearth the morally relevant circumstances that are decisive in determining its resolution. Take the case of Nancy Cruzan. She, like Karen Quinlan, was also in a permanent vegetative state. But Nancy could breathe on her own. She did not need ventilator support. Her life was being prolonged by medically assisting nutrition and hydration. In order to move from the clear case of Karen Quinlan to the more complex case of Nancy Cruzan, casuistry focuses on similarities and differences between the cases. The cases are linked by the proportionate/disproportionate means standard which helps us to interpret the elements of each case. When we put the Cruzan case in the neighborhood of the Quinlan case and compare the two, we unearth the morally relevant circumstances that become decisive in determining the outcome. Here is where the details of the circumstances count.

How is the case of Nancy Cruzan, regarding medically assisting fluids and nutrition, sufficiently similar or different from the paradigm case of ventilator assistance, whose resolution was accepted as a model? Can we say that medically assisting fluids and nutrition are like ventilator support in that they are both forms of medical treatment? Are both patients dying? Whereas most patients dependent on ventilator support die when the ventilator is removed, Karen Quinlan did not, to the surprise of everyone. But without medically assisting nutrition and hydration, the patient in a permanent vegetative state is sure to die. But in either case, further intervention provides no benefit beyond the mere prolonging of life in a permanent unconscious state. So we ask the question of consequences, "Is that benefit enough?" At this point, two of our strategies now interact—consequentialism and casuistry.

To reach a resolution, Jonsen and Toulmin say that it takes an experienced and prudent person to see how close the details of the new case are to those of the paradigm case so as to determine whether it can be resolved in the same way. So making the comparison of cases and answering the question of consequences requires a third method as well—virtue. Prudence is a precondition for determining whether to treat or not to treat. Casuistry recognizes that only those who can discriminate between real differences will have a proper feeling for what love demands.

The case-based method of casuistry is appealing in many respects. One appealing feature is that it respects what everyone knows—namely, each case is different. The motto of casuistry as seen by St. Thomas is that "actions should be considered differently in view of different conditions of the person, of time, and other circumstances."[9] Casuistic reasoning includes many complementary considerations which pertain to the circumstances of a case, such as who is acting, with what loyalties, beliefs, and duties, where something is being done, when, how, what else can be done, and what consequences follow from different courses of action. No wonder much of professional ethics works with this kind of method. It best appreciates the way circumstances play an integral role in moral judgment.

Casuistry also avoids an inflexible use of principles. Casuistry recognizes that moral decisions are seldom made by way of syllogistic deductions from principles. The logic of casuistry is inductive and intuitive. The resolution of a case comes from the impression made by juxtaposing principles and circumstances as one moves by analogy from the paradigm case to the new case at hand. Thinking along with principles and comparing circumstances of analogous cases requires the skill of catching the nuances that make each case different. For this reason, casuistry requires a person with experience, prudence, and a discerning sensibility for what is fitting. This calls for a person of virtue. The kind of person we are will limit what we discern as important in the case. Only accumulated experience of how cases get resolved in line with the bigger picture and purpose of moral striving will give us the practical wisdom that a casuist needs in order to do moral analysis.

Another attractive feature of casuistic analysis is that it appreciates the possibility of a variety of opinions on a complex case. It recognizes that there is not just one solution to a dilemma and that moral resolutions are often not *certain* conclusions. There is a range of acceptable solutions, more or less probable. Casuists have room for conscientious differences of opinion. The strength of a probable opinion derives from the internal reasons given, and it derives from the significance of recognized authorities who support it. Casuists do not seek a compelling truth from a deductive argument that has rigidly clear lines. Casuistry seeks, rather, a position that can be *reasonably* held because it fits what we already know from other similar cases.

Casuistry also has its limitations. It relies on a paradigmatic case as the common ground for comparison. But in our pluralistic society, where do we get a consensus on paradigms? For example, is a premature infant morally closer to a normal newborn whose life should be saved? Or, is it more like a terminally ill patient for whom one may decline life support measures? Even if we could agree on the paradigm, we still need to decide what the relevant features of this new case are so that they can be compared to the paradigmatic one.

Because casuistry deals with particulars, it can lose sight of the big picture and the purpose of moral striving. When this happens it can become lax and situationalist. This is what gave casuistry a bad name in the past. Its susceptibility to laxism and situationalism makes some suspicious of casuistry as a reliable method in ethics. This suspicion will be confirmed or canceled by the breadth of experience and depth of prudence of the one doing the casuistry. While casuistry depends a great deal on the character of the one comparing cases, casuistry itself does not ask the big question of what kind of person we ought to become.

VIRTUE

After lecturing on a serious issue in American life, T. S. Eliot was asked, "What are we going to do about the problem you have discussed?" He replied, in effect, "You have asked the wrong question. You must understand that we face two types of problems in life. One kind of problem provokes the question, 'What are we going to do about it?' The other kind poses a subtler question, 'How do we behave towards it?'" As Eliot implied, the first type of problem would be quick to invoke the previous methods in ethics, which focus on the situations of choice, principles, obligations, and rights. The second type of problem, however, poses a different challenge. It is not to find something to do, but to find someone to be.[10] This is the challenge of virtue ethics which emphasizes the agent who performs actions and makes choices. The distinction between doing and being does not create a dichotomy. Who we are spills over into what we do, and what we do tends to make us into the kinds of persons that we are.

Casuistry already put us into the realm of virtue. When comparing cases, our character limits what we discern as differences. A truthful character is the precondition for truthful moral knowledge. Moreover, the situation we get into is a manifestation of the kind of person we are. What might be a moral dilemma for one person is not for another because of the differences in character.

In the opening scenario, Arthur Winner struggled more with disclosing the cover up than did Julius Penrose. Arthur Winner knew that embezzlement is wrong and that anyone involved in it ought to be reported. But he couldn't bring himself to act on what he knew to be right. He lacked courage. With that, we are dealing more with his character and virtue than we are with the principles he espoused. The person of character has the courage of his or her convictions and is willing to take an unpopular stand if it means preserving integrity.

Virtues are character traits which we have acquired by practice and which dispose us to act in ways that would fulfill our highest potential. We draw on virtue ethics when we call for honesty, courage, loyalty, respect, truthfulness, patience, compassion, and the like. Virtues such as these dispose us to act in ways that make us good, for they are rooted in the desire to be loving. Virtue ethics is less concerned with solving problems and more concerned with the sort of persons we have become and aspire to be and with the communities we have created or want to be part of. Virtue ethics moves us away from focusing on problems and actions to focusing on our attitudes, motives, perspectives, ideals, beliefs, feelings and communities of influence. Virtue ethics affirms that, in the end, we choose the way we do because the choice fits who we are and want to become. In this sense, character decides for us.

Virtue ethics contends that virtues give us a cognitive advantage to know what is right and an emotional predisposition to do it. Cognitively, we speak of virtuous people as having a "nose" for what is right. Virtues influence how a person assesses what is going on. The ideal virtuous person knows what is right without thinking about it. Emotionally, virtuous people will want to do what is right and avoid what is wrong because virtues make us affectively committed to certain values. The ideal virtuous person has a passion for values.

The virtuous person, who has already developed the habit of being at ease with human relationships and is sensitive to people, for example, has an interior compass pointing to what fits a person in need. Right actions come somewhat spontaneously to those who have formed good habits. I recall a physician who responded to a situation of conflicting values by following her gut feeling and clinical hunch. All the rest of us were trying to determine which principle ought to be given priority. She, who had already nurtured a perspective that saw the other in need as neighbor and who had established a commitment to acting for the patient's total good, had the moral instinct for what to do. She did not begin by appealing to any particular principles to tell her what to do. Our principles confirmed her action as right, but they were not her first recourse. Well-established habits were. That's the way it is with virtuous people. Character decides for them.

One of the great advantages of virtue ethics is that it forces us to look at the larger moral picture beyond problems and actions. Virtue ethics also includes attitudes, motives, feelings, and ideals. It reminds us that we not only expect people to act in a certain way, but we also expect them to have certain feelings, attitudes, and ideals to inform their actions. For example, if someone donates blood out of duty to a family member about to have surgery, we would not think that as praiseworthy as doing so with a feeling of sympathy for them.

Moreover, we need to give more attention to virtues today because so much of our work is filled with ambiguity that principles do not adequately clarify. Then again, many of us have become so specialized that few people can truly oversee our work. Or, we work so much in private that no one is there to correct us when we begin to go astray. The less possibility there is of being scrutinized, the greater the need to be virtuous. William F. May once said that the best way of telling whether we are virtuous or not is by noticing the way we act when no one is looking to influence or to correct us.[11] Virtue makes us alert to the moral claims of a situation even when no one is watching.

Virtue ethics, however, has its own set of difficulties. In relation to actions, for example, their rightness or wrongness does not rest on character alone. People of good character can still do the wrong thing. Our actions must be measured against consequences and principles as well as virtues. Character and virtue may influence our assessment of a situation and dispose us to act in a certain way, but we also need to consider principles and consequences to determine the appropriateness of an action.

Another difficulty with virtue ethics is that virtues must be defined in relation to some good or end which the agent intends to achieve. But we have no religious or philosophical consensus about the meaning, purpose, or value of human life that can give us a common end, or vision of the good. Furthermore, we have no common agreement on how to measure the content of a virtue—is it from a religious conviction, a professional standard, the culture, the person in power? Nor do we have common agreement on whom we ought to hold up as our model of being a good person in our profession. Which character type or list of virtues are appropriate for our profession? Could we come to a consensus on such a list?

FEMINIST ETHICS

Feminist ethics is not monolithic. It is very diverse, sharing many perspectives.[12] I want to draw on the perspective of the feminist ethics of caring. It insures that we illumine the relational dimension of moral experience, for it affirms that we are deeply interdependent persons. The feminist ethics of caring has more interest in acting on behalf of persons with whom one has a significant relationship than in acting on behalf of one's own benefit, for it knows that individual choices affect the freedom and well-being of others.

In the opening scenario, a hint of this method is evident in the appeal that Julius Penrose makes to Arthur Winner's attachment to his daughter and wife as relationships he could protect by saying nothing about the embezzlement. He said, "You have a daughter to educate; you have a wife.... You'd be sorry, I'm sure, to see either without proper provision."

Unlike the principlist perspective that sometimes encourages an isolated world of individual rights, the feminist perspective promotes an understanding of the self based on relationality. A feminist ethics of caring would want us to be sure to include socially oriented principles, such as mutuality, fidelity, sensitivity, solidarity, empathy, nurturance, and caring. As a result, personal autonomy is not taken as an absolute. Feminist ethics of caring focuses on responsibility for the ties that bind people together. It appreciates the role of moral emotions in making a judgment and it acknowledges that the moral enterprise is thoroughly communal. Thus, it requires sympathy and compassion rather than dispassion; it is more interested in attachment than in detachment; in reconciliation rather than in winning; in liberating rather than dominating.

An example of a feminist method influencing a legal case is the first trial of the Menendez brothers in California. Two brothers admitted to killing their parents. The male-led prosecution based its strategy upon the violation of rules prohibiting murder. They sought justice in the form of punishment for violating the rules. The defense, led by female lawyers, based their case on the history of abuse by the parents which drove the brothers to kill them out of fear for their lives. The relational context provided justification for the act. The jury split along gender lines. Men favored clear-cut breaking of rules; women considered the relational context that made the murders understandable. This argument, however, did not carry the day in their second trial.

In medical ethics, a feminist method is evident in the case of the incompetent elderly person whose wishes are known but whose children disagree about what course to follow. A principlist who absolutizes autonomy would act immediately according to the patient's preferences. A feminist commitment to caring and to relationships, however, will go to great lengths to hear from all the children before making a decision, believing that it has a duty to the family network as well as to the patient. Similarly, in cases involving seriously ill newborns, feminist arguments are likely to focus on decisions for the family as a group in which relationships exist and on how the decision will foster or destroy those relationships. The feminist commitment to preserving relationships would reflect the family's preference about whether and how the newborn could be sustained within existing relationships.

This commitment to caring and preserving relationships, however, is not limited just to women. It shows itself in anyone who tries to be inclusive of all those involved in the decision, and it pays close attention to the depth and quality of personal relationships that exist in a person's life and to how these will be affected by a decision. One of the great advantages of the feminist method is that it has an acute sensitivity to the needs of particular others in concrete circumstances. This point of emphasis takes seriously the role of emotions in moral judgment for it requires the cultivation of those capacities necessary to enter imaginatively and empathetically into the world of the person being cared for. But the emotional base of sympathetic perception, motivation, and imaginative projection can make us partial to those who are close to us and blind to caring for those at a distance. In order to avoid unfair patterns of responsibility, feminist ethics needs some way of determining which of all the expressed needs are the ones most morally demanding.

Moreover, the feminist method is also inclusive of the ties that bind us. It does not focus just on the isolated individual. But just how many people we are to include in the network of relationships is always a question. Ideally, we ought to consult all those who might be affected by the decision before reaching a moral decision. The process makes this method cumbersome and time consuming. If we are too rigid about including everyone, we may never resolve anything. Yet striving to be inclusive, and insisting that heartfelt caring ought to characterize everything that goes on when dealing with persons are qualities of this method that we do not want to lose.

CONCLUSION

These, then, are five of the leading methods used in ethics today. I offer them as complementary methods, not as rival alternatives. No single one provides a universally appropriate way of determining how to love well amid the conflicting claims in our professions and in our lives. Together they witness to the pluralism of moral thought and to the complexity of moral experience which Norbert Rigali's historically conscious, relational model of ethics has recognized. In addition, these methods can be roads disciples of our day might travel in order to reach the full flowering of love which fidelity to God and service to our neighbor demand. In this way, ethics and spirituality converge to inform the ways of discipleship for today.

I think that one of the challenges that will continue to lie before us in the new millenium is to be both citizens and disciples in the world. On the one hand, we will need to let our religious convictions inform our citizenship, such as our conviction that God is love and that the moral life must be guided by the love which we see Jesus express in his obedience to God and in his service to others. On the other hand, we will need to be able to use a public language to express the demands of discipleship, such as the language of the five methods which I just reviewed. As the Catholic tradition has in the past, so I believe it will continue in the future to draw on these resources of faith and reason to inform the way of discipleship in a new age.

NOTES

1.   Hereinafter, I will refer to normative method simply as method.

2.   Some of the outstanding contributions in this regard are from his articles in *Chicago Studies* and include "Human Experience and Moral Meaning," 13 (1974), 88–104; "Christian Ethics and Perfection," 14 (1975), 227–40; "After the Moral Catechism," 20 (1981), 151–62; "The Future of Christian Morality," 20 (1981), 281–89; "The Unity of Moral and Pastoral Theology," 25 (1986), 225–32; "The Story of Christian Morality," 27 (1988), 173–80; and "Models of the Person in Moral Theology," 32 (1993), 177–85.

3.   James Gould Cozzens, *By Love Possessed* (New York: Harcourt, Brace & World, Crest Books, 1957), 524–37.

4.   Tom L. Beauchamp and James F. Childress, *Principles of Biomedical Ethics* (New York: Oxford University Press, 1994, 4th ed.).

5.   Thomas Aquinas, *S.T.*, I–II, q. 94, a. 4.

6.   For a collection of essays that offer various critical perspectives on relying too heavily on principles in ethics, see Edwin R. DuBose, Ron Hamel, and Laurence J. O'Connell, *A Matter of Principles? Ferment in U.S. Bioethics* (Valley Forge: Trinity Press International, 1994).

7.   Perhaps the most significant book to focus this revision is Albert R. Jonsen and Stephen Toulmin, *The Abuse of Casuistry* (Berkeley: University of California Press, 1988). For a collection of essays contributing to the revived interest in casuistry, see James F. Keenan and Thomas A. Shannon, eds., *The Context of Casuistry* (Washington: Georgetown University Press, 1995).

8.   Albert Jonsen, Mark Siegler, and William Winslade, *Clinical Ethics: A Practical Approach to Ethical Decisions in Clinical Medicine* (New York: McGraw-Hill, 1992, 3rd ed.).

9.   Aquinas, *S.T.*, I–II, q. 18, aa. 10–11.

10. As cited in William F. May, *The Patient's Ordeal* (Bloomington: Indiana University Press, 1991), 3.

11. William F. May, "Professional Ethics: Setting, Terrain, and Teacher," in Daniel Callahan and Sissela Bok, eds., *Ethics Teaching in Higher Education* (New York: Plenum Press, 1980), 231.

12. For an overview of the variety of feminist ethics, see Rosemarie Tong, *Feminine and Feminist Ethics* (Belmont, CA: Wadsworth, 1993).

The Fundamental Polarity of Moral Discourse

Joseph A. Selling

Every time one attempts to speak about or explain morality, any time one makes a moral statement, "she is basically a moral person" or "that is an immoral act," one engages a language that is, at its most basic level, ambiguous. There are several reasons for this. The most common source of ambiguity is linguistic. While the discipline of moral discourse can and perhaps should be carried out only through the use of well defined terminology, agreed upon and shared by persons who are well informed on the subject, the fact remains that morality itself is the concern of every human person. This is not only desirable, it is most appropriate that every member of a community or society has the opportunity to address moral issues. However, the average person may not always use vocabulary in a consistent or even commonly accepted manner. For better or worse, the major portion of terminology used by the professional ethicist simultaneously is—and must be—the common property of a moral society.

Another reason why every moral statement will exhibit ambiguity is because even at the level of professional discussion there are several schools of thought about exactly how morality comes about or should be practiced. Hugely different opinions have frequently vied for attention throughout the history of moral philosophy. Even religiously inspired morality—or theological ethics—admits of widely divergent opinions. Some theologians insist that morality is dictated by original documents, as in the case of Christians, the Hebrew and Greek scriptures. Others rely upon historical precedent, tradition or some instance of authority to determine the authenticity of one kind of moral approach over another. Still others appeal to reason to provide some form of insight into God's providence, the inherent structure of creation, or natural law, as the source of moral wisdom.

These various schools of thought on theological ethics have been more or less evident throughout history, although the amount of controversy they might have generated was not always evident. Roman Catholic Christianity, for instance, had a tendency to suppress divergence of opinions and sought to establish a standard form of moral theology from the time of the counter-reformation. This standardization, which gave the impression of conformity[1] right up through the age of the moral manuals or handbooks until the 1950s, was shattered by the accomplishments of the Second Vatican Council (1962-65). During that historic event, the Church recognized the drastic need for reform within moral theology, a reform that was so long overdue that its completion still has not been achieved.

The work of a moral theologian like Norbert Rigali could almost be read as a barometer for the development of moral theology in the post-Vatican II era. Having come to grips with the problem of redefining theological ethics at the end of the 1960s,[2] Rigali understood the challenge of finding alternative paradigms.[3] Having concentrated some of his earlier analysis on the moral act as such,[4] he had the insight that moral discourse needed to go beyond this single aspect[5] and to address the core of moral discourse in general.[6] The work that Rigali did on fundamental ethics touched upon some of the most important questions of post-Vatican II theology. Nevertheless, the Catholic milieu which had been so accustomed to standardization in moral theology was not well equipped to deal with the ambiguities that had emerged. The divergence of opinions that surfaced in the post-conciliar era frequently led to divisions rather than enrichment in moral discourse.[7] These divisions were most manifest on the level of methodological discussions and can be illustrated with several examples.

DIVERGENCES IN CONTEMPORARY THEOLOGICAL ETHICS

Deontology and *teleology* seem to constitute the sharpest of these divisions, although neither of these so-called systems has its foundations in religious ethics.[8] Teleology, an ethical theory (method) that begins with the definition of the "end" of human action, appears to be a hallmark of Aristotelian philosophy and was eventually imported into Western Christian thinking by Thomas Aquinas. Deontology, on the other hand, which is a theory (method) based upon "duty," could be traced back to Platonism which provides the foundation for a knowledge of absolutes. However, the philosophical godfather of deontology is, of course, Immanuel Kant, who provided the foundations for the modern version of this theory. These two "systems" appear to represent the opposite poles of a spectrum that remain irreconcilable, despite some attempts to combine the two.[9]

Another methodological division that springs to mind is that between *basic goods theory* and *proportionalism*. It is difficult to determine which of these "systems" came first, and, somewhat ironically, both claim their origin in the writings of Aquinas. The leading proponent of basic goods theory is Germain Grisez who seems to have laid the foundations for this approach in his 1964 book on contraception.[10] According to this—largely Anglo-Saxon—school, what is considered '(a) good' is what contributes to "human flourishing" and hence needs to be pursued and protected. Of all human goods, there are seven or eight[11] that are so "basic" that none of them may ever be harmed, undermined or sacrificed to any degree. These "basic goods" are fundamentally *not* comparable with each other, i.e., we may never choose one over the other.

Proportionalism, on the other hand, has European roots[12] and appeals to Aquinas' notion of volition (orientation, intention, and subsequent choice of action) rather than his illustration of natural law (basic goods theory relies heavily on *S.T.*, I-II, q. 94, a. 2). This theory refers to what it calls an "ethics of responsibility" that starts with attitude (virtue) and culminates with prudential judgment (due proportion: concrete action appropriate for realizing a value decision). The recognized founders of this approach include Louis Janssens (Louvain), Josef Fuchs (Rome) and Frans Böckle (Bonn). The ideoogical differences between these two schools are rather large and sometimes acrimonious,[13] so that also here reconciliation appears to be nearly impossible.

A third methodological division is most commonly referred to as an *ethics of faith* versus *autonomous ethics*.[14] The first claims that Christian ethics is explicitly religious and contains foundational elements that are not discoverable in any other context. Thus, the Sermon on the Mount (Mt 5-6) inspires an explicit way of life that is maintained by the tradition of a specific narrative that serves to create and sustain a moral community (Alasdair MacIntyre, Stanley Hauerwas).[15] In contrast to this we find autonomous ethics (Alfons Auer)[16] that maintains the competence of reason (cf. Rom 2:14-15) to acquire moral knowledge and to work out the detailed distinctions that are necessary for building an ethical method (Jack Mahoney, James F. Keenan).[17]

Perhaps because this third division seems to presume a fundamental divergence on the important question of whether moral discourse is dependent upon a body of religious truths or faith propositions, reconciliation between these two schools also appears to be extremely difficult.

One could cite other examples of divergences if not divisions in contemporary moral discourse, such as the debate between an "ethics of justice" and an "ethics of care."[18] One of the more telling illustrations of ambiguity occurs not between different systems but within a specific theory of morality that has generally come to be known as "revisionist" moral theology. The ambiguity is intimated with the distinction between goodness/badness and rightness/wrongness.[19] The former refers to attitudes and intentions and is addressed by the formal or fundamental norms: be virtuous (be just, be honest, etc.). The latter refers to behavior and is addressed by the concrete material norms: do this (right behavior), do not do that (wrong behavior).

This distinction is highly reminiscent of the divergences that I named above. Teleology, proportionalism, autonomous ethics and an ethics of care emphasize attitudes or dispositions. The moral goals to be reached are explicated in general terms, while the problem that the ethicist deals with in great detail and analysis is the manner of achieving those goals, the means to the end, as it were. Deontology, basic goods theory, faith ethics and an ethics of justice emphasize actions and behavior. From this perspective, moral goals are achieved—and only achieved—by right living, by doing the correct thing. Whereas the former approach focuses on the end while the bulk of its analysis is directed toward the means, the latter focuses on human action, while the bulk of its analysis is directed toward describing the best possible model of moral life (being dutiful, natural, holy, or just).

THE SIGNIFICANCE OF THESE DISTINCTIONS

It is probably not too difficult to accept this description of ambiguity. These distinctions may even help us classify the various divisions in contemporary moral discourse, or at least those present in Catholic moral theology. However, my question has continued to be whether these distinctions do not have some greater significance. Understanding the nature of the divergences, could they not be bridged? Could not the ambiguities be explained and ultimately overcome? My question became all the more acute with my meditations upon the encyclical of John Paul II on moral theology, *Veritatis Splendor*.[20] That document appeared to take one side in the debate between the various schools of thought, favoring an objective moral approach and rejecting a so-called *teleologism*[21] or attitudinal approach to moral theology. What is more, the entire structure of the encyclical appeared to claim its basis in the New Testament, beginning with the story of the young man who approaches Jesus and asks "What good must I do to have eternal life?" (Mt 19:16-22). The answer to this question is apparently very simple: "keep the commandments."

Over the years I have developed a certain familiarity with this story, interpreting it as one of the fundamental building blocks of Christian ethics. However, the scriptural passage with which I usually begin is not that of Matthew but the parallel passage from Luke. It is only in Luke's gospel that the question occurs twice. The scenario that occurs later in Luke (18:18-23, followed immediately with a discussion of "who will be saved" in vss. 24-30) is found earlier in Matthew (19:16-22, followed by the same discussion in vss. 23-30) as well as in Mark (10:17-22, followed by vss. 23-31). Simultaneously, the earlier citation of the question in Luke (10:25-28, followed exclusively in Luke by the story of the Good Samaritan) is paralleled later in Matthew (22:34-40) and in Mark (12:28-34). In this alternative instance, however, Matthew and Mark report a different question being posed to Jesus, "which is the great commandment?" The passages are parallel because the answer is the same, "Love God ... and love your neighbor as yourself" (cfr. Dt 6:4-5 and Lev 19:18b).

Certainly betraying my own prejudice, I begin my exposition on New Testament ethics with the primacy of the "love command," noting that although it is obvious that living in love means keeping the commandments, it remains a perennial question "which of the commandments is the most important." I used to think that this other question was secondary, again betraying my understanding of ethical method. I now realize that it is not secondary, but neither is it primary. In fact the whole approach of visualizing primary and secondary questions is misleading because the simultaneous presence of several approaches to moral thinking is not merely gratuitous, it is essential to the very existence as well as the structure of moral discourse.

Having looked at these passages literally hundreds of times, it never struck me until very recently that there is a fundamental polarity in the gospel narration. The simple fact is that to the same question (hence Luke's version of the narrative which repeats the same question), there are two, equally valid replies. The New Testament presents two approaches to morality, not one. What is significant about this is that these two approaches are not reducible. The evangelists did not and could not edit these two approaches into one, more simple model. In fact, reflecting upon the gospel as a whole, I suggest that it is rife with ambiguous, contrasting and divergent opinions about morality. The Sermon on the Mount is attitudinal and teleological in nature, as are the stories that relativize the importance of the law, such as whether to cure on the Sabbath (Mt 12:9-14). In contrast, Jesus has come to fulfill the law, and not one iota of the law will be changed (Mt 5:18-20). The prostitute and the polyandrist are told to stop sinning and to uphold the law. We are taught to render to Caesar what is Caesar's, and so forth.

The exposition of New Testament ethics in light of a theory of polarity remains a formidable task. I have no intention of even initiating that project here. Nor did I come to the understanding of polarity in moral discourse through my studies of the New Testament. The importance and pervasiveness of polarity, namely the irreducibility of different approaches to morality, occurred to me while attempting to explain a classical moral theory that is typical of, although not necessarily exclusive to, the Catholic moral tradition. I will recount that process here because I believe that it provides a clear, even visual, explanation that will then open the way to investigating the real significance of this finding.

THE ELEMENTS OF MORALITY

The Western Christian tradition of moral discourse has recognized for centuries that morality consists of several elements, each of which must be present and accounted for before one can confirm that a truly moral statement (or judgment) is being made. The tradition has even—mistakenly, I believe—referred to these elements as the *sources* of morality, a proposition that has been enshrined in the doctrine of the *tres fontes moralitatis* (TFM).[22]

These elements ("three sources") of morality may initially be named with the simple terms: object, end and circumstances. Classically, the three elements refer to three insights into what has come to be designated "morality": something that is done, expressed, brought about or prevented from happening (the object) in the real world that admits not only of constancy but of contingency as well (the circumstances) by a human person who is free, conscious and motivated (the end). All three elements must be accounted for if we are really speaking of a "moral act." Paradoxically, however, and this is the source of a great deal of confusion, it is possible to speak of each one of these elements individually in terms of its moral *relevancy*.

A "moral object" can be distinguished from a non-moral or indifferent form of activity that may become morally relevant through the addition of specific circumstances (e.g., sleeping vs. sleeping-on-the-job) but which itself contains no inherent moral relevance. To have relevance for morality, such objects must contain some identifiable aspects of benefit or harm for living, supposedly sentient creatures. Examples might include almsgiving (helping the poor) and mutilation (causing physical harm). If one were to refer to these "moral objects" merely as morally-*relevant* objects, I think a great deal of confusion and disagreement could be avoided in moral discourse. Nonetheless, there remains the theory that some actions (objects) are, in and of themselves, "intrinsically evil" and hence immoral, no matter what (further?) circumstances or motivations are added to their description. This remains a stumbling block to dialogue among moralists that can only be overcome, I think, with the following reflection.

"Moral circumstances" are perhaps the most difficult to define because they are simultaneously the most illustrative and most elusive of the elements of moral discourse. Some would say that it is impossible to describe any human action (object) without at least implying some presumption of circumstance. This would go a good distance toward explaining the meaning of "intrinsic evil," such as when one realizes that *murder* involves not simply killing but *unjust* killing.

Still, one must admit that even an unjust killing might amount to something less than murder if, for instance, the perpetrator of such an act is insane, ignorant, or operating without freedom. At best, then, we should only speak of morally-*relevant* circumstances, although the more circumstances one tries to attach to the description of what is taking place, the more one feels they are getting close to a genuinely moral statement in every sense.

Perhaps the most likely element to serve as a candidate for bearing the full weight of morality is the end, expressed as the "moral intention" of the acting person. Traditionally, one is said to perform a moral act at the moment of commitment to some act or omission, regardless of whether that commitment is actually carried out; "one who lusts after another in one's heart has already committed adultery" (Mt 5:28). All this is very well and good, until one uncovers the complexity of human motivation. I once encountered a very pertinent example of this while doing research on the topic of suicide.

> In suicide, perhaps more than with any other mental content, the distance between the conscious intention offered verbally and what actions and attitudes reveal about more significant unconscious intention is a crucial datum for explanation and understanding. *A suicidal thought is not a suicidal wish.* Every thought is a trial action, itself a compromise of instinctual impulse and defense. *A suicidal wish is not a suicidal intention.* Not every wish is intended yet for action. *A suicidal intention is not a suicidal attempt.* Intentions are subject to further intrapsychic testing—actually, a series of tests. *A suicidal attempt is not yet the act of suicide.* Indecision and compromise formation continue. *Even a suicidal act is not yet suicide.* The intention is still not unequivocal, or its results assured. Finally, there is suicide. Even here there is not always finiteness, especially now that there is a question of when death actually occurs.[23]

In the end, it is meaningful to speak of morally-*relevant* intentions (ends), just as it is to consider morally-*relevant* objects and morally-*relevant* circumstances, in one's efforts to carry on moral discourse. At the same time, it appears to be a case of jumping the gun to assign full moral qualification to any one of these three elements, independent of the other two. It is here that we come to a first glance at the interpretive key for understanding the ambiguity of moral discourse. The two expressions, "moral" and "morally-relevant," are largely interchangeable, and ordinary, day-to-day language does not distinguish them at all.

This observation, however, explains only a potential linguistic confusion and addresses only the level of ambiguity, not polarity. To gain an insight into the latter, we need to consider an important but hitherto overlooked dimension of these elements of morality.

THE ORDER OF PRESENTATION

Throughout the handbook tradition the theory of the TFM appeared to exhibit the characteristic of an absolute moral criterion when it was combined with another relevant, but not necessarily connected, theory that seems to have originated with Pseudo-Dionysius: *bonum ex integra causa, malum ex quocumque defectu*.[24] Briefly, what this principle means is that for some *thing* (n.b., not necessarily a moral activity) to be good, it must be good in every one of its aspects or dimensions. If there is one, single aspect that introduces evil into the thing being considered, then one must conclude that it cannot rightly be called "good."

One can consider the radicalness that this introduces into moral discourse when this principle, *ex integra causa*, is applied to the TFM. When we admit that morality consists of at least three, seemingly independent elements—object, circumstances, and end—*ex integra causa* would dictate that even a minor flaw in any one of these elements would disqualify it as a candidate for moral goodness. Thus, a hugely philanthropic action is "made immoral" by the motive of pride, while the most altruistic motives can never be invoked to justify even a slight evil. All the circumstances of human activity need to be considered and judged to be good if one is ever to act in a moral way. The one exception to this rule appears to be the circumstance of effect or consequence,[25] which another principle (double effect)[26] neatly divides into "direct" and "indirect,"[27] so that only direct or "indirect-but-disproportionate" consequences will make a difference.

While the notion of the TFM might have developed into a valuable tool for shedding light on the complex world of moral discourse, in combination with *ex integra causa*, it was converted into a weapon for moral judgment and condemnation. Seemingly, that principle could be invoked at any time and from any perspective. As a result, it appeared to render irrelevant what I consider to be the most important aspect of the TFM theory itself, namely the order in which one presents these three elements for consideration in the context of moral discourse.

Considered in the abstract and held hostage by *ex integra causa*, it appears to make no difference whatsoever how the three elements of morality are presented and analyzed. My thesis is that it makes all the difference in the world how one considers these elements because one will (have to) look at them differently depending upon the question one is asking.

Whatever may have been the original formulation of the TFM,[28] the practice of confession helped to shape the structure of its presentation into the form: object-circumstance-intention.[29] The evolution of the TFM provides a clear example of practice leading theory. With a view to being a spiritual healer, the priest-confessor first heard about the penitent's deeds (the object) with or without some detail about which the confessor might eventually inquire in order to determine the gravity of the matter (circumstances), followed by the most pertinent question of all, "why did you do such a thing?" (intention).

Although this evolution occurred in service to confessional practice, the same priest would most likely also have the task of preaching about morality, in which the same scheme would prove to be very handy. What is moral and immoral? What is going on out there? What kinds of activity should one avoid at all costs? The evident answer is acts: theft, fornication, telling untruths, showing disrespect, being disobedient, using profanity, gambling, drinking too much, neglecting one's duties, and so forth. The *preacher* saw all these things very clearly and denounced them for what they are: evil. The *confessor*, on the other hand, though frequently the same person, had to be more nuanced in his evaluation, and realized that circumstances had to be considered before one could really pronounce upon immorality.

Similarly, the same priest-confessor knew that behind every act and set of circumstances there was a person who could be malicious, misguided, ignorant, perhaps even virtuous. Ultimately, one's intention was the deciding factor, although in the context of the confessional what was being determined was not evil or wrongdoing but responsibility and guilt (moral evil or sin).

What the confessor and the preacher had in common was that they were looking for the same thing and asking the same questions: Where is sin? What is immoral? In such an atmosphere, the TFM became solidified in its expression and order of presentation: act-circumstance-end.

AN ALTERNATIVE PERSPECTIVE

There is, however, a very different way of looking at moral life, a way that might be used by the spiritual director, and almost certainly would be used by someone for whom the mere identification of sins is of relatively little importance.[30] This is a morality of ideals and inspiration. It looks first at "the moral life" as an integrated whole, not something fragmented into acts, circumstances and ends. The questions being asked here are: How is one to be moral? How can one lead a moral life?

The answer to these questions begins with the consideration of who I am and who I want to become—who we are and who we wish to become?[31] In other words, it begins with intentionality—both the deepest and most inward orientation of the person (fundamental option) and the existential determination of oneself through the choice and expression of a way of living (virtue or vice). This question about attitude, however, remains literally "immaterial" unless it is placed very concretely into the context of one's life situation or circumstances. This is precisely why the Sermon on the Mount, inspirational as it is, cannot be translated directly into activity. We lack the knowledge or presumption of whose life is being inspired. Saying that the peacemakers are to be considered "blessed" (Mt 5:9), does not help us identify the work of peacemakers, who may be diplomats, negotiators, policemen, psychotherapists, pacifists, protestors or infantrymen. Trying to be financially responsible means different things to a consumer, a salesperson, a banker, an accountant, a builder or a business manager. What it means to be chaste is different for the married, the unmarried, and the committed celibate.

Life-circumstances are the place where our attitudes are situated. They take their meaning from the total context of one's life while they give substance and materiality to the intention one chooses and pursues. Only in this context of "materialized intention" is it meaningful to speak about moral activity in a personal sense. In doing so, we realize how *human activity* is something more than a merely disembodied "action," it represents the manifestation of the whole person, inspired by a basic orientation expressed in a specific intention in the context of one's life circumstances.

In asking this question, how is one to be moral, then, what we see unfolded is the dynamic of the TFM, *but in precisely the opposite direction* as that employed by the confessor and preacher. It constitutes looking at the same "reality," but from a completely different point of view. In fact, with a slight alteration of vocabulary, recognizing the important affinity of synonyms, the whole project of moral discourse reveals its simplicity in the following diagram.

What is morality?
What is moral/immoral?
What is to be done/avoided?

> .... > .... >

event	circumstances	end/ethos
action	reality-questions:	intention
decision	who, what, when,...	attitude
judgment	life-situation	orientation

< .... < .... <

How to be moral?
What is the moral life?
Can one have moral feelings?

Each of the elements will be described slightly differently, depending upon the point of view one is taking. What is most important here is: Which question is one asking?

What I find even more striking is that in daily life, which is rather distant from the abstraction of ethical theories, most people do not simply ask one question or the other, they ask *both* questions. In fact, we *must* ask both questions if we ever hope to be moral persons and to build moral communities. Yet, the way or the priority with which these questions are asked will have a significant impact upon the perspective one formulates with respect to moral discourse as a whole. This might be made clearer with a visual example.

Picture the diagram written on a blackboard. Standing to the left, one poses the question, what is moral or immoral? What one sees immediately or most closely are the events or actions, the (projected) results of a moral decision having been made. Beyond these are the circumstances of those events, those elements which might help to fill out the picture. In the distance one could inquire into all the possible, but still unknown, intentions of the moral agent. This is the perspective of the confessor; but it is also the perspective of the preacher or anyone who is attempting to point out what is to be done and what is to be avoided.

Now walk over to the right side of the board and ask, how is one to be moral? The immediately evident answer to the question is to examine one's basic attitude or orientation with respect to how one lives one's whole life. Morality emanates from the heart, from the deepest core of who we are and who we wish to become. This is an important characteristic of the Christian tradition in particular, although not necessarily exclusive to it. One's attitude, however, must always be fleshed out in the context of one's life-circumstances. As illustrated above, being a peacemaker will be embodied quite differently by the diplomat or the foot-soldier. The actual judgment or decision one makes about specific behavior remains quite distant from the place where one is standing when asking the initial question. This is the perspective of the moral educator, counselor or spiritual director. It is also the dominant perspective of the moral agent for the majority of time. It may be referred to as the "intentional" approach to morality.

At first glance, this contrast of perspectives may cause confusion. Understanding that confusion merely explains the origin of what we have already observed as ambiguity. However, I believe that this understanding can take us much further and reveal an even deeper level of interpretation. Through it, we can finally grasp the fundamental *polarity* of moral discourse.

POLARITY AND MORAL DISCOURSE

For one reason or another, the majority of Western philosophy has been extremely uncomfortable with the notion of paradox. Perhaps it is an exaggerated appreciation for the principle of non-contradiction; perhaps it is some form of anxiety about living with unresolved conflict. Whatever it is, most western thinkers seem to be driven to resolve conflict, to reduce incompatibilities, to search for a lower common denominator or a higher synthesis. Some philosophy is even built upon the very idea of thesis and antithesis resolved into some sort of synthesis. Epistemology is reduced to dialectic, with the promise of ultimate, if not absolute, truth.

This approach, however, is not the only possible one. A number of western thinkers, from John Scotus Erigena[32] to Allen Watts,[33] have been capable of integrating the insights of eastern philosophy and proposing a much different view of things: how to deal with seemingly incompatible and conflicting observations. The same has been observed in some modern Christian writers, notably Samuel Taylor Coleridge and John Henry Newman.[34] What these writers have in common is the ability to accept the notion that two or more even widely differing ideas can be held at the same time. What is more, they realized that the simultaneous presence of differing ideas could present the foundation of a new idea that is neither synthetic nor reductionistic. This new idea, in fact, remains de-

pendent upon the tension between the different elements *not* being resolved. This is "polarity."

I suggest that moral discourse, or the attempt to say something
meaningful about the phenomenon we call morality, is fundamentally
polar because it consists of bringing together various elements that can
be neither synthesized into a single concept, nor reduced to a single,
common element, without destroying the structure of morality itself
(e.g., substituting it with either good intentions or legal rules). To address moral questions, one must be concerned with the disposition of the
person or persons[35] called upon to respond to a given issue or situation.
Simultaneously, one (both the responding person and the observer) must
be concerned with the facts, givens or objective elements (objects) of
issues and situations, lest the moral endeavor constitute nothing more
than a solipsistic fantasy.

It is important to note that not only on the practical level but also on
the theoretical (systematic) level both moral questions have to be asked,
both perspectives must be accounted for, if we hope to achieve moral
insight—even morality itself. Neglect the givens or objective elements,
and the exercise is one of wishful thinking. Neglect the intention or resolve (goal, aim, purpose, end) of the person(s), and the exercise is one
of mere legislation. One without the other is incapable of achieving
moral insight; one aspect stated without taking account of the other is
not moral discourse but disembodied abstraction.

Fundamentally, at its deepest level and within its very constitution,
moral discourse is polar. It incorporates seemingly incompatible elements but it does not resolve the tension between these elements without
ceasing to be moral discourse. This is why (western) philosophy has
never succeeded in the construction of a singular ethical method. Teleology responds to the question, how can one be(come) moral? It does
not, of itself, sufficiently address either the material circumstances of an
individual's life or the so-called objective possibilities or limitations of
the given human situation. Contrarily, deontology responds to the query,
what is (im)moral? It does not, of itself, acknowledge the importance of
the subjective engagement on the part of real, historical, existential persons who must sort out the complex details of their existence and experience. Both these methods are morally-*relevant*, but neither, by itself,
can provide a sufficient foundation for moral discourse.

Other theories of ethical method implicitly recognize the need to acknowledge the polarity of moral discourse, but because they begin with
one specific aspect or question they present the impression of one-

sidedness. Thus, basic goods theory begins with the question, what is moral or immoral—implying that the objective elements, which are certainly morally-*relevant*, might be sufficient to establish grounds for moral judgment and action. From the other direction, proportionalism begins with the question, how can one be moral—implying that personal commitment, anchored in the fundamental option, which is certainly morally-*relevant*, will be sufficient to inspire persons to make the correct judgment about the more concrete elements of actual behavior.

The extent to which each of these theories presumes that both poles of the moral enterprise ultimately will be addressed, they may function sufficiently in the practical realm of moral decision-making. However, as long as those aspects which are merely presumed to be accounted for and are not explicitly articulated as necessary considerations (which may happen as a result of the enthusiasm to emphasize one of the poles as a point of departure), the theory will fall short of establishing the entire range of perspectives necessary for moral discourse.

The polarity of moral discourse should make us aware that unless we are willing to rethink our epistemological bias (non-contradiction, the felt need to choose one perspective *or* the other), it will remain impossible to grasp the simple complexity of the interrelations of all the elements of morality. This remains true to the extent that one embraces one of the two poles or perspectives exclusively. Thus, seen from the perspective of the object(s) of moral behavior, circumstances remain independent, as do the intentions of acting persons, to be considered or not, as a kind of optional judgment. In contrast, starting with moral intention, circumstances become a necessary condition ("materialization"), for describing the landscape of moral life and decision-making, but their contingency may be easily exaggerated. Neither circumstances nor acts in themselves (objects, events) can be judged *morally* before the entire picture is complete. As long as these perspectives are considered to be mutually exclusive, in that the choice of one becomes the exclusion of the other, the hope of achieving moral consensus in the contemporary Christian community will remain elusive.

What we need to aim for is an understanding of polarity in which the different perspectives simultaneously maintain their significance and interact with other elements of the discourse.[36] Thus the person with a given morally-relevant orientation (attitude, intention) will always be looking beyond circumstances to analyze human acts (events) for their potential appropriateness for embodying their goals or purposes. We examine actions *from* an attitudinal perspective.

At the same time, attitudes themselves are chosen and reinforced *through* behavior. We learn by doing. This is an observation that has particular import for moral development and moral education. What we learn through behavior influences later behavioral choices which, in their turn, will have an impact upon learning once again. In place of cause and effect, linear thinking, the recursive process of human understanding continuously turns back upon itself to construct a truly human reality in which the agent is both participant and observer.[37] Thus, in moral discourse, the insights of recursive thinking reveal that moral conclusions, norms, or laws originate not outside of us but through a process that we continuously carry out in dialogue with the whole human community.[38]

POLARITY AND RECURSIVE FEEDBACK

What is left to consider is the creative dynamics of moral discourse as a polar system. We have seen that much of that discourse breaks down into placing an emphasis on one of two poles, either the subjective, intentional, and goal-oriented perspective of constructing a moral lifestyle or the objective, event oriented perspective of describing the content of moral activity. The simultaneous presence of these two dynamics can function as a feedback system in which the moral sense continuously (recursive) comes back on itself for re-examination (feedback).

The dynamic of intentionality presumes and supports human freedom and autonomy. Maximizing freedom, including options and choices, creates room for experimentation, questioning existing structures and seeking ways to liberate human persons from the bonds of conformity. Eventually, however, this strategy encounters the limitations of human experience which have been thematized in structures, institutions, laws, and norms. This encounter simultaneously stretches the boundaries of human possibility and encroaches upon the borders that may have been erected too protectively.

The dynamic of searching for objectivity presumes and supports human identity and solidarity. Drawing upon the wisdom of the past from all sources (religion, history, narrative, authority, structure, jurisprudence), it realizes that not only do we become what we do but the very construction of human identity is dependent upon opportunities that are presented to us from outside ourselves. We are given a language, a culture, and a complex set of customs and institutions that create the very possibility for human interaction. Further, this approach serves best to protect the individual: 'your freedom ends where my being begins.' It matters not to my well-being whether you are well-intentioned or ill-willed. What matters is that you respect the conventions of the moral community and behave accordingly. The outlines of human behavior created by normativity provide a touchstone of objectivity that sustains the fabric of human social living.

After the reaction to the overly objectified approach of the textbooks of moral theology resulting in a strong emphasis upon human intentionality and creativity, today we are witnessing another reactive emphasis upon the precedence of behavior over intention. First we act, then we thematize; first we follow the rules, then we begin to grasp what the rules stand for. Or to put it again into ethical language, heteronomy, the formulation and imposition of norms, precedes autonomy, the self-direction of the moral agent.

This may be true in the chronological sense, but in the logical sense the precedence is exactly the opposite. Without autonomy there is only legalism not—necessarily[39]—morality. Getting beyond the heat of the contemporary debate and the shifts that have taken place in the history of moral discourse, we must always remember that both dynamics must be present, and they must remain in tension, challenging and limiting each other. The entire enterprise of moral discourse is and must always be engaged precisely as a polar system.

NOTES

1.   The standardization of moral theology after the counter-reformation was never complete or absolute. One immediately thinks of the probabilist controversies of the seventeenth and eighteenth centuries and of the attempts to reform moral theology in the late nineteenth century. See Bernard Häring, *The Law of Christ*, E.G. Kaiser, trans. (Westminster: Newman, 1963), v. 1, 22–33; and Charles E. Curran, *The Origins of Moral Theology in the United States: Three Different Approaches* (Washington, DC: Georgetown University Press, 1997).

2.   "Moral Theology: Old and New," *Chicago Studies* 8 (1969), 41–57; and "On Christian Ethics," *Chicago Studies* 10 (1971), 227–47.

3.   "Human Experience and Moral Meaning," *Chicago Studies* 13 (1974), 88–104; "Morality and Historical Consciousness," *Chicago Studies* 18 (1979), 161–68; and "Evil and Models of Christian Ethics," *Horizons* 8 (1981), 7–22.

4. "The Moral Act," *Horizons* 10 (1983), 252–66; and "Sin in a Relational World," *Chicago Studies* 23 (1984), 321–32.

5. "Moral Pluralism and Christian Ethics," *Louvain Studies* 13 (1988), 305–21; and "Models of the Person in Moral Theology," *Chicago Studies* 32 (1993), 177–85.

6. "Reimaging Morality: A Matter of Metaphors," *The Heythrop Journal* 35 (1994), 1–14.

7. Raphael Gallagher, "Change and Continuity in the Human Condition: The Implications of *GS* paras. 4–10 for Moral Theology," *Studia Moralia* 35 (1997), 63–66, has drawn attention to the polarization that has occurred in moral theology since the time of Vatican II. He suggests that this polarization is most evident between the schools of "autonomous morality" and "faith ethics," although it can be identified in association with other foundational ideas as well. Gallagher's purpose with this reference is to point out how much work still needs to be done on the ecclesiological background of moral theology, that is, understanding the church not as an unchanging institution but as the historically situated sacrament of salvation. The present essay suggests that polarization occurs when we fail to recognize the irreducible polarity of moral discourse itself.

8. See Todd Salzman, *Deontology and Teleology: An Investigation of the Normative Debate in Roman Catholic Moral Theology* (Leuven: University Press, 1995). Salzman's book (555 pp.) is about as close as one can come to the definitive work on the subject. In his study, Salzman demonstrates how this terminology was borrowed from C.D. Broad, *Five Types of Ethical Theory* (London: Routledge & K. Paul, 1930), and introduced into Roman Catholic moral theology by Bruno Schüller, "Typen ethischer Argumentation in der katholischen Moraltheologie," *Theologie und Philosophie* 45 (1970), 526–50; see also "Typen der Begründung sittlicher Normen," *Concilium* 120 (1976), 648–54, transl. as "Various Types of Grounding for Ethical Norms," in C.E. Curran and R.A. McCormick, eds., *Readings in Moral Theology No. 1: Moral Norms and Catholic Tradition* (New York: Paulist, 1979), 184–98.

9. See, for instance, Charles E. Curran, "Utilitarianism and Contemporary Moral Theology: Situating the Debates," *Louvain Studies* 6 (1976–77), 239–55; and Lisa Sowle Cahill, "Teleology, Utilitarianism, and Christian Ethics," *Theological Studies* 42 (1981), 601–29.

10. Germain Grisez and John Wright, *Contraception and the Natural Law* (Milwaukee: Bruce, 1964).

11. Having surveyed Grisez's work in five publications between 1964 and 1987, during which he explains or makes reference to the "basic goods," I have found variations both in the number and the order in which they are presented. The most elaborate explanation is found in *The Way of the Lord Jesus, Volume One: Christian Moral Principles* (Chicago: Franciscan Herald Press, 1983),

122–25.

12. See Bernard Hoose, *Proportionalism: The American Debate and its European Roots* (Washington, DC: Georgetown University Press, 1987).

13. In a glossary at the end of *The Way of the Lord Jesus*, Germain Grisez describes proportionalism as "a mistaken theory of moral reasoning..."

14. See Vincent MacNamara, *Faith and Ethics: Recent Roman Catholicism* (Washington, DC: Georgetown University Press, 1985).

15. Alasdair MacIntyre, *Whose Justice? Which Rationality?* (London: Duckworth, 1988); and Stanley Hauerwas, *A Community of Character: Toward a Constructive Christian Social Ethic* (Notre Dame, IN: University of Notre Dame Press, 1981).

16. Alfons Auer, *Autonome Moral und christlicher Glaube* (Dusseldorf: Patmos , 1971)

17. John Mahoney, "The Challenge of Moral Distinctions," *Theological Studies* 53 (1992), 663–82; and James F. Keenan, "The Return of Casuistry," *Theological Studies* 57 (1996), 123–39.

18. The justice-care debate refers to the reaction to the theory of moral development by Lawrence Kohlberg, "Moral Stages and Moralization: The Cognitive-Developmental Approach," in T. Lickona, ed., *Moral Development and Behavior: Theory, Research and Social Issues* (New York: Holt, Rinehart and Winston, 1976); and by Carol Gilligan, *In a Different Voice: Psychological Theory and Women's Development* (Cambridge, MA: Harvard University Press, 1982). For a review of the literature on this topic, see Lisa Sowle Cahill, "Feminist Ethics," *Theological Studies* 51 (1990), 47–64; and Susan A. Ross and Mary Catherine Hilkert, "Feminist Theology: A Review of Literature," *Theological Studies* 56 (1995), 327–52.

19. The good/right, bad/wrong distinctions first appear to play an important role in Catholic moral theology in the work of Louis Janssens in his seminal article, "Ontic Evil and Moral Evil," *Louvain Studies* 4 (1972), 115–56. At first, the distinctions that Janssens was making were often responded to with the puzzling observation that 'the good may not be separated from the right.' Eventually, however, the distinction became a topic of study itself. See, for instance, James F. Keenan, *Goodness and Rightness in Thomas Aquinas's Summa Theologiae* (Washington, DC: Georgetown University Press, 1992).

20. See "The Context and the Arguments of *Veritatis Splendor*," in J.A. Selling and J. Jans, eds., *The Splendor of Accuracy: An Examination of the Assertions made by Veritatis Splendor* (Kampen/Grand Rapids: Kok-Pharos/Eerdmans, 1994/1995), 11–70.

21. John Paul II, *Veritatis Splendor* (Vatican City: Libreria Editrice Vaticana, 1993), §§ 71–75. As far as I can tell, the encyclical has coined a term, *teleologism*, which had not been used before. One could be tempted to draw a parallel with Leo XIII's condemnation of *americanism*, which apparently no one

had ever heard of before the publication of *Testem Benevolentiae* in 1899.

22. Although my first exposure to moral theology came from what could be called the extremely late manual tradition (John Ford and Gerald Kelly, *Contemporary Moral Theology* (Westminster, MD: Newman Press, 1964), the significance of the TFM did not strike me until I saw it mentioned in passing by Josef Fuchs, in his very important article, "The Absoluteness of Moral Norms," *Gregorianum* 52 (1971), 415–58.

23. Leo Rangell, "The Decision to Terminate One's Life: Psychoanalytic Thoughts on Suicide," (expanded version of an address given on 27 May 1987) *Suicide and Life-Threatening Behavior* 18 (1988), 30.

24. Frequently, this is the form of the principle as it is usually rendered in the manuals of moral theology. Reference is usually given to Thomas, *S.T.*, I–II, q. 18, a. 4, ad 3, "...quia quilibet singularis defectus causat malum; bonum autem causatur ex integra causa, ut Dionys. dicit 4 cap. Div. Nom.." The original phrase from *The Divine Names*, PG 3, cc. 729–30, is, "...bonum ex una integraque causa exsistit, malum autem ex multis partialibusque defectibus." Note that the context of the expression is the question of theodicy, not morality.

25. "Circumstances" refer to any number of factors surrounding human activity. It is only in the debates about the so-called theory of "consequentialism" that effects or consequences have been singled out and given so much attention. Thomas, referring to Tully and Aristotle, *S.T.*, I–II, q. 7, a. 3, names eight circumstances: time, place, mode of acting, what, why, about what, who and by what aids. See Johannes Gründel, *Die Lehre von dem Umständen der Menschlichen Handlung im Mittelalter* (Münster: Aschendorffsche, 1963). Richard M. Gula, *Reason Informed by Faith: Foundations of Catholic Morality* (New York: Paulist, 1989), 267, very aptly refers to these as "reality-revealing questions" (who, what, when, where, why, how, what else, and what if).

26. The "principle of double effect" (PDE) has received a great deal of attention since Peter Knauer, "The Hermeneutic Function of the Principle of Double Effect," in Curran and McCormick, eds., *Readings in Moral Theology No. 1*, 1–39 (originally published as "La détermination du bien et du mal moral par le principe du double effet," *Nouvelle revue théologique* 87 [1965], 356–76), brought our attention to what he considered to be a key idea for the whole of morality.

27. In the handbook tradition, direct and indirect were used as physical, and especially temporal terms, referring respectively to what one did (direct) and what flowed from what one did at a later point in time or because of the intervention of factors outside of the control of the acting person and effecting their action after it was performed (indirect).

    Knauer proposed that the tradition assigned the term direct to that which flowed from the intention of the agent and indirect to that which remained outside of that intention ("indirectly intended" meant *praeter intentio-*

nem, beyond intention). He then suggested that the definitions of what was directly intended or indirectly (not) intended were dependent upon whether there was present a *commensurate reason*: "I say that an evil effect is not directly intended only if there is a commensurate ground for its permission or causation" (6).

Classically, the term direct referred to that which was actually done (an act) and indirect referred to that which was accomplished by omission. Later events or effects that flowed from either act or omission (what the PDE means by indirect effects) were designated with the term "voluntary *in causa*."

28. Again, although many would like to trace the formulation of the TFM to *S.T.*, I–II, q. 18, the debates that have continued on the issue for more than 700 years would seem to indicate that its formulation is more a myth than a tenable hypothesis. Salzman, *Deontology and Teleology*, 271ff., suggests that the notion of considering multiple aspects of human acts to make moral judgments was introduced by the Fourth Lateran Council (1215) when it imposed the practice of the yearly confession of one's sins to a priest, who was admonished to be attentive to the circumstances of sin as well: "Sacerdos autem sit discretus et cautus...diligenter inquirens et peccatoris circumstantias et peccati...."

29. See my essay *"Veritatis Splendor* and the Sources of Morality," *Louvain Studies* 19 (1994), 3–17.

30. One could refer here to a moral theologian who is not a confessor or even a priest. However, the divisions need not be so drastic. Indeed a priest-confessor who recognized this insight even before the council was Bernard Häring, *The Law of Christ*, 3 vols. (Westminster: Newman, 1963).

31. See J.A. Selling, "The Human Person," in Bernard Hoose, ed., *Christian Ethics: An Introduction* (London: Chapman, 1998) 95–109. A word needs to be said here about the notion of *person*, what has come to be known as the "human person adequately considered." On the one hand, "person" must always be understood as "person-in-community." The idea of person merely as individual is completely untenable within the context of moral discourse, for being human always admits of a social dimension. On the other hand, too many considerations of morality, the moral act, or the moral agent—including the development of the TFM and its use in the moral handbooks—have fallen into this individualist way of thinking. I will suggest further on that what is attributed to "person"—not just individual—here is also attributable to groups of persons and that it is meaningful to speak of social act(ion)s, social circumstances (culture) and even social intention (*ethos*).

32. A very interesting discussion of Erigena's contribution to Western thought is found in an as yet unpublished work by Marcella E. Sires, *Knowledge, Reality and Behavior: An Investigation of the Constructivist Paradigm* (Katholieke Universiteit Leuven, thesis for the degree of M.A. in Family and

Sexual Sciences, 1990), 22–28. Some other references are available in Gordon Leff, *Medieval Thought: St. Augustine to Ockham* (Harmondsworth: Penguin, 1958), and Vladimir Lossky, *The Mystical Theology of the Eastern Church* (London: Clarke & Co., 1957).

33. See Michael C. Brannigan, *Everywhere and Nowhere: The Path of Alan Watts* (New York: Peter Lang, 1988), 87–95.

34. See Terrence Merrigan, *Clear Heads and Holy Hearts: The Religious and Theological Ideal of John Henry Newman* (Leuven: Peeters, 1991), 7–19. The simplest example of polarity is the phenomenon of magnetism. Without the irreducible poles of north and south, positive and negative, magnetism does not exist.

35. As indicated above, this understanding can function not only on the individual level but on the level of social ethics as well. Consider the act of capital punishment. This can only be understood in the context of a broader range of circumstances (a society with or without prisons, an aggressive criminal urgently representing a clear threat to others, the presence or absence of alternative methods of restraint and/or punishment). It also begs the question of the present or dominant ethos of a society (exactly how high or low on the scale of valuing is the importance or worth of human life). One could also reverse the order or priority of questions on the level of social ethics, asking first about the dominant ethos of a group, then investigating the circumstances that may promote or frustrate that ethos. Finally, decisions will have to be taken and actions performed, either in the form of actually doing something or formulating guidelines (laws) for the behavior of individuals.

36. One might like to suggest that the two perspectives being represented here actually describe the subject area of two distinct disciplines. The attempt to describe the moral relevance of actions and events is dealt with in normative ethics while the attempt to describe the core of the moral life itself falls within the realm of spirituality. Tempting as this distinction may be, we should recognize that this approach has been tried and found wanting, for the two disciplines ultimately either become detached from each other or are collapsed into a single, all encompassing perspective. See Kevin T. Kelly, *Conscience: Dictator or Guide?* (London: Chapman, 1967), 119–29.

37. For a most interesting collection of essays on constructivist thinking and recursive feedback, see *Radical Constructivism, Autopoiesis and Psychology*, a special issue of *The Irish Journal of Psychology* 9 (1988).

38. This dialogue, of course, is not bound by time, since the tradition of any community is a valuable resource of moral insight. The idea that this dialogue is not only trans-cultural but inter-religious is affirmed by *Dignitatis Humanae*, § 3: "Truth is to be sought after in a manner proper to the dignity of the human person and his social nature. The inquiry is to be free, carried on with the aid of teaching or instruction, communication, and dialogue. In the course of

these, men explain to one another the truth they have discovered, or think they have discovered, in order thus to assist one another in the quest for truth. Moreover, as the truth is discovered, it is by personal assent that men are to adhere to it."

39. In Kohlberg's theory of moral development, the conventional stages of conforming one's behavior to the law is not only a valid plateau of moral motivation, it is probably the location of the vast majority of people. This, however, does not make it sufficient to describe what morality and moral living will mean to the ethicist and what it should mean to the mature community. See Rigali, "Reimaging Morality: A Matter of Metaphors," 1-14.

Natural Law, Acts and Persons

Bernard Hoose

In spite of the blurring of differences between Catholic and Protestant approaches to matters of morality that has occurred in recent times, there are still Protestants, it would seem, who are more than a little wary of Catholic appeals to natural law. There is, of course, a fairly long history to such wariness. Catholics have long been accused of handing ethics over to the philosophers and of relying upon corrupt human reasoning. The classical Protestant tendency to turn instead to the Bible for moral guidance, however, has also run into difficulties in the last century or so. Those Protestants who would seek to rely upon Scripture for their moral teachings must face the issues arising from the development of biblical scholarship, initially within Protestantism itself. They too, it would seem, have to resort to fallible human reasoning when they come to the job of biblical interpretation. A way out of this apparent impasse, however, is provided by adopting a divine command approach which is devoid of all appeal to human reasoning powers. There are various types of divine command theory. God may, for instance, directly assist the individual Christian in the reading of Scripture. Alternatively, God may directly instruct the individual about the rightness or wrongness of certain actions in a particular situation, without any reference to Scripture. Something like the latter form might be thought necessary when dealing with such thoroughly modern issues as organ transplants and genetic engineering, which are simply not dealt with in the Bible.

A divine command approach which bears some resemblance to the latter type, but which also maintains a certain biblical connection is that kind of situation ethics theory according to which, in any given situation, love (*agape*) will tell the agent what to do. Love is the only absolute and the only guide. There is apparently no question of taking sections of Scripture out of context in such a system. Indeed, in adopting it, one might claim to be adopting the most basic and all-encompassing of biblical themes. In spite of its obvious initial attraction, however, no theory of this kind gets an easy ride from most moral theologians nowadays. One reason for this is undoubtedly the history of Christianity, which abounds in examples of apparently saintly (and therefore loving) people who simply got things very wrong in the ethical sphere on occasions, in spite of the fact that they obviously believed the contrary.[1] Critics of situation ethics thus say that we need more than a vague guarantee of love's guidance. And yet, in spite of the vagueness, one has a nagging feeling that love really ought to be enough. After all, even when the sophisticated arguments have been presented, is it still not the case that an all-embracing commandment really is found in the call to love God and neighbor? Perhaps the truth of the matter is that, in each situation, we really are instructed very precisely by love, but simply do not clearly hear what love is saying. Such an explanation would fit in with the 'already but not yet' theories of redemption. We are already saved, but the effects of corruption are not yet quite overcome. Whatever may or may not be the truth of all this, it appears that in our present plight we need some guidance from other sources (sources that we can actually hear) about what is and what is not good for humans. In other words, it seems that we need to turn to natural law thinking after all.

In this present period of revival and discovery in the sphere of virtue ethics, however, much has been said and written about an excessive concentration by moral theologians in earlier debates on acts rather than persons. In such an atmosphere it might be thought that any attempt to lay emphasis on the importance of natural law in the ongoing conversation among moral theologians is a retrograde step. After all, as Norbert Rigali once put it, "Even 'natural law' has frequently seemed to be ultimately no more than a law of doing or not doing when its 'primary precept' was formulated: *bonum est faciendum et prosequendum, et malum vitandum.*"[2] Rigali, however, goes on to point out that, if we adopt a more contemporary standpoint,

> natural law can be clearly seen as referring directly and primarily to human life, personal existence, as the unity and whole that it is rather than to human acts or even the sum-total of human acts. It can be seen as the law of being and becoming; for it is the "dynamically inviting possibility" confronting human freedom, "Become what thou art," in which "man's 'self' presents its demands to an 'ego' consciously realizing itself."[3]

Rigali, it will be noted, sees the foregoing description emerging in a contemporary view of natural law. Now, expressions such as "contemporary view," and "contemporary standpoint" tend to convey the impression that all—or at least the vast majority—of the participants in current debate about natural law would be content with such a description. That may well, of course, be the case, and such a distinct possibility—dare one say likelihood—could lead us easily to the conclusion that the sometimes fiery and acrimonious exchanges on the subject of natural law encountered in modern debate (especially within the ranks of Roman Catholicism) are much ado about very little indeed. Another possibility, however, is that the above description is open to somewhat different interpretations. It might, for instance, still be thought possible to maintain the static approach to natural law taken by the writers of numerous documents on sexual ethics emanating from the Vatican, and yet still agree with Rigali. Needless to say, someone with a thoroughly static approach might have more than a few difficulties dealing with such matters as "the dynamically inviting possibility confronting human freedom." Although the basic difference between the approach of the Catholic magisterium to natural law and that of so-called revisionist moral theologians is usually described in terms of static and dynamic approaches (the magisterium being said to adopt the former and the revisionists the latter), most commentators nowadays, it seems, admit that the magisterium is open to change and development in natural law when it deals with various matters beyond the sphere of sex and sexuality. Examples are seen in encyclicals devoted to questions of social ethics. In other words, in that sphere (and perhaps others), it adopts a dynamic approach to natural law (in the sense of an approach that is open to the possibility of change and development in ethics). It is most specifically in the sphere of sexual ethics that the magisterium is accused of adopting a static approach. Could it not be, then, that one who adopts such a mixed approach to natural law (static here, dynamic there) might accept dynamism and even notable differences in human becoming and yet still declare that "you will hamper the process of becoming who you are if you perform certain acts in any circumstances"? Most revisionists, of course, are reluctant to talk about acts being always wrong without taking all the morally relevant circumstances into account. They also point out that it is impossible for us to know here and now all the possible circumstances that could arise in the future.[4] This, however, leads us back into a debate about acts rather than persons. And yet, it seems to me that, unless we face up to the differences of approach to the subject of natural law in regard to acts, we cannot easily pass on to a discussion of natural law and the human person at a truly deep level.

THE ROOTS OF DISAGREEMENT

Natural law thinkers have run into several crises in recent centuries, and some of those crises, it would seem, have remained in existence largely because of a deep seated, though not always openly acknowledged, disagreement about precisely what natural law thinking should be. Sometimes, for instance, discussion about natural law takes place in such a way as to create the impression that, no matter how cleverly words are disguised, what is being proposed is that humans should simply conform to a given order. They should not interfere with nature. In response to such an approach, Cynthia Crysdale writes:

> To admonish people to conform to a given created or-
> der, when their constitution is such as to orient them to-
> ward the transforming of themselves and their worlds, is
> to stifle human flourishing and overlook the role of hu-
> man value and action in history. On the other hand, to
> promote unreflective intervention in the created world
> as if there were no conditions limiting such intervention
> is to sabotage, as we now realize, the very existence of
> the species itself.[5]

Most moral theologians who resort to a natural law approach to ethics, one imagines, would agree with Crysdale, but where do we go from here? Again most of us, it seems, would agree that, at a basic and very general level, natural law thinking involves reflecting upon what we are. Such reflection—which is largely a reflection upon our own and other people's experience of what it is to be human—leads us to see what tends to promote human flourishing and what tends to detract from it.[6] So far so good, but any attempt to specify what happens beyond that vague description will almost certainly lead to disagreement. At least insofar as the Catholic tradition is concerned—and probably much further afield—the most influential figure in regard to the formulation of what are widely regarded as the basic principles of natural law thinking is, of course, Thomas Aquinas. The most basic principle of practical reasoning identified by him is often described in terms of our awareness that we should do good and avoid evil. Columba Ryan describes this

initial principle as "the bent of the will to the good." This bent he further
describes as natural, "not in any sense contrasted with rational, for it is
not blindly impulsive, but natural in the sense of being an ineluctable
tendency of our human make-up."[7] Most people, one imagines, would
agree with Ryan's assertion that, at this most basic level, it makes sense
to say that nobody can be devoid of knowledge of natural law. He
considers it very doubtful that any human being (whatever he or she may
actually claim) could ever be devoid of this basic sense of right and
wrong. If such a person were to exist, he opines, that person would
forfeit all claims to being human. Indeed, he or she would be in the
moral order the equivalent of a lunatic or infant in the order of theoretic
truth—"and even lunatics and infants have at least the radical capacity
for, in the one case, acceptance of the rules of reasoning, and in the
other, discrimination between good and evil."[8]

Thus far, then, we have little reason for disagreement, but, as is well
known, Aquinas endeavored to put flesh on the bones of his theory by
moving on to what we might call a second level of first principles. Here
he discussed three classes of inclination to good: 1) the inclination to
good in accordance with the nature humans share with all substances; 2)
the inclination to good in accordance with the nature humans share with
animals; 3) the inclination to good according to the nature of reason,
which Aquinas saw as specifically human.[9] The first of these classes or
levels has traditionally been seen as a basis for the ethics of life and
death issues (such as suicide and self-defense), whilst the second has
been seen as a basis for sexual ethics. The third class refers to our
natural inclination to know the truth and to live in social groups.

In recent times various commentators have seen grounds for disagreement with Thomas in this threefold distinction. They accept that
there may be, for instance, some sort of analogous relationship between
canine[10] sexuality and that of humans, but they are more than a little
wary of pushing the analogy too far—a trap into which, they suspect,
those who exercise the Catholic magisterium may have fallen on more
than one occasion. Some at least are of the opinion that matters of life
and death, along with issues of sex and sexuality, are best dealt with in
Thomas's third category. Everything about human behavior, they
believe, comes under the heading of the human inclination to good
according to the nature of reason.

Even if we were to accept Aquinas's three categories, however, it
does not follow that we could immediately base prohibitions of suicide,
artificial contraception and lying on those general inclinations to good.
This point is made by Ryan, who points out that such prohibitions would

have to be based on principles of such a form as "some arrangements should be made for the preservation of life," "some for the organization of the family" and "some for the organization of society." He goes on to say that precisely what those arrangements are to be will result from further experience and enquiry.

> The natural law has different levels; basically it consists of those highest principles which are simply given and indemonstrable—whether as the rules of moral conduct or as the primary axioms of an entirely general moral awareness; but it comprises also anything which may be derived, by way of conclusion, from such axioms, and which may serve in turn as principles in reaching individual decisions as to conduct. In this way, the natural law is indefinitely extendable, as we come into fuller and fuller possession of what we see to be derivable from the original premises. But, and it is important to notice this, such development is not to be had without constant reference to a wider and more sensitive assessment of experience; nor is it to be had without danger of making mistakes, and without exacting enquiry.[11]

Ryan goes on, however, to suggest that, when the Catholic magisterium invokes natural law in its moral teaching, it does not do this by way of appeal to evidence so much as by way of affirmation. Guided by the Holy Spirit, he writes, the magisterium does not confine itself to what can be known only through divine revelation. It also affirms other matters which can, in principle, be known by human reason. What is thus taught is incumbent upon all humans if they would truly fulfil themselves as humans. The discovery of the why and the wherefore is left to theologians, philosophers, sociologists and statesmen.[12] Claims such as this are, of course, another source of disagreement among moral theologians and philosophers concerning the natural law. In a recent book, Frank Mobbs argues that natural law lies outside the object of the magisterium's authority and that, in teaching on it while claiming "divine authority to bind to belief," the magisterium has acted *ultra vires*. As a consequence, teachings of the magisterium on that subject are not to be counted as teachings of the Catholic Church. "When, like Paul VI in *Humanae vitae*, an organ of the magisterium is attempting to teach definitively, but not teach *revelata*, then it is teaching *ultra vires*: teaching in an area in which it has no divine authority." The reason why the magisterium can teach erroneously, he explains, is that Christ promised to keep it from error only when it is teaching what he taught. Mobbs does not, of course, argue that the magisterium should withdraw from all discussion of non-revealed morality. When it does so, however, it would do well, he feels, to imitate St. Paul: "I have no command of the Lord, but I give you my opinion..."(I Cor 7:25).[13] A very large percentage of Catholic moral theologians, one imagines, would be inclined to agree with Mobbs.[14] If the lack of a serious theological argument were not enough to lead one to discard the case for the claims of the magisterium, the impressive list of mistakes in moral teaching on its part over the centuries would be a serious obstacle to accepting that it has any special kind of authority in regard to natural law.[15] Moreover, it would seem that Gerard J. Hughes is right in thinking it unhealthy for us to expect authority to shield us from moral uncertainty. Hughes also points out that appeals to teaching authority and to tradition tend, in practice, to short-circuit the need for proper enquiry and argument that will withstand criticism in open debate. "These," he says, "are the normal human means to the attainment of truth, which we ignore at our peril."[16]

Such denial of certainty that could come from magisterial statements, however, leads us back to the uncertainty and, indeed, the possibility of mistakes referred to by Ryan. If we accept that ethics is to be based on a study of human nature in its natural environment, it follows, says Hughes, that, at root, ethics is an empirical study. We make discoveries about it in the same way that we make discoveries about physics, astronomy, psychology and medicine. Previously held conclusions in these sciences will be called into question by further information when it is acquired. A similar process occurs in ethics. In other words, our ethical conclusions are provisional. They are open to revision. "In short, it is implicit in a natural law approach to ethics that our view of what is ethical will change as our knowledge of human nature develops." Needless to say, Hughes points out that he is not suggesting we should expect wholesale revision to be an everyday experience. Major changes in scientific theory are rare. So too, in the sphere of ethics, we would not expect to find that our entire approach has been radically mistaken, "but we might well discover that in notable ways we had an inadequate grasp on how we ought to live."[17] Ryan, moreover, points out that we can be no surer of the results of our practical reasoning than we can be of those of our theoretic reasoning when we seek to reach speculative truths. We may encounter a good deal of confusion and disagreement when pursuing detailed conclusions within the body of natural law. We should not, however, be any more disconcerted at this, he says, than is the case when we are beset by perplexities in our pursuit of truth.[18]

Ryan also notes that, in spite of the weight of tradition claiming absolute immutability where natural law is concerned, Aquinas himself seems to have indicated the possibility of development. In a passage in the *Summa theologiae*, for instance, Thomas holds that, although the first principles are immutable, natural law may change in regard to subsequent precepts because of some special causes that hinder the observance of those precepts in some cases.[19] Ryan points out that, although Thomas has only individual cases of exception in mind, it could be asked whether his ideas could, in principle, be enlarged to cover wider "exceptions."[20]

Thus we are left, it would seem, with provisionality and revisability where moral norms based on natural law are concerned. Bruno Schüller addressed this issue some years ago. There are, he noted, elements of both change and continuity in human beings. A distinction must therefore be made between moral norms that are based on humanity's unchangeable metaphysical nature and norms that are grounded in humanity's changing historicity. "Precisely to the extent that man's being changes with time must the applicable ethical norm also change in every case." Schüller then provides some examples. Children, he notes, owe love, reverence and obedience to their parents until they come of age. At that point, the duty to obey ceases. He puts this in more abstract terms, saying that, the obligations of the growing person change because his or her being changes. Schüller then turns to the New Testament admonition that wives be subject in all things to their husbands. He sees this as presupposing a lack of "age" on the part of the wife. This, at least as far as most of the Western world is concerned, is no longer valid. The model for the relationship between husband and wife today is one of equal partners, not one involving subjection and one-sided superiority. He goes on to point out that there is no problem of relativism here. The spousal relationship has changed and so too, therefore, have the appropriate ethical precepts.[21]

In short, Schüller speaks of change in humans and change in human relationships. It is perhaps worth noting, however, that sometimes the change that occurs might be seen as resulting from a development in *knowledge* about what it is to be human which, *in turn*, helps bring about a change in relationships. Thus we might say that our knowledge of what it is to be a female human has changed in recent decades. We have reflected upon women's experiences of being women rather than upon a very limited and limiting definition of womanhood produced (apparently by a man or men) a long time ago within a patriarchal system. We can thus say that our knowledge of what it is to be human (most specifically in this case, but not exclusively, a female human) has developed in some ways. In reflecting upon our nature, therefore, we are reflecting upon knowledge of that nature which differs in significant ways from the knowledge possessed by those who went before us. That, however, is not all that has happened. Our appreciation of what it is to be a woman has had the effect of altering both our attitudes to relationships between men and women and the relationships themselves, the marital relationship being an obvious example. Thus we arrive at Schüller's second example.

This leads us on to the question how we can know if traditional moral precepts are valid today. Schüller suggests that the more general and abstract moral principles are, the more reason we have to consider their having timeless validity. We have more reason to consider timebound (and, therefore, to re-examine the demands of) prescriptions that are concrete and detailed. In view of the fact that all moral precepts are to be justified by the God-given being of humanity, he continues, it must in principle be possible, in the here and now, to perceive their continuing validity from that given reality.[22]

Without detracting in any way from these thoughts of Schüller, it might be apt to point out that we do not all readily behave in the way he suggests we should. In a recent work, Hughes notes that most moral theologians and philosophers are unwilling to stray far from the received wisdom of the church or society with which they identify. It has been said often, and with some justice, he notes, that the theoretical accounts supplied by such scholars are tailored to a defense of the status quo. "We tend to identify human fulfilment with what we have learnt is human fulfilment, for men, or women, Europeans, or Amazonian villagers."[23] Hughes makes no specific mention of the Catholic magisterium in this context. It could, however, be suggested that magisterial documents display a tendency to defend a particular interpretation of Aquinas's presentation of natural law—one which, perhaps, has come to be regarded as traditional. It could also be suggested that, whereas Schüller speaks of moral norms that are based on humanity's unchangeable metaphysical nature, the magisterium at times seems to speak of norms that are based on humanity's supposedly unchangeable *biological* nature. Surely a little reflection would suffice to reveal that this is a difficult position to defend even if we ignore the possibility of change through genetic engineering that is lurking in the background.

Although it would seem that, where natural law thinking is concerned, some degree of disagreement is almost inevitable, it would also seem that much of the tension in recent years within the ranks of Roman Catholicism on this subject has resulted from the kind of lack of openness in debate referred to by Hughes. More specifically, it seems to the present writer and, one imagines, numerous others, that clinging to what the magisterium apparently sees as the "traditional" way of approaching the subject of natural law hinders progress. Aquinas's threefold division of the human inclinations towards the good seems to be both unnecessary and misleading. We clearly do not share all aspects of our sexuality with all the other animals. Some of them, for instance, indulge in sexual activity at a certain time of year in order to produce offspring. Humans make love. The other species, moreover, do not share one and the same sexuality. There are numerous differences among them. Bearing such matters in mind, then, it seems to me that we should restrict ourselves to a reflection upon what is truly human.[24] In doing so, we may have to accept that Aquinas presumed a little too much knowledge about our inclinations to the good, perhaps most specifically in the sphere of sex and sexuality. Abandoning the threefold approach of Aquinas and the restricting interpretations of his thought that have perhaps prevailed in recent times in magisterial circles will not, of course, solve all our problems. Clearly, we find ourselves in a situation in which different groups of scholars approach natural law differently. This situation, however, is far from chaotic. As Hughes notes, the various theories are not *wholly* different. Most of them, moreover, call attention to aspects of us that truly exist and have to be taken into account. "They are often partial rather than false, needing to be thought through in relation to one another rather than simply rejected." Although we have not lost our bearings, he says, we need to learn how to live with complexity and a fair amount of uncertainty.[25]

Many may feel that two schools of thought in particular would do well to heed Hughes' words about thinking theories through in relation to one another. The schools concerned are one based largely on the thought of Germain Grisez, on the one hand, and those who have come to be known as proportionalists, on the other. Having sought to discover what fulfils human beings, Grisez concludes that there are certain basic human goods which can also be described as aspects of persons. He lists the following: life, health and safety, or bodily well-being; knowledge and aesthetic experience ("having a firm hold on reality, knowing the truth, seeing the world's beauty and enjoying it"); some degree of excellence in work and play ("skillful performance —'work'— done not for some other reason but for its own sake, and play, by which the self expands into the world"); self-integration ("the elements of the self are at peace with one another"); authenticity ("there is harmony among one's abilities, judgments, choices and behavior—one sees and chooses what is good and acts appropriately on its behalf"); interpersonal harmony: living in peace with other people, friendship, neighborliness; and harmony or peace with God ("the relationship of reverence and friendship which is religion").[26]

Members of the proportionalist school of thought also tend to be natural law thinkers. In other words, they too discover their values (human goods or values) by reflecting upon what it is to be human, upon what makes humans flourish. Not surprisingly, perhaps, some have been known to adopt similar lists of basic goods to those used by Grisez and other members of his school. The main point of disagreement between the two schools concerns Grisez's claim—based, one assumes, on natural law thinking—that, when a person is making moral choices, he or she should choose inclusivistically. In other words, the values in the options not chosen must be acknowledged. They must in no way be downgraded. Grisez lists eight "modes of responsibility," the application of which will ensure such inclusivistic choosing. These include not being deterred by laziness or lack of enthusiasm from acting for basic goods and not being moved by hostility to freely accept or opt for the impeding, damaging or destruction of any one of the goods.[27] The most controversial item in the list, however, and the main source of disagreement with the proportionalists, is the call never to act directly against one of the basic goods. "One should not be moved by a stronger desire for one instance of an intelligible good to act for it by choosing to destroy, damage or impede some other instance of an intelligible good, whether that same one or another." We find this mode of responsibility coming into play, says Grisez, when we are tempted to do evil so that good may result.[28]

By way of example, he cites the case of a neonate who has Down's Syndrome. Because, if the baby lives, it will cause many problems for its parents, they decide to let it starve to death, after first sedating it.[29] Other cases discussed by Grisez, however, are more debatable. In one of his books, for instance, he raises the issue of lying to a known murderer in an effort to save the life of the potential victim. Even if you were certain you were speaking to a murderer, he says, you would not be acting as love requires if you lied in an effort to save the life of the potential victim. He accepts that lying does not always violate a right of the person deceived. However, it is impossible to lie, he claims, "without choosing the self-alienation which, opposed as it is to self-integration and authenticity, is sufficient to make lying wrong." Aware that many will find it strange that deadly force could be justifiable in such circumstances, Grisez argues that "deadly force can be used to defend the innocent without choosing the death which, because it is opposed to life, makes intentional killing always wrong. Moreover, using deadly force does not impede community as lying does."[30]

Proportionalists are not convinced by such arguments. In general, they hold that the various basic goods (life, knowledge, etc.) are nonmoral goods, whilst death, pain, ignorance, etc. are nonmoral evils. Nonmoral evils, they say, should be kept to a minimum, but it is simply not possible in this life to eliminate them. Sometimes, in promoting human flourishing, we have to make choices between goods. To do otherwise would be to detract from human flourishing. This, however, says Grisez, amounts to deciding that one good outweighs the other, and that involves doing the impossible because the basic goods are incommensurable. For some years now, members of Grisez's school of thought have seen this apparent incommensurability as a major weak point in proportionalist theory.

The present author has pointed out in partial response that, sometimes at least, what appears to be a conflict between goods or values is not such. An example could be a case in which it is thought that a friendship will be lost if one tells the truth. Suppose Albert makes it clear to Richard that he will continue to be his "friend" only on condition that Richard does not disagree with his ideas regarding some matter (in the sphere of politics, science or whatever). There may be a great deal at stake if the truth to be told by Richard is of great importance to those who would hear or read it and if Richard is tempted to pretend that he believes something else merely in order to preserve his "friendship" with Albert. In such a case, however, friendship is not really on offer. A friend does not love me only on condition that I agree with his or her pet theory. Whether the matter is serious or trivial, only truth is at stake. There is no conflict with friendship.[31]

Although other similar examples could be given, the fact remains that, in some cases at least, it seems difficult to describe the dilemma confronting the moral agent as anything other than a conflict between what Grisez and many others would call basic human goods. The claim that such goods are incommensurable, however, is not the final word on the subject. Some years ago, Grisez and Boyle noted that consequentialists do not perceive this incommensurability. They perceive the goods according to a uniform standard, which, Grisez and Boyle's readers are led to conclude, does not exist.[32] If we were to resort to the language of mathematics, we might say that Grisez and Boyle appear to be saying that the basic goods have no common denominator. Mathematical terminology in such a context can, of course, be misleading, and most proportionalists, one imagines, would agree that value is not a quantifiable standard. One proportionalist who stated just that but also that he still believed comparisons are possible is Edward Vacek. If comparisons were not possible, he said, we would not be able to claim that human beings are more valuable than stones. Vacek also made the observation that humans are not mere computers which can handle data only if they are reducible to multiples of a common denominator.[33] The expression "common denominator," however, also has a figurative, non-mathematical usage which could help in our discussion of "a uniform standard." *The Oxford Dictionary* defines this meaning as a "common feature of members of a group." This meaning is important for our purposes. In fact, a denial of its applicability to the basic human goods would amount to an argument against Grisez's basic thesis that the goods are aspects of persons. In an unpublished paper, the British Passionist John Kearns has pointed out that the basic human goods do have a common denominator in that they are all *human* goods. This insight takes us back to the basic notion that what matters is *human* flourishing, not the flourishing of individual goods or values. As the present author has noted on more than one occasion, there is a danger of viewing the goods as separate entities like Platonic Ideas.[34] When united to Kearns' insight, a reminder that they are not such leads us back to the basic notion highlighted by Hughes that, at root, ethics is an empirical study. We need, therefore, to learn from human experience which kinds of choices best promote human flourishing in various types of situations. If we wish to talk in terms of human goods, it seems we must say that, inevitably, in different situations, right choosing will involve different mixtures or cocktails of goods. On rare occasions, as new knowledge about what it is to be human becomes available and/or as new insights result from the ongoing reflection upon human experience of what it is to be human, we may have to revise our ideas about which cocktails are the best in particular situations.

If we apply such thinking to Grisez's case of lying to a murderer, we will need to look at human experience of telling the truth and of telling untruths in such circumstances. It could be argued that such experience indicates that, at least in certain circumstances, telling an untruth would be the cause of action most likely to promote human flourishing or prevent further damage. Needless to say, Grisez accepts that telling the truth would not be the right course of action in the case under discussion, but, because he also believes that lying would not be right, he suggests other courses of action, such as maintaining silence and, under certain conditions, mental reservation. Experience may well indicate that, in certain circumstances, the employment of one of these other methods would be more likely to promote human flourishing than would lying. Experience may also show, however, and I think it does, that maintaining silence often amounts to telling the truth, because the person asking the question is easily able to guess why no reply is being made. Mental reservation, on the other hand, demands that the user be quickwitted. Moreover, it is not likely to work a second time with the same inquirer. As for Grisez's comments about deadly force, upon consulting experience, we find that it is more than difficult to see why Grisez should claim that its employment "does not impede community as lying does." The fact is, it would seem to me, that sometimes, regrettably, we find ourselves in situations in which human flourishing is best protected (or least impeded) either by telling an untruth or by resorting to force.

WIDENING THE SCOPE OF NATURAL LAW

One thing that we would do well to admit at this stage is the fact that, in spite of what was said in the introductory paragraphs of this chapter, most of what we have discussed so far has been limited to the usefulness of natural law thinking in determining the rightness or wrongness of acts. That would seem to have been necessary in order to prepare the ground for further discussion. Even if we were to consciously restrict our discussion to that sphere of interest, however, we would still be well advised to include some discussion of the human person. Indeed, Rigali notes that, "as Catholic tradition undergoes transformation through historical consciousness, the abstraction, human nature, has been increasingly replaced as the criterion of morality by the human person."[35] Here he refers more specifically to the work of Louis Janssens, who lists eight dimensions of the human person "integrally and adequately considered." Thus Janssens described the human person adequately considered "as essentially (1) a subject, (2) corporeal, (3) being-in-the-world, (4) directed towards other persons in interrelationship, (5) member of a social group, (6) oriented to God, (7) historical and (8) unique."[36]

Even if one were to claim that a concept such as the human person adequately considered is merely a tool which adds some precision to the concept of nature, one would be granting a great deal. However, it could also be claimed that a consideration of the human person adequately considered could lead beyond what many would consider to be the boundaries of natural law thinking. A concentration on human nature as such could lead us to limit our reflection only to what all humans have in common. A consideration of the person as unique, on the other hand, could go far beyond that. So, too, could a consideration of the fact that, as members of social groups, human persons are cultural and, to that extent at least, different.

What we most need to note in the shift from acts to persons, however, is the fact that it tends to put the spotlight on the moral goodness or badness of persons as the central issue in moral theology. Some years ago Josef Fuchs took up this theme. The rightness of our inner worldly behavior, he wrote, can be called *moral* rightness only in an analogous sense.

> For "moral" in its proper and formal sense refers only to persons and their free attitudes and decisions, but, because personal moral goodness contains concern for the well-being of the human world as its moral task, it urges "right" activity within this world; and only because of this relationship between personal goodness and material rightness, this rightness is also called moral rightness. Of themselves, material moral norms of behavior say only what belongs to right human behavior in the various areas of human life; but they add an appeal to the moral goodness of the person to incarnate itself in this world of space and time only through behavior which has been judged as right. Only the added appeal to moral goodness is therefore, in this formal sense, directly moral, and not the judgment on innerworldly activity.[37]

Inevitably, in what follows there will still be some reference to our attempts to reach awareness of the objective rightness or wrongness of acts because it is in striving to reach such awareness and to do what they see to be right that human persons express their goodness and incarnate it, as Fuchs might put it, "in this world of space and time." Throughout, however, we shall be considering chiefly the development of truly human life, truly human persons and truly human relationships. As Rigali points out, even if our moral theology is only mediately and secondarily (not immediately or directly) concerned with deliberate acts or laws of human behavior, it still has to be involved in the discussion of human acts. We will discover, however, adds Rigali, that such a moral theology has both more and less to say about acts than was the case with the classical worldview. It has more to say in the sense that the meaning of an act will be viewed explicitly within the context of a personal existence which is located in history. It has less to say in the sense that, if it is seen as merely one limited expression of the human life, a human act often requires a good deal less attention than moral theologians have been wont to give it.

> The frequently excessive and even obsessive concern with acts of the classical worldview can be seen, for example, in the notion: "All directly voluntary sexual pleasure is mortally sinful outside of matrimony," "even if the pleasure be ever so brief and insignificant." Such a doctrine can be conceived only through a total failure to recognize that *vita humana*, not *actus humanus*, is the primary locus of the *humanum* and, therefore, of morality.
>
> *Vita humana* (*vita personalis, vita moralis*) is a reality far greater than acts or the sum-total of acts. *Vita humana* is, for example, a vocation, a profession, a marriage, the "causes" to which one commits oneself, the organizations to which one belongs, a "life-style" and much more. Above all, *vita humana* is a network of personal relationships and a developmental process involving many different stages of personal growth. All this and more is the *vita humana* that must be the focal point of the new moral theology of the future.[38]

In pursuing this matter further, however, it would seem necessary to clarify a basic point. More than once in this chapter I have talked about the need to spell out, confront and compare various interpretations of natural law. It may be thought by some, however, that in highlighting the importance of such matters as culture and personal uniqueness I (and, perhaps, Rigali and others to whom I have referred) have abandoned discussion of natural law altogether. In response, a point worth noting immediately is that several scholars in recent years have pointed out that the term "natural law" is an inadequate one. Indeed, however suitable it may have been considered by philosophers and jurists in ancient times, there is a case for saying that it was already inadequate in some ways when Aquinas wrote on the subject. Certainly, what we are discussing is not law in any of our usual senses of the word. What we are concerned with when we use the term "natural law" is getting in touch with wisdom and applying it in the moral sphere. What, then, of "natural" and "nature"? *The Oxford Dictionary* lists several meanings for "natural," including "of or concerned with or according to nature," "provided or produced by nature," and "conforming to ordinary course of nature." For "nature," among other definitions, we find "phenomena of the physical world as a whole," "physical power causing these," "thing's essential qualities," and "person's or animal's innate character." Often in the past, it seems, natural law thinking has concerned itself with the "essential qualities of a thing" definition of nature. The "thing" being considered, however, has not been the individual human. There has been a tendency to concentrate on what all humans have in common. In view of the fact that we have an enormous amount in common, such a process has more than a little importance. It is also important to bear in mind, however, that there are various aspects of our being that we do not have in common with all other humans. There is a good deal, for example, that extraverts do not have in common with introverts, and vice versa.[39] Noting the importance of this distinction, which has been highlighted in recent times among proponents of Jungian psychology, some people have noted that certain writers of books in the sphere of spirituality are (or were) introverts. In some cases, advice given and observations made by some of those writers may ring true for other introverts, but not for extraverts. If this proves to be the case, should not writers on spirituality and teachers in that sphere bear in mind the fact that there are various valid personality types (as, I believe, many now do), and not assume that everything that has proven to be of value to them will be of value to all other human beings? Clearly this is the case. It would seem, then, that an increase in knowledge about what it is to be human (in this case, resulting from advances in the field of psychology) can reveal differences among human beings. These differences must be taken into account in natural law thinking. What promotes human flourishing in one person will not necessarily have the same effect in others. Some acknowledgement of this was perhaps given in the past in regard to the differences between men and women, although many may now feel that some of the differences acknowledged were not real ones, and that not all of the real ones can yet be identified. Advances in psychology, however, would seem to indicate that, in the process of acknowledging that there are significant differences among human beings, we should be prepared to acknowledge differences other than those that exist between the sexes.

Having raised the subject of sex and sexuality, however, it is worth noting at this point that something analogous to what we have said in regard to personality types could, perhaps, be suggested in regard to types of sexuality. It may be further suggested that, in discussing types of sexuality, we need not limit ourselves to a consideration of sexual orientation. Having said this, however, it is also worth noting that we should beware of the temptation to conclude too much from the mere fact that certain types of sexuality exist—even if they have a genetic basis, and are, in that sense, natural. In order to spell things out a little, we might consider the possibility that tendencies to pedophilia have a genetic source or arise in some other way that allows us to consider them as 'natural' in some sense. Clearly, however, in determining the rightness or wrongness of sexual activity performed by pedophiles, one needs to take into account not only their sexual tendencies, but also the effects of their sexual activity upon the children involved. Human experience would seem to indicate that such effects can be disastrous. Moreover, when considering the significance of the fact that an aspect of a person's sexuality may be caused genetically or be in some other sense 'natural,' we should bear in mind that something similar may prove to be the case in regard to tendencies to violence and other kinds of behavior which we normally label as 'criminal.' In view of the fact that a certain amount has been written in recent times about the possibility of homosexual tendencies having a genetic basis, this last remark could, perhaps, be construed as an argument against homosexual activity. It is certainly not intended as such. It does, however, serve to show that a genetic argument, on its own, does not suffice to prove the acceptability or otherwise of homosexual behavior. What needs to be determined in this case is whether or not human experience shows that homosexual activity can contribute to human flourishing. As in the case of hetero-sexual activity, of course, we also need to determine the circumstances in which such flourishing can or cannot occur. Again experience can be invoked to assess, for example, the importance of committed relation-ships. In short, it would seem that we still need to reflect a great deal upon human experience in the sphere of sex and sexuality. We have a long history of jumping to conclusions where such matters are concerned. It would be a pity to merely add to that list of hastily reached conclusions.

Although perhaps not as basic as the matters just discussed, cultural factors, as we have already noted, should also be taken into account when we are trying to determine what tends and does not tend to promote human flourishing in given circumstances. Also already noted, but more basic, is the question of the uniqueness of each and every individual human person. Here we enter into a sphere of controversy. Many may feel an almost instinctive urge to resist any attempt to suggest that what is right for most people is wrong for a certain individual. The urge to resist may, moreover, be even stronger when it comes to suggestions that what is wrong for most people may be right for a certain person because he or she is unique is some way. Nevertheless, the possibility exists. At a deeper level, however, we need to bear in mind that there is a positive side to the developmental process of human life, not just a series of decisions and choices concerning what is and what is not considered to be permissible. This takes us back to Rigali's observation about the meaning of an act being viewed within the context of a personal existence located in history. There is, and indeed has to be, a certain creativity with regard to vocation, life-style, relationships as well as all the other matters mentioned in the above quotation from Rigali concerning human life, and, of course, much more besides. There has to be uniqueness here, and any theory of natural law that failed to recognize, and indeed to emphasize the importance of, such uniqueness could produce only a deformed version of the wisdom that we seek. In a later work, Rigali echoes Michael Himes[40] in seeing the human person, first and foremost as "a creative participant in history." The mature moral life, therefore, is "to be understood in images of creation, creative process, and the person as creator." Further on he writes:

> Morality understood as creation not only brings together personal and social morality; it unites them both to environmental morality. What is to be created is the self and society and the world they will inhabit. What is to be created is, moreover, interpersonal relations, family, community and culture in all its dimensions. In its breadth, the secular metaphor of creation reflects something of its sacred counterpart. And in reflecting its sacred counterpart, morality understood as creation is joined to religion: for the mature Christian, morality is being united with God in the ever ongoing work of creation in search of the Kingdom of God.[41]

The real source of human personal goodness is, of course, love, that love of God which is poured into our hearts through the Holy Spirit (Rom 5:5), who is love. Everything we do should be done in love (I Cor 16:14). Love (*agape*) is the activity of the Holy Spirit in the core of our personalities. That love can never be sterile. As Häring puts it, "Belief in the Holy Spirit whom Jesus Christ has sent us, the Spirit who renews the hearts of men and the face of the earth, means creative and liberating participation in ongoing history."[42] Moved by love, then, the natural law thinker strives to incarnate goodness "in this world of space and time only through behavior which has been judged as right," and he or she arrives at that judgment about rightness after appropriate reflection within the community upon human experience of being human. This is part of "the ever ongoing work of creation in search of the Kingdom of God." Human reason is, of course, corrupt, but not totally so. It is also graced, because the love of God has been given to us. There will be struggles and there will be mistakes because we are not yet complete, but the fact remains that there is an "already" as well as a "not yet." Nevertheless, the Protestant wariness with which we began this chapter is not totally to be dismissed. "It is only at the End that there will be fulfilment. Recognising this ensures that we are temperate in our expectations and have the humility to acknowledge that ultimately wholeness is the gift of God, not the achievement of humanity."[43]

Accepting that point, let us turn again to Rigali, who, in an essay to which we have not thus far referred, speaks of the historical consciousness of morality.

> Centered on human persons in history, historically conscious moral theology understands humanness and morality accordingly. The norm of morality is not human nature but the historical human person, to whom grace and virtue are not adventitious but intrinsic. The heart of morality, consequently, is the self-realization of the human person in history through virtue (vice), character, faith, world-view, community, friendship, commitment, political involvement, relationships, etc. as well as through the intellectual-volitional-affective activity and outward action that constitute the act of deliberate will. In a word, the realm of morality is concrete human persons as self-actualized in history.[44]

This sums up succinctly much of what I have tried to say in this chapter. I am sure, however, (especially bearing in mind what he says about love in other writings), that Rigali will have no objections to my adding a rider to his comments about self-actualization in the light of what was said above concerning the place of *agape* in the moral equation. Without the gift of love, no truly creative self-actualization can take place. Moral goodness is an impossibility if love is absent. Without love no amount of natural law thinking will be truly productive.

NOTES

1. An example referred to in recent years by more than one moral theologian is that of St. Bernard of Clairvaux, who preached the Second Crusade. In a letter to the English he declared that, in return for taking up arms in God's cause, they would be rewarded with pardon of their sins and everlasting glory (Epist. 391). *The Letters of Saint Bernard of Clairvaux* (London: Burns & Oates, 1953), 460–3.

2. Norbert Rigali, S.J., "Christ and Morality," *Concilium* 110 (1978), 15.

3. *Ibid.* His citations are apparently from Louis Monden, *Sin, Liberty and Law*, Joseph Donceel, S.J., trans. (New York: Sheed and Ward, 1965), 31.

4. Pope John Paul II wrote that we should reject the thesis that it is impossible for us to classify as morally evil according to its object the deliberate choosing of certain types of behavior or certain specific acts without taking into consideration the intention of the agent taking the choice and all of the foreseeable consequences of the act for everybody concerned. (*Veritatis Splendor* [Vatican City: Libreria Editrice Vaticana, 1993], § 79) This thesis he attributed to teleological and proportionalist theories. The term 'object' here seems to be understood as the action devoid of all circumstances and intention. Several authors have pointed out, however, that, without knowledge of relevant circumstances and intentions, we cannot accurately describe an action. Cutting someone with a knife, for example, could be a murderous act, an act of self-defense, part of a surgical operation, and any one of many other possibilities. Thus, responding to the Pope, Richard McCormick said he believed all proportionalists would agree that the object renders some acts intrinsically evil, "if the object is broadly understood as including all the morally relevant circumstances." ("Killing the Patient," *The Tablet* 247 [1993], 1411, emphasis his). For a fuller discussion of this point, see Bernard Hoose, "Circumstances, Intentions and Intrinsically Evil Acts," in Joseph A. Selling and Jan Jans, eds., *The Splendor of Accuracy: An Examination of the Assertions made by Veritatis Splendor* (Grand Rapids: William B. Eerdmans Publishing Co., 1995), 136–52.

5. Cynthia S.W. Crysdale, "Revisioning Natural Law: From the Classicist Paradigm to Emergent Probability," *Theological Studies* 56 (1995), 480.

6. Gerry Hughes, "Natural Law Ethics and Moral Theology," *The Month* (March 1987), 100, puts it thus: "The central feature of the natural law tradition is a conviction that the way in which we should live our lives is to be discovered by coming to understand the kind of beings which we are, and the ways in which we interact with our environment."

7. Columba Ryan, "The Traditional Concept of Natural Law: An Interpretation," in Ronald P. Hamel and Kenneth R. Himes, eds., *Introduction to Christian Ethics: A Reader* (New York: Paulist Press, 1989), 420.

8. *Ibid.*, 421.

9. Thomas Aquinas, *S.T.*, I–II, q. 94, a. 2. Ryan classifies the three sets of goods as "the good of individual survival, biological good, and the good of human communication." (*Ibid.*)

10. Feline, equine, murine, or whatever.

11. Ryan, "The Traditional Concept of Natural Law," 422.

12. *Ibid.*, 425. Ryan uses the word 'Church' where I have employed 'magisterium.'

13. Frank Mobbs, *Beyond Its Authority: The Magisterium and Matters of Natural Law* (Alexandria, NSW, Australia: E. J. Dwyer, 1997), especially 2–3, 297, and 301.

14. There are, of course, those who question the extent of the magisterium's authority even where *revelata* are concerned. Discussion of such matters is, however, beyond the scope of this chapter.

15. Various examples of errors can be found in Bernard Hoose, *Received Wisdom: Reviewing the Role of Tradition in Christian Ethics* (London: Geoffrey Chapman, 1994) and "Circumstances, Intentions and Intrinsically Evil Acts."

16. Hughes, "Natural Law Ethics and Moral Theology," 102.

17. *Ibid.*, 100–101.

18. Ryan, "The Traditional Concept of Natural Law," 422–23.

19. *S.T.*, I–II, q. 94, a. 5. In an endnote, Ryan refers to an article in which Michael B. Crowe points to several passages in which Aquinas talks of human nature itself as being subject to change and of natural law being variable as a consequence. ("The Traditional Concept of Natural Law," 427, n. 36.) The article in question is "Human Nature—Immutable or Mutable," *The Irish Theological Quarterly* 30 (1963), 204.

20. Ryan, "The Traditional Concept of Natural Law," 424.

21. Bruno Schüller, "Can Moral Theology Ignore Natural Law?" in Hamel and Himes, eds., *Introduction to Christian Ethics*, 411.

22. *Ibid.*

23. Gerard J. Hughes, "Natural Law," in B. Hoose, ed., *Christian Ethics: An Introduction* (London: Geoffrey Chapman, 1998), 55–56.

24. This does not, of course, exclude attempts to understand the nature of other creatures which might aid us in respecting them.

25. Hughes, "Natural Law Ethics and Moral Theology," 102.

26. Germain Grisez and Russell Shaw, *Fulfillment in Christ: A Summary of Christian Moral Principles* (Notre Dame, IN: University of Notre Dame Press, 1991), 55. In another work the possibility of a non theistic approach appears to be accepted in reference to the final good in the list, which is there described as peace with God or the gods, or some non-theistic but more than human source of meaning and value. See Germain Grisez, John Finnis and Joseph Boyle, "Practical Principles, Moral Truth and Ultimate Ends," *The American Journal of Jurisprudence* 32 (1987), 107f.

27. *Ibid.*, 86–93.

28. *Ibid.*, 93.

29. *Ibid.*

30. Germain Grisez, *The Way of the Lord Jesus: Vol. II: Living a Christian Life* (Quincy, IL: Franciscan Press, 1992), 406–407.

31. For a fuller discussion see Hoose, *Received Wisdom?*, 168ff.

32. Germain Grisez and Joseph Boyle, *Life and Death with Liberty and Justice* (Notre Dame, IN: University of Notre Dame Press, 1979), 354.

33. Edward Vacek, "Proportionalism: One View of the Debate," *Theological Studies* 46 (1985), 304.

34. Hoose, "Proportionalists, Deontologists and the Human Good," *The Heythrop Journal* 33 (1992), 180, and *Received Wisdom?*, 167–68. Grisez says that he does not claim that the goods have an independent existence, "as if they were Platonic Ideas." (G. Grisez and R. Shaw, *Beyond the New Morality* [London: University of Notre Dame Press, 1974], 71). It has appeared to me, however, that members of both schools, including, perhaps, the present writer, have, at times, displayed a tendency to treat them as such.

35. Rigali, "Reimaging Morality: A Matter of Metaphors," *The Heythrop Journal* 35 (1994), 2.

36. *Ibid.* Janssens' original work is to be found in "Artificial Insemination: Ethical Considerations," *Louvain Studies* 8 (1980), 3–29.

37. Josef Fuchs, "Moral Truths—Truths of Salvation?" in *id.*, *Christian Ethics in a Secular Arena* (Washington, DC: Georgetown University Press, 1984), 52.

38. Rigali, "Christ and Morality," 17–18. The citations are from Heribert Jone, *Moral Theology* (Westminster, MD: The Newman Bookshop, 1956), 146.

39. Matters are further complicated by the fact that some people are extreme extraverts or introverts, some are slightly extravert (or introvert) and many are found at various points on the 'scale' in between. Extraversion and introversion are not, of course, the only factors taken into account by psychologists who work with the notion of personality types.

40. See Michael J. Himes, "The Human Person in Contemporary Theology: From Human Nature to Authentic Subjectivity," in R.P. Hamel and K.R. Himes, eds., *Introduction to Christian Ethics*, 59.

41. Rigali, "Reimaging Morality: A Matter of Metaphors," 11–12.

42. Bernard Häring, *Free and Faithful in Christ: Volume Two: The Truth Will Make You Light to the World* (Slough: St. Paul Publications, 1979), 432.

43. Michael Adie, *Held Together: An Exploration of Coherence* (London: Darton, Longman and Todd, 1997), 12.

44. Rigali, "The Uniqueness and Distinctiveness of Christian Morality and Ethics," in Charles E. Curran, *Moral Theology: Challenges for the Future* (New York: Paulist Press, 1990), 85.

METHOD AND THE CATHOLIC MORAL TRADITION

Purity of Heart and the Christian Moral Life

Mark O'Keefe, O.S.B.

More than twenty years ago, in an article entitled "The Fragmented Christian Life," Norbert Rigali argued that the authentic renewal of moral theology required reconceiving the Christian moral life and therefore also reconceiving the science that studies it.[1] The Christian life had come to be understood as consisting in two separate parts: on the one hand, the moral life with its concern for the demands of the natural law and the "life of the commandments" and, on the other, the spiritual life with its concern for "striving for perfection." Moral theology studied the former and ascetical theology studied the latter; but just as the separation in the Christian life must be overcome, so too for the separation of the two disciplines:

> Like Humpty Dumpty, the Christian life has to be put together again. The rediscovery of the unity of the Christian life is the great and urgent task that faces both moral and spiritual theology today.[2]

It can be argued that this theme has persisted throughout Rigali's writings, informing particularly his frequent focus on the question of the specificity of Christian morality.[3]

In the present article, I join many other contemporary moral theologians in taking up Rigali's challenge, specifically by reclaiming the patristic and monastic theme of "purity of heart" (*puritas cordis*) as relevant to and revelatory of the shape and direction of the Christian moral life. Although it is a theme little discussed today outside of monastic circles, the reality expressed by "purity of heart" is at the very core of the traditional understanding of the Christian spiritual path. Today, it finds parallels in contemporary moral and spiritual discussions of desire, asceticism, conversion, and love. After an examination of *puritas cordis* and its affinity to the vision and goals of a Thomistic moral and spiritual theology, I will briefly examine some parallel contemporary themes in order to shed light on the concept of purity of heart. By doing so, I hope to show that today's reflections have been, in some ways, anticipated by the patristic and monastic theologians.

I begin, then, by simply presupposing the universal call to holiness announced by the Second Vatican Council and the unity of the Christian life as a "striving for perfection" asserted by Rigali more than twenty years ago. Christians are called to be holy—and nothing less. They are invited into a life of prayer and of self-giving love for God and for other persons. It is my purpose in this article to show that the attainment of moral goodness as the essential foundation of the life of holiness requires a "purified" heart. This purity of heart consists in desires and subsequent choices that are ordered, integrated, or transformed in the process (conversion) of striving (asceticism), with the help of grace, to attain a truly selfless (kenotic) love after the model of Jesus. The purified heart, then, entails the transformation of the Christian's character, the shaping of his or her moral agency. It is foundational for a life conformed to God in love and in deep and sustained prayer to which every Christian is called.

"BLESSED ARE THE PURE OF HEART"

In the introduction to a book on the monastic approach to contemplation, Cistercian Michael Casey offers a summary statement of the meaning and central place of purity of heart in the monastic spiritual tradition. He summarizes well the patristic-monastic reflections on the topic and introduces a number of themes that will be discussed below:

> The key idea that is common to these teachers [Augustine, Cassian, Benedict, Gregory, and Bernard] is that contemplation is possible only for those who have *puritas cordis*: an undivided heart. The act of communion with God is one which engages the whole person and calls upon all the interior energies. It can occur only when these energies are working together, when inner disharmony has been overcome and unity reigns within. Such a state is not achieved quickly but only by the grace of God and the labor of decades. It involves a radical conversion of life and persevering will to live in accordance with the Gospel. Spiritual growth is thus

seen as a matter of progressively purifying the personal center of will and knowledge, eliminating inner division and becoming more intent on seeking the one thing necessary.[4]

The concept of "purity of heart" in the Christian spiritual tradition is rooted in the earliest monastic and patristic sources. *Apatheia*, or "purity of heart" (*puritas cordis*) as it came to be called in the Latin West, is a concept at once both spiritual and moral. As Casey suggests, it consists of a calming or ordering of one's affective life, seen as essential to any serious growth in the life of deep prayer. This "ordering" is both formed by and manifested through the life of overcoming sin and vice, growing in virtue, and being shaped by love. For patristic and monastic theologians, purity of heart was the necessary foundation for contemplation as well as for a truly free and selfless loving. Although later spiritual theologians did not use the term *puritas cordis*, the reality to which it points is at the heart of any authentic growth in the Christian spiritual life.

Clement of Alexandria was the first Christian theologian to use the Stoic term *apatheia* to speak of a goal of the Christian life. Showing the influence of some of the Stoic ideal of passionlessness, Clement understood *apatheia* to be "the full possession, under the influence of divine contemplation, of the affective faculties, so that disordered passions are resolved in a state of abiding calm."[5] *Apatheia*, then, was closely tied to the life of contemplation as a necessary foundation. If a life of contemplation was to be attained, then the Christian's affective life and the choices made in regard to his or her affections would have to be duly ordered.

Origen, while using the term *apatheia* much less than Clement, was the first theologian to concern himself with identifying successive stages in the maturing Christian life.[6] He spoke both of a three stage development (which would eventually be called the Three Ways of purgation, illumination, and union) and of a two stage development involving *praktikos* and *theôria*—that is, what would later be called the "active" life of overcoming sin and growing in virtue and the "contemplative" life. Origen, then, played an important role in identifying the developing pattern of ascetical preparation for a contemplative or properly mystical life. The attainment of purity of heart is at the center of this "ascetical" foundation for a life of deepening communion with God and of a selfless love of other people. Again, while later spiritual theologians would not always use the language of "purity of heart," it is clear that the reality it signifies has always been seen as essential to authentic growth in the Christian life.

Evagrius Ponticus took from Clement the theme of *apatheia* and from Origen the identification of stages in the Christian life. For Evagrius, *apatheia* was the "key-stone" of the ascetical preparation for attaining the goal of Christian perfection. While dependent on Clement's reflections on *apatheia*, Evagrius gave the concept a more human character and a more biblical foundation (related to the "fear of the Lord").[7] For him, *apatheia* was a "relatively permanent state of calm" that arises "from the full and harmonious integration of the emotional life, under the influence of love."[8] *Apatheia*, then, is not a matter of attempting to level or flatten human emotion for a complete indifference toward others (as the Stoic ideal or the English derivative "apathy" would imply). Rather, *apatheia* is a state in which God and other people can be truly and freely loved because the agent is free of the disintegration of the emotional life that makes truly generous, other-regarding love impossible. As John Eudes Bamberger summarizes:

> For Evagrius it is unthinkable that a man should aspire to be united with God in pure prayer without first cleansing his heart fully. Only when he has attained *apatheia*, a state of abiding calm deriving from full harmony of the passions, can he speak of perfect charity. Only when he has perfect charity can he hope to know God.[9]

It was John Cassian who brought the concept of *apatheia* from the East to the heart of Western monasticism as "purity of heart." A Western monk who traveled and studied extensively in the East, Cassian translated the concept of *apatheia* with the Latin words *puritas cordis*. In changing the term, he may have been quietly distancing himself from Origen and Evagrius, some of whose works had become suspect. More positively, Cassian was establishing the concept more firmly in the Gospel: "Blessed are the pure in heart, for they shall see God" (Mt 5:8). The change in terminology also further removed the concept from the Stoic sense of passionlessness.

For Cassian, purity of heart is an intermediate or proximate goal. It involves a "personal integration, a single-heartedness, due to a lack of inner division."[10] The growing attainment of this state is the necessary foundation for attaining one's true end: participation in the reign of God.[11] Negatively, purity of heart involves the avoidance of vice and the

systematic uprooting of sin; positively, it is related to, or even identical
with, love. For Cassian and the subsequent monastic tradition, a "purified" heart is not *less* able to love; in fact, it is the only heart that can
truly and freely love without selfishness. As Cassian says: "Purity of
heart is acquired by the flowering of the virtues, and the perfection of
apostolic charity is possessed by means of purity of heart."[12] It is, then,
the effort to attain purity of heart and charity that gives meaning to all
moral effort. This can be said to summarize Cassian's "moral theology."[13]

Saint Benedict secured a central place for the theme of purity of
heart in Western monastic spirituality by encouraging the regular reading of Cassian's work. As it developed in Benedictine spirituality, purity
of heart takes on a meaning similar to "detachment" in the thought of
John of the Cross or of "indifference" in the work of Ignatius Loyola.
All of these terms can be (and have been) misunderstood to encourage a
Stoic-like passionlessness and the suppression of all desire and of "particular loves." Instead, properly understood, they point to the essential
integration of desire and choice in any maturing Christian life that is
growing both in virtue and in a sustained and deep life of prayer. In
short, purity of heart, detachment, or indifference involve the development of a greater and deeper freedom as the properly moral preparation
for the mature Christian life.[14]

"PURITY OF HEART IS TO WILL ONE THING"

Clifford Williams has largely captured the meaning of purity of heart in
a spiritual reflection entitled *Singleness of Heart: Restoring the Divided
Soul*.[15] Throughout, Williams shows the influence of the collection of
"edifying addresses" of Søren Kierkegaard entitled *Purity of Heart is to
Will One Thing*.[16] In fact, the patristic and monastic reflections on purity
of heart are indeed concerned with a "singleness" of heart in which all
desires are not suppressed, but ordered into the Christian's deepest desire and will for God. The traditional meaning of purity of heart can be
said to involve "willing one thing."

To speak of a moral life directing the will to the "one thing necessary" suggests immediately an affinity with the moral life as conceived
by Thomas Aquinas. For him, the Christian moral life is a life directed
to the attainment of communion with God, an ultimate end that is attained by ordering all choices and dispositions, empowered by charity,

to this one goal. As Servais Pinckaers has recently summarized the moral theology of St. Thomas: "This is the main theme of all his moral treatises: the ultimate end—and corresponding intentionality—which draws human acts together and forms them into a dynamic unity ordered to a single end."[17]

In the course of Pinckaer's analysis of Thomistic moral theology, he contrasts two different interpretations of freedom. "Freedom of indifference" is a post-Thomistic view of freedom that sees natural inclinations and affections as a hindrance to the authentic exercise of freedom. (In the present context, we can see how the concept of *apatheia* or *puritas cordis* could be mistakenly interpreted in this light.) On the other hand, as Pinckaers shows, for St. Thomas, authentic freedom is a "freedom for excellence" that takes up the natural inclinations in the positive pursuit of God. Aquinas analyzed the range of the human affective life and showed how the various natural inclinations or affections are meant, under the guidance of the virtues, to serve the positive development of the Christian moral life.[18] Authentic freedom in living the Christian moral life directed to God is served by properly ordered desires.

A contemporary moral theology, therefore, that points Christians in the direction of purity of heart would find ample affinity to the moral theology of St. Thomas. Purity of heart, properly understood, is precisely the attainment of a broadly and deeply virtuous life which does not ignore or suppress our natural inclinations and affections but orders them to the free pursuit of our truest end: communion with God and with other persons in God. The growing attainment of purity of heart, then, can be seen as the center of a Thomistic view of the Christian moral life. To speak of purity of heart, in other words, is to speak with St. Thomas, of the person of virtue whose entire life is empowered, directed, and shaped by love.

THE ORDERING OF LOVES AND OF DESIRE

Diogenes Allen has defined purity of heart as "the acquired ability to gather more and more of our scattered desires into focus as we come more and more to desire the good that God seeks to give us...."[19] As we have said, authentic purity of heart does not involve the suppression of desire but rather the proper ordering of desire. A renewed appreciation of desire and affective elements of the Christian life have become a recent focus of both moral and spiritual theologians—for example: a work entitled *Virtuous Passions: The Formation of Christian Character*[20] by moral theologian G. Simon Harak as well as *Befriending Our Desires*[21] and *Jesus, The Liberator of Desire*[22] by spiritual theologians Philip Sheldrake and Sebastian Moore, respectively. A brief examination of the contemporary theological discussions of desire will shed further light on the concept of purity of heart and its relevance for contemporary moral theology.

Of course, an appreciation of the important role that desire plays in the moral and spiritual life is not a modern discovery. Desire and love were a frequent topic of Augustine's reflections. For Augustine, the ordering of loves is the heart of the moral preparation for the contemplative life. This ordering consisted precisely in the purification of the affections.[23] Of course, disordered desire, on the other hand, would lead a person to turn away from God and toward a created good (*aversio a Deo per conversionem ad creaturas*)—Augustine's definition of sin.

Twelfth century theologians, immersed in the writings of Augustine and in line with the late medieval fascination with the topic of love, also focused a good deal of attention on the "ordering of loves" (*ordinatio caritatis*). The mystics and theologians of the twelfth century were neither inherently suspicious of desire itself ("loves," broadly considered) nor naive about the effects of sin precisely as it impacted our natural inclinations. Still, their attention was focused less on avoiding passions than on harnessing them to serve their most desired end.[24] They sought to encourage the energizing and harmonizing of the natural human affections toward the attainment of the love and enjoyment of God.[25] As McGinn summarizes: "Ordered love, then, means not that we have to choose *between* God and creatures, or to reject totally the body and the material world, but rather that we need to put all our affections and desires in the proper relation."[26]

Despite this earlier appreciation of the place of ordered desire, the Christian tradition has also manifested, at various times, a deep suspicion of desire, at least in the moral life. At times, denial of desire and of the body and its "urges" seemed to be the ideal. Precisely in the effort to eradicate any dualistic distortions of the past that disparaged all affective responses, contemporary moral and spiritual theologians have been attempting to reclaim the proper role of affections in the Christian life. Different theologians use different terms with different nuances of meanings—desires, passions, affections, loves—but, for our purposes, the word "desire" can be used to capture the experience of attraction that precedes choice and action. In a more holistic age, contemporary theologians are quick to agree that the goal of the moral and spiritual life must not be the attempt to deny or suppress desire, as if it was evil in itself.

At the same time, of course, experience tells us that sin makes it necessary to integrate "disordered" affections in order to grow both morally and spiritually. Both the experience and theology of original sin point to the need to order desires to their proper end. However "disordered concupiscence" is to be understood, it is clear that human beings are born with a tendency to allow desires to become disordered, leading to choices that cannot be integrated with a life directed towards relationship with God. Therefore, even a more positive appreciation of desire cannot blind us to the task—and even the struggle (*askesis*)—involved in the right ordering of our desires.

Contemporary theologians use a variety of terms to speak of the task of re-orienting desire. Just a brief mention of a few terms will indicate the richness of the discussion. To speak of "purifying" or "schooling" desire suggests that desire made unruly or confused by sin must be tamed, formed, or educated. "Ordering" or "integrating" desire suggests that it need not so much to be controlled or suppressed, but rather to be put at the service of some greater pursuit or some higher value.[27] "Transforming" or "transfiguring" desire suggests, more, that desire is to be re-constituted by or "taken up" into some higher or greater value.[28] Sebastian Moore has suggested that authentic desire must be "liberated"—not a liberation *from* desire but the liberation *of* desire. It is in this sense that Moore speaks of Jesus as the liberator of our deepest and most authentic desire.[29]

Promising in its breadth of meaning is Philip Sheldrake's suggestion of the need to "focus" desire. Disparate and superficial desire must be focused in the desire for God that emerges from our truest self. The "focusing" of desire is at the heart of authentic asceticism.[30] Wordless prayer is most basically the experience of focused desire for the presence of and communion with God.[31] Discernment is nothing other than a focused attentiveness, in the midst of the distractions from within and from outside the person, to our most authentic desire.[32]

The attainment of purity of heart, then, can be described precisely as a focusing of desire. We are created with a radical incompleteness which is the source for a desire that is the foundation of all desiring and that can be fulfilled only by God. Because of sin—original and personal—we find ourselves with disparate and sometimes conflicting desires that lead us to choices, some good and others evil. A "purified" heart is a heart in which desire has been ordered, focused, or integrated into a passionate seeking after God. The purified heart is, in fact, a passionate heart—filled with single-hearted passion for God. As G. Simon Harak has said:

> All our delights, all our passions must be aligned, must
> be caught up in the one great, most rational passion for
> God. That is, we must see that all the things which de-
> light us, delight us because they are related to, partake
> in, the being and goodness of God.[33]

THE UNIFIED SELF AND CONVERSION

To speak of disparate desires that need to be integrated already suggests an experience of the self as divided, in need of unifying. As we have seen, Clifford Williams has spoken of the pursuit of "singleness of heart" and of the task of "restoring a divided self" as the authentic Christian path. Michael Casey described purity of heart as the pursuit of an "undivided heart."[34] Indeed the purification of the human heart involves an increasing unity gradually attained by grace-filled effort. In short, as Benedictine spirituality has consistently affirmed, the attainment of purity of heart is a matter of a life of continuing conversion (*conversatio morum*).

In his classic discussion of conversion, William James spoke of conversion as a healing of a "divided self."[35] One of the classic narrative descriptions of this experience is offered in Saint Augustine's *Confessions*, when he asks God to give him chastity "but not yet." In fact, there is a fundamental division within the human person, a division between a "false" self and one's true self. At times, this division is experienced—sometimes, at some critical junctures in life, quite intensely—and an authentic conversion represents an important if not complete triumph of the true self. The person's true self becomes more the center of choice and action. The ongoing task of the Christian life can be described as a continual conversion understood as the more complete triumph of the true self over what is false in us. This positive movement brings an increasing inner consistency, a more undivided or pure heart.

In his classic characterization of religious conversion as an "otherworldly falling in love" that overflows into other conversions, Bernard Lonergan has pointed to the unifying effect of a real experience of conversion.[36] The deepening conversion seeks to order all of one's self into the pursuit of God, creating a sense of a greater singleness of heart, so that all is subordinated or taken up ("sublated") into this search. This sense of radical subordination of everything to the living out of one's otherworldly love is captured in Jesus' metaphors for God's reign: finding the treasure hidden in the field or the pearl of great value and selling all that one has in order to buy it (Mt 13:44–46).

The seeking after an increasingly unified self through conversion is also reflected in discussions of the positive fundamental option. The deepest and most authentic purpose of one's freedom is to "choose" God; and a life fundamentally directed to God seeks an ever greater integration of all of one's desiring, choosing, and acting consistent with one's fundamental option. In other words, conversion as the foundation of a positive fundamental option is not only a matter of a decisive turning toward God but, even more, it is the ongoing process of integrating all one's exercises of freedom into the deepest disposing of oneself to God. The growing attainment of purity of heart is both a life of continual conversion and the ongoing integration of the fundamental option for God.

A RENEWED ASCETICISM

As we have seen, because of the effects of original sin and of our personal sin, desire must be ordered. The struggle (*askesis*) to order desire has traditionally been called asceticism. The Christian tradition has consistently maintained the importance of ascetical discipline on the path to holiness. "Purgation" was seen as one "stage" in the threefold Christian journey of purgation, illumination, and union; but it was also seen as essential to every stage of the Christian life, though ever deeper and more "spiritual." Until recently, it was the discipline of ascetical theology that studied the purgative aspects of the Christian life as the ground for a contemplative life; and, as we have seen, it is clear for early Christian authors that the attainment of purity of heart is essentially an ascetical path. Ascetical theology overlapped therefore with moral theology's discussion of overcoming sin and growing in virtue.

While ascetical practice at some times in the past has been seen as a "mortification" of the sinful body and its desires, in fact, asceticism simply serves a positive goal. The clearest "natural" parallel is seen in the rigorous preparation of athletes to attain victory in competition.[37] St. Paul exploits this parallel in speaking of the rigorous Christian preparation to attain the prize of eternal life (1 Cor 9:24–27; Phil 3:12–14). The ascetical task is simply the effort to order our desire to attain that purity of heart which represents the life of virtue and the foundation of prayer. Because of sin, this effort involves struggle and the experience of self-denial.

Asceticism can take the form of a self-imposed program to order desire through some traditional ascetical practice like fasting. This can legitimately be called "mortification," though not in the sense of the death of any authentically human desire or in any denial of the goodness of what is authentically human. What must die is what is false in ourselves (the "false self"), reflected in Jesus' challenge to "deny oneself" and to "die to self." We can also speak of the asceticism involved in making those sometimes difficult choices in our daily lives that will serve the growth of habitual dispositions to good choices, that is, virtues. Further, we can speak of the asceticism of a genuine act of self-giving love that goes against our selfish inclinations. Saint Bernard of Clairvaux once said that the common life is the greatest penance (*vita communis poenitentia maxima*), and this odd-sounding dictum reflects accurately Saint Benedict's emphasis on the ascetical value of living in community with other imperfect and sinful persons. Of course, the same can be said of the daily struggle to meet the challenges of marital, familial, and business life—the "asceticism of everyday life."[38] In fact, contemporary discussions of asceticism, without denying the value of self-chosen forms of self-denial, emphasize the importance of accepting the everyday challenges of living one's vocation and commitments with a spirit of generosity, self-forgetfulness, and joy.

In whatever form, authentic asceticism always has an instrumental value; it aims at a good beyond itself. By ordering desire, asceticism liberates freedom from the tyranny of disordered desires. Asceticism, then, serves the freedom by which we "choose" God. The purity of heart that is attained by a sustained asceticism serves love.

CHRISTIAN LOVE: THE KENOTIC SHAPE OF THE PURIFIED HEART

Authentic purity of heart serves love. Love is the heart of an authentic Christian morality. Norbert Rigali states this truth emphatically:

> Only when this [Christian] love is seen to be a participation in the selfless love of Christ, by which he was totally devoted, even unto death on a cross, to the good of others according to the will of his Father, will the Church be in the right position to accept the idea that

her morality is basically love rather than adherence to
law and the thesis that love is, in the final analysis, the
only real moral absolute.[39]

In this affirmation, Rigali puts himself firmly in the company of
Augustine and his famous dictum "love and do what you will." Certainly, the moral theology of Aquinas, centered on virtue, understood
charity to be the "form of the virtues." (More emphatically, Augustine
and Bonaventure, following him, argued that virtues are so many forms
of love.) Traditional spiritual theology sought a life illuminated by charity, reaching its fullness, not in any mystical states but in the "perfection
of charity." But Rigali goes further than placing love at the center of an
authentic Christian morality. He identifies love as essentially self-
giving. The specific Christian morality, he says, is precisely a morality
of *kenosis*—that is, of self-emptying or self-renunciation—after the
model of Jesus in doing the will of God.[40] Authentic Christian love, after
the model of Jesus, is essentially self-transcending, self-giving, and self-
forgetful.[41]

But if, as Rigali has argued, kenotic (self-emptying) love is the
deepest meaning of the Christian life, then we see that the enemy of the
Christian life is selfishness, self-centeredness, and self-seeking. And, in
fact, disordered desire is inherently selfish. From our truest self, created
in the image of a triune God who *is* love, arises our deepest and truest
desire for intimate relationship with God. This relationship is fulfilled in
receiving God's gift of self in Jesus through the Holy Spirit and freely
giving one's life completely in return. The ordered desire of the purified
heart leads to those choices that serve our deepest desire; disordered desire serves only a false self, preventing the full giving of ourselves to
God and to others.

As we have seen, Evagrius and John Cassian maintained that purity
of heart is the necessary foundation for love. A proper understanding of
love as essentially kenotic helps us to see why this is so. A purified heart
is a heart freed of selfish, disordered desire which is the obstacle to
authentic love. The pure heart is a heart that is truly free to love. In fact,
because Christian love is essentially a self-giving, it requires a heart in
which the false self has been vanquished and selfish desires quieted. It is
not surprising that both Evagrius and Cassian saw *puritas cordis* both as
the parent of love and equivalent to it. Nor is it surprising that the attainment of a truly self-giving love requires an ongoing, lifelong process
of conversion—the ascetical struggle to focus desire in our most basic
and most deeply authentic desire for God.

To see the relationship of purity of heart to a kenotic love is to see how *puritas cordis* is essential to authentic community life, whether political, monastic, or familial. The danger in offering reflections on the heart, desire, conversion, and asceticism is that they can tend merely to reinforce an individualistic perspective that has characterized moral and spiritual theology until very recently. In fact, however, a proper understanding of the meaning of love and of purity of heart breaks open the social nature of these reflections. It is not enough to say that the human person is inherently social. We must see how it is possible for human persons to live together authentically in interpersonal and social relationships. Sin and the selfishness that grounds it undermine the possibility of a healthy common life of persons. On the other hand, by promoting a spirit of self-giving, authentic love and the purity of heart that are its foundation make authentic relationships possible. Purity of heart, then, makes possible the genuine flowering of the human social nature in increasingly other-regarding relationships.

CONCLUSION

Moral theology, Norbert Rigali has long and consistently argued, must be renewed by a re-conception of the Christian life itself. The Christian life is aimed at communion with God, and so moral theology cannot content itself with minimums (the "life of commandments") nor only with the precepts that flow from the natural law, whether construed in a classicist or historically conscious sense. Moral theology must serve the Christian's pursuit of the "perfection" that is attained through love, and therefore moral theology must be reunited with ascetical theology.

In the present article, I have tried to examine one aspect of bringing together contemporary moral theology and an important traditional theme from spiritual theology. To understand purity of heart as a goal of the Christian life is to offer a key to understanding the shape of an authentically Christian moral agency. In fact, purity of heart can be understood as the life of virtue unified by love, a life truly free to offer itself to God and to neighbor. We can find, therefore, in this patristic-monastic concept a tool for further enlightening the contemporary reappropriation of an authentic Thomistic emphasis on virtue in the Christian moral life, aiming always at a deeper relationship with God.

Of course, a potential problem in the position taken by Rigali is the fact that many Christians do not understand their moral lives to be directed toward communion with God and therefore closely connected with a spiritual life aimed at the holiness to which God calls them. The danger is, then, that a moral theology conceived as Rigali suggests will appear removed from the ordinary, mundane lives of the average Christian who knows nothing of a universal call to holiness. Ironically, moral theology would appear to be elitist—as spiritual theology had once been.

The response to this concern is the response that Rigali has consistently offered: Christian morality is for Christians. The task is not to develop a moral discipline by which the well-intentioned person (Christian or not) can live out an existence that does not violate the moral law; rather, the challenge is to help all Christians to see the fullness of life to which they are called and to re-conceive moral theology so that it can truly serve this pursuit. Rigali has done a great service to the contemporary discipline of Catholic moral theology in offering this challenge so consistently throughout his published works. This statement does not deny the value of a natural law moral theology that allows moral dialogue with non-Christians, but it is to say that the Christian moral life aims at holiness.

Certainly, many Christians do not see the fullness of the final goal of their efforts to be good and to act rightly. They content themselves, therefore, with far less than what God is so graciously offering to them. Nonetheless, the task of Christian moral theology cannot be simply to offer a structure by which Christians live well the "lesser" life to which they believe themselves to be called. Rather, it is the task of moral theology to challenge, guide, and empower Christians to seek the fullness of life that a loving God offers to them. Only then will moral theology live up to the challenge given it by the Second Vatican Council to "throw light on the exalted vocation of the faithful in Christ and their obligation to bring forth fruit in charity for the life of the world."[42]

NOTES

1. Nobert Rigali, S.J., "The Fragmented Christian Life," *Cross and Crown* 27 (1975), 352–59.

2. *Ibid.*, 357.

3. In his earlier works, Rigali addresses the issue of whether or not there is a "distinctively Christian ethic" ("Christian Ethics and Perfection," *Chicago Studies* 14 [1975], 238). In later works, however, he clarifies that what is at stake in the discussion is whether or not there is "a specifically Christian moral-

ity." He makes important terminological distinctions between 'specific' or 'unique' and 'distinctive' on the one hand, and 'ethics' and 'morality' on the other hand (see "The Uniqueness and the Distinctiveness of Christian Morality and Ethics," in Charles E. Curran, ed., *Moral Theology: Challenges for the Future* [New York: Paulist Press, 1990], 74-76).

4. Michael Casey, *The Undivided Heart: The Western Monastic Approach to Contemplation* (Petersham, MA: St. Bede's, 1994), v.

5. John Eudes Bamberger, ed. and trans., *The Praktikos: Chapters on Prayer* (Spencer, MA: Cistercian, 1970), lxxxiii.

6. Bernard McGinn, "Asceticism and Mysticism in Late Antiquity and the Early Middle Ages," in Vincent L. Wimbush and Richard Valatasis, eds., *Asceticism* (New York: Oxford University, 1995), 62.

7. Bamberger, *The Praktikos*, lxxxii–lxxxiii.

8. *Ibid.*, lxxxiv.

9. *Ibid.*, 49.

10. Michael Casey, "*Apatheia*," in Michael Downey, ed., *The New Dictionary of Catholic Spirituality* (Collegeville, MN: Michael Glazier/Liturgical, 1993), 50.

11. Columba Stewart, "The Monastic Journey According to John Cassian," *Word and Spirit: A Monastic Review* 15 (1993), 33–35.

12. John Cassian, *Institutes* 4.43, quoted by Bernard McGinn, *The Foundations of Mysticism: Origins to the Fifth Century*, vol. 1 of *The Presence of God: A History of Western Mysticism* (New York: Crossroad, 1991), 220.

13. McGinn, *The Foundations of Mysticism*, 219.

14. Philip Sheldrake, *Befriending Our Desires* (Notre Dame, IN: Ave Maria, 1994), 88.

15. Clifford Williams, *Singleness of Heart: Restoring the Divided Soul* (Grand Rapids, MI: William B. Eerdmans, 1994).

16. Søren Kierkegaard, *Purity of Heart is to Will One Thing*, Douglas V. Steere, trans. (New York: Harper and Brothers, 1948, rev. ed.).

17. Servais Pinckaers, *The Sources of Christian Ethics*, Mary Thomas Noble, trans. (Washington, DC: The Catholic University of America Press, 1995), 222.

18. *Ibid.*, 222–23, 327–99.

19. Diogenes Allen, *Spiritual Theology: The Theology of Yesterday for Spiritual Help Today* (Cambridge, MA: Cowley, 1997), 81.

20. G. Simon Harak, *Virtuous Passions: The Formation of Christian Character* (Mahwah, NJ: Paulist, 1993).

21. Philip Sheldrake, *Befriending Our Desires*.

22. Sebastian Moore, *Jesus: The Liberator of Desire* (New York: Crossroad, 1989).

23. McGinn, *The Foundations of Mysticism*, 258–62.

24. Casey, "*Apatheia*," 50.

25. Bernard McGinn, *The Growth of Mysticism: Gregory the Great through the Twelfth Century*, vol. 2 of *The Presence of God* (New York: Crossroad, 1994), 155.

26. *Ibid.*, 219.

27. Harak, *Virtuous Passions*, 91.

28. Kallistos Ware, "The Way of the Ascetics: Negative or Affirmative?" in Wimbush and Valatasis, eds., *Asceticism*, 8–13.

29. Moore, *Jesus*, 19–21.

30. Sheldrake, *Befriending Our Desires*, 24.

31. *Ibid.*, 50–52.

32. *Ibid.*, 91.

33. Harak, *Virtuous Passions*, 79.

34. Casey, *Undivided Heart*, v.

35. William James, *The Varieties of Religious Experience* (London: Longmans, Green, and Co., 1902), 166–258.

36. Bernard Lonergan, *Method in Theology* (New York: Herder and Herder, 1972), 237–43.

37. Jean Leclerq, "Asceticism: A Permanent Value in Monasticism Today," *Word and Spirit: A Monastic Review* 13 (1991), 9–14

38. Elizabeth A. Dreyer, "Asceticism Revisited," ch. 9 in *id.*, *Earth Crammed With Heaven: A Spirituality of Everyday Life* (Mahwah, NJ: Paulist, 1994), 136–49. See also Lawrence S. Cunningham and Keith J. Egan, *Christian Spirituality: Themes from the Tradition* (Mahwah, NJ: Paulist, 1996), 105–22.

39. Rigali, "Love and Christian Morality," *Homiletic and Pastoral Review* 76 (1976), 64.

40. *Id.*, "Christian Ethics and Perfection," 238.

41. Edward Collins Vacek, *Love, Human and Divine: The Heart of Christian Ethics* (Washington, DC: Georgetown University Press, 1994), 63–66, 170–86, 208–15.

42. Second Vatican Council, *Optatam Totius* (Decree on the Training of Priests), in Austin Flannery, ed., *Vatican Council II: The Conciliar and Post-Conciliar Documents* (Collegeville, MN: Liturgical Press, 1975), § 16.

Spirituality and Morality: What's the Difference?

James F. Keenan, S.J.

My title is a play on words. On the one hand, by emphasizing the two fields as distinct, I ask about the differences between the two fields and the historical significance of their being distinguished from one another. On the other hand, by emphasizing the two fields combined, I ask about the impact of integrating the two fields.

No one has with greater diligence and intelligence argued for this integration than Norbert Rigali.[1] In the aftermath of Vatican II, Rigali consistently invoked its mandate that moral theology "should draw more fully on the teaching of the Holy Scripture and should throw light upon the exalted vocation of the faithful in Christ and their obligation to bring forth fruit in charity for the life of the world."[2] Consequently, he saw that only a theology that integrated morality and spirituality could animate the ethical lives of Vatican II Christians. How then is Rigali's argument so challenging and promising?

FORMALLY DISTINGUISHING THE FIELDS OF PRACTICAL THEOLOGY

Since the sixteenth century, the Roman Catholic moral theologian defined moral theology precisely as distinct from spirituality (or ascetical theology as it was known during those centuries). Consider, for example, the Jesuit Thomas Slater, the most important English speaking moral theologian at the turn of this century and the author of the first moral manual published in English. In 1908, in the preface of that manual he defined the limits, the scope and the aim of his work.

> Here, however, we must ask the reader to bear in mind
> that manuals of moral theology are technical works in-

tended to help the confessor and the parish priest in the discharge of his duties. They are as technical as the textbooks of the lawyer and the doctor. They are not intended for edification, nor do they hold up a high ideal of Christian perfection for the imitation of the faithful. They deal with what is of obligation under pain of sin; they are books of moral pathology. They are necessary for the Catholic priest to enable him to administer the sacrament of Penance and to fulfill his other duties.

After describing spiritual or ascetical theology as the study of the "lofty ideals of life," Slater added, "Moral theology proposes to itself the humbler but still necessary task of defining what is right and what is wrong in all of the practical relations of Christian life."[3]

In another work, Slater wrote that the object of moral theology "is not to place high ideals of virtue before the people and train them in Christian perfection...its primary object is to teach the priest how to distinguish what is sinful from what is lawful...it is not intended for edification nor for the building up of character."[4] He was not alone in expressing the differences between spiritual and moral theology. Thirty years later Henry Davis wrote: "it is precisely about the law that Moral Theology is concerned. It is not a mirror of perfection, showing man the way of perfection." Nonetheless, he added that the priest/confessor for whom Davis wrote, ought not to "put before his people...the standard of Moral Theology alone; he must lead his people to aim at Christian Perfection."[5] Ascetical theology helped devout persons pursue Christian perfection; moral theology assisted priests in their role as confessors.

Those who wrote ascetical theology also defined their fields in opposition to moral theology. In his *Institutiones Theologiae Mysticae*, (1774), Dominikus Schram held that ascetical theology was "not content to deal with the sins to be avoided, but goes beyond them to consider man's moral life as perceptible by the counsels to such a degree that he attains, through exalted virtue, the union of the created will with the Divine Will."[6]

Though the two fields of moral and ascetical theology were distinct, they were neither separate nor competitive. Their relationship with one another was assured in three ways. First, along with canon law and liturgy, they were complimentary services provided in the broader framework of practical theology. Moral and ascetical theology were integrated, not in their respective fields or the text books that came out of those fields, but rather in the practical ministry of theology. Adolphe Tanquerey who made a point of distinguishing the two, at the same time insisted on an organic unity (among: dogmatic, moral and ascetical theology) throughout the science of theology.[7]

Second, the organic unity in the understanding of theology was implicitly testified to by the theologians themselves who wrote in both fields. In this century, along with Tanquerey, other moral theologians like Reginald Garrigou-Lagrange[8] and Bernard Häring[9] wrote important works of ascetical theology. In fact, since the sixteenth century, theologians wrote in both fields. Robert Persons, for instance, is a classic example, having written both a moral casuistry book (1582) for the English missionaries and one of history's most famous ascetical works, *The Christian Directory* (1582).[10]

Finally, though the moral manuals affected the lives of all Catholics, while the influence of the ascetical works pertained to a much more specific audience of devout Christians, the two fields came together precisely in the lives of these devout Christians. The books of ascetical theology helped lay and religious readers have a context for understanding the entire scope of their relationship with God. Even though their confessors still resorted to the moral manuals, those who read the ascetical works understood their sins not just as those acts needing penance and absolution but also as signs of the brokenness of their relationship with the Lord. The ascetical works, then, did not contradict or lessen the importance of sin as it was understood in the moral manuals, but rather amplified that understanding. In fact, ascetical works often endorsed the practice of frequent confessions. Thus, though the written matter from the two fields was dramatically different, those works were integrated in the life of devout Christians who depended on both.

SUBSTANTIALLY DIFFERENT FIELDS OF PRACTICAL THEOLOGY

The two fields of moral and ascetical theology were, nonetheless, remarkably different. Concerning the moral manuals, a first distinctive feature is their singular importance in Christian life. Recognizing that Christ won our salvation and that grace was and is given to us, the Church held that the only way this salvation could be lost was through sin. Furthermore, since people sin often, the common theological presupposition was the belief that the masses were going to hell. Thus, the confession of one's sins and re-entering the state of grace was key to a person's salvation and no practice was more important for a Christian than to be sure that one's sins were forgiven.[11] Second, the role of the confessor was so specifically concerned with the removal of sin, that he had to determine with precision the specific sin and the appropriate penance that was due.[12] The manuals were therefore concerned with naming the objects of activity that were sinful.[13] Stemming from the penitential and later confessional manuals that spanned from the sixth to the sixteenth century, the casuistic moral manuals of the sixteenth to the twentieth century were solely concerned, then, with defining what was and was not sinful.[14] Third, in these manuals clearly the objects of activity were described under specific categories, often under the seven deadly sins or as infringements of the Decalogue.[15] In these categories though intentionality was somewhat engaged,[16] the point of departure was always the "exterior act." Thus, in these manuals, sin was found not in the person or her intention, but rather in an action that the penitent should always avoid. Fourth, at best, then, these manuals were designed to keep the person from becoming worse: they aimed to control the person, particularly her passions, or what we today call feelings. There was little interest in personal improvement. Finally, because these were professional works they were written in Latin, to train and assist priest confessors.[17]

Books of ascetical theology were about perfecting one's relationship with God. In their first point of departure from the manuals, they were optional; unlike the matter of the moral manuals, if one did not attend to growing in perfection, one could still be saved. Second, since one was perfecting what was within, these books did not concern particular external actions to be avoided but particular internal dispositions to be developed. Third, while the moral manuals tried to control the passions, the ascetical texts tried to engage them. Passions became the positive engines of growth in these works. Fourth, with such development in mind there was both an end point, Christ, and a way, discipleship. Discipleship language provided both an affective relationship with Christ and, inasmuch as a disciple is a follower, a dynamic motif of movement. Inviting the reader into a deep relation with Christ, ascetical works called attention to the reader's deep interiority, prompting her to give her whole heart and life to Christ. Fifth these works were enormously positive about human capabilities and carried none of the pessimism that influenced the moral manuals. The hope that underlined these texts was about the possible, not the probable: they described what the human being could become, not that she would probably be damned. Finally, they were written for the laity and religious in the vernacular.[18]

While the language of virtue appeared in both types of theological works, they had different tasks. The moral manuals referred to virtues (to the extent that they did) as supporting the agent's attempts to control herself and to avoid sin. They promoted an obedience of the will to Church commands, the prudence of finding a good confessor, a spirit courageous in the face of temptation, and a temperate disposition to curb the dangerous passions. They were meant to restrain the agent and were hardly expressive of human flourishing. In the ascetical books, however, the virtues were designed to move the agent not away from sin, but closer to the Lord. They were to promote, enhance, and deepen the reader's ability to follow the Lord. Courage was to face danger as an advancing disciple; prudence was to discern how to advance in perfection; and temperance was about how one could more fervidly deny oneself so as to be more intimate with God.

THE ROOTS OF ASCETICAL THEOLOGY

"The twelfth century has long been seen as a turning point in the history of Latin spirituality," claims Bernard McGinn. "There can be no argument that the twelfth century was fascinated with the mystery of the human person as *imago Dei* and brought to the study of this mystery a systematic ordering mentality not seen before." Through Abelard's insistence on the conscience, Bernard of Clairvaux's location of the image of God in human freedom and Richard of St. Victor's understanding of the interpersonal human subject as an image of the three-personed God, the theologians of the twelfth century developed a powerful relational anthropology as a base for their spirituality.[19]

Caroline Walker Bynum agrees with McGinn: "No period was ever busier creating structures for its piety than the twelfth century."[20] Like McGinn she too examines Bernard of Clairvaux, who with "other 'new monks' stress discovery of self- and of self-love- as the first step in a long process of returning to love and likeness of God, a love and likeness in which the individual is not dissolved into God but rather becomes God's partner and friend."[21] Bernard's spirituality as well as his contemporaries's drew deeply from the scriptures and cultivated in a particular way a devotion to the humanity of Jesus, which moved readers into greater intimacy with Jesus and with those who shared the devotion.[22] In developing a highly relational anthropology, then, the twelfth century never compromised the person and in fact discovered "the self, the inner mystery, the inner man, the inner landscape." Nonetheless, the discovery of the self did not mean the endorsement of individualism; as Bynum argues, the twelfth century "also discovered the group in two very precise senses: it discovered that many separate 'callings' or 'lives' were possible in the church, and it elaborated a language for talking about how individuals became a part of them (the language of 'conforming to a model')."[23]

Into the thirteenth century these insights flourished and developed into three long-standing beliefs. First, inasmuch as union with Jesus undergirded ascetical theology, charity became the premier virtue for the pursuit of perfection. Thomas Aquinas, for instance, insisted that the perfection of the Christian life consisted chiefly of charity.[24] With regard to the charisms of religious life in the thirteenth century, he noted that the perfection of charity is the end of religious life[25]: religious life was instituted to obtain perfection by exercises whereby the obstacles of charity are removed.[26] Those exercises are the stuff of the religious life, "a training school for attaining to perfection in charity."[27]

Perfection, as even Thomas noted, was not simply for those in the newly formed religious communities. In fact Thomas stated that religious life was no guarantee for the life of perfection.[28] Even the famous thirteenth century debates and suspicions about the worthiness of the new mendicants basically did not dispute that charity, in whosever life, was the virtue for ascetical perfection.

Second, the twelfth-century foundational self-understanding of the practicing Christian as *imago Dei* so ennobled the human that it dared her to develop as a goal for life, union with Jesus. But in the thirteenth century both this foundation and this goal forged a bridge: the *imitatio Christi*. Being in God's image, the thirteenth century devout Christian dared to imitate Christ so as to draw closer to him.

The imitation of Christ flourished through a variety of texts and practices. As Giles Constable notes, that invitation to imitate in turn produced a self-understanding of the devout Christian as a disciple. "After the twelfth century the ideal of the imitation of Christ increasingly entered the main stream of late medieval spirituality and became equated with following Christ and, more generally, with the Christian way of life."[29] This prompted a powerful interest in Christ's earthly life, which generated works such as the *Meditations on the Life of Christ* (c. 1265) as well as the *Lives of Christ* by Michael of Massa and Ludolf of Saxony (c. 1348-68). "The most influential exposition," however, was the early fifteenth century *imitatio Christi* (1491) which "summed up and handed on to later generations much of the spiritual teaching of the twelfth and thirteenth centuries."[30] The devotional practice of imitating Christ begins, then, in the twelfth century and continues until the present as a devotional means to finding the way to perfection in union with God.

Third, these spiritualities led to coherent lay and religious groups. Lay groups, for instance, often incarnated the charism of a particular religious order and from that particular spirituality developed a series of practices that were aimed to help their own members. Thus, in the thirteenth century 'Third Orders' affiliated with religious communities like the Dominicans and Franciscans developed. Later, confraternities, modeled on the 'Third Orders,' emerged and, in time, promoted not only their own devotional practices but also works of charity that were aimed to serve those outside of the membership. This combination of devotional practices for the members and the practice of corporal works of mercy for outsiders became the structure for many confraternities.[31]

THE SPECIFIC CONTRIBUTIONS OF ASCETICAL THEOLOGY

In light of these roots, what can ascetical theology contribute to moral theology today? I want to suggest that ascetical theology fundamentally *amplifies* our understanding of the moral life. This occurs in several ways. I will specify only ten of these.

First, the ascetical texts were so decidedly *based on Scripture* that the difference between these texts and the moral manuals is striking. When Vatican II admonished moral theologians to draw more fully on the Scriptures, they had nothing in their own tradition of four hundred years to turn to as a reference point. In practical theology, only ascetical theology grew out of a Scriptural foundation. Thus, fifteen years before the Vatican II, when Fritz Tillmann published his landmark work in moral theology on the disciple of Christ, readers sometimes associated the text with ascetical and not moral theology.[32] This work, which integrated a Scripture based investigation into a discipleship ethics, became foundational for the later major innovators of moral theology.

Second, the ascetical texts *animated* the reader's devotional and moral practices. These texts motivated persons to confess their sins, not only for the sake of salvation, but also for greater union with the Savior. Without these texts, moral practices were animated by fear of damnation; with them, they were animated by the pursuit of Christ. Thus, they provided a relational context for the motivation of moral practices. In turn, the moral life became considered by the devout as a response to the initiative from God in their spiritual relationship with Christ. Being moral meant being a grateful disciple.

Third, ascetical theology's powerful interest in anthropology prompted moral theology to be concerned not simply with external actions that were to be avoided, but also with *a character to be developed*. Thus, Thomas Aquinas' interest in the virtues in the thirteenth century is not simply due to the retrieval of Aristotle. Rather, the virtues emerged earlier in the ascetical theology of the twelfth century that conceived and nourished the religious movements that developed at that century's close. That theology, via the *imitatio Christi*, guided the new religious orders into their relationships with Christ. Thomas, like others in the newly established Franciscan and Dominican orders, grew up in a culture that promoted the virtues as the vehicle for the devout disciple; and he, like others, introduced them into his moral theology.[33]

Fourth, the ascetical texts also introduced *positive exercises* into the life of the Christian not only for devotional practices but also for acquiring those virtues. While the moral manuals directed persons away from (sinful) actions, the ascetical texts directed readers to the practice of actual concrete positive exercises. As de Guibert notes, asceticism means, "to make someone adept by exercises."[34] Exercise becomes key, then, for understanding the development of the ascetical and virtuous personality. In fact, Aquinas used the word "exercise" basically to convey growth in two areas of life: in the ascetical schools of perfection and in the acquisition of the cardinal virtues.[35]

This point is not simply important for moral theory. The training of persons in the school of perfection helped them understand through experience that just as they could take specific steps to pursue ascetical union with God, so could they take steps to grow in moral character. The exercises of the schools of perfection gave concrete lessons for developing virtuous character.

Fifth, the moral life was no longer understood by the devout Christian as the simple avoidance of sin. Rather, whenever (whether in the thirteenth or the twentieth century) ascetical theology has amplified moral theology, the latter defined itself as primarily interested in *the increase of charity*. This increase was accomplished both by devotional practices and by corporal works of mercy. These modes of growing in discipleship by prayer and good deeds became the measure of the moral worth of the devout. Failure in these practices became confessional matter as well. That is, the ascetical manuals in a way prompted the moral manuals to incorporate not only the seven deadly sins which were the sins of those minimalistically Christian but also the sins of the devout. Their sins may have been a failure to be attentive in prayer, an inability to fast as much as they could, or a failure to donate sufficient alms. The ascetical books actually altered and broadened the moral manuals to not only consider the sins by which we are damned, but also the sins by which we falter in the pursuit of discipleship.

Sixth, ascetical theology introduced *moral effort or striving* as a key concept for capturing the moral goodness of the agent. This notion of striving was rooted in ascetical theology's overriding interest in charity.[36] Striving particularly manifested itself in the ascetical theology that accentuated the metaphor of the struggling soldier, which appeared in many texts, including Erasmus's *Enchiridion Militis Christiani* (1519) or Lorenzo Scupoli's enormously popular *Spiritual Combat* (1603).[37] When moral theology also appropriates the concept of striving, it locates the cause of striving, charity, in the heart of the disciple. This turn to the heart conveys the goodness of deep human desire, captures human aspiration and longing, and finally prompts moral theology once again to talk about love.[38]

Seventh, likewise ascetical theology presented the *passions positively*, not as sources of sinful inclinations, but as the force that when properly trained would assist the devout Christian in the way of the Lord.[39] This shift was only accomplished when a positive anthropology (*imago Dei*), a positive goal (union with Christ), and a positive way (*imitatio Dei*) provided the framework that the energy of humanity had to be understood as at least potentially positive.

Eighth, just as the ascetical texts would foster *union with Jesus Christ*, devout Christians could also interpret their moral lives as disciples who seek union with the Lord. The intimacy that ascetical theology proposed was consistently evident in their texts, whether it be Johannes

Lanspergius' *Epistle from Jesus to a Soul* (c. 1526) or Ignatius of Loyola's *The Spiritual Exercises* (1522). The end of ascetical theology eventually became also *the end of moral theology*.

Ninth, the ascetical works also prompted *an attentiveness to the ordinariness of life*. Though ascetical works began as little more than prayer manuals, in time they became meditations that pursued union with Christ in one's ordinary existence.[40] The engagement of ordinariness demonstrated the comprehensiveness of the scope of ascetical theology; in ordinariness ascetical theology encountered humanity completely. For that reason, the *imitatio Christi* aimed to depict the ordinariness of Jesus' human life. That ordinariness is well-captured elsewhere in the very successful *The Christian Man's Guide* (1630) by Alfonso Rodriguez which went through fifty editions and was translated into twenty-three languages: each of the two treatises are entitled "The Perfection of Our Ordinary Actions." Aquinas captured the inclusiveness of the ordinary and applied it to the moral life when he insisted that every human action is a moral action.[41] The ordinary rescues moral theology from its restricting tendency to study only sinful or controversial actions.

Tenth, as they developed, the ascetical manuals specifically *addressed the occupations and vocations* of their readers. This specificity is well conveyed, for instance, in a recent essay that investigates the prayers for midwives at the time of childbirth.[42] Nowhere was the particular vocation of the reader more specifically treated, however, than in the lives of the saints. In ascetical literature the saint became an exemplar for readers trying to live out their vocations. One pair of saints who became incredibly comprehensive was Martha and Mary who were often depicted together so as to uphold the necessity of both active and contemplative vocations.[43] In general, the saint served to encourage the reader to pursue a life of holiness in her specific field of life.[44] In moral theology, also, the saint became a paradigm as well, a living embodiment of the virtues in the person who concretely follows Christ in her/his vocation.[45]

In each of these ways, then, ascetical theology amplified the scope, competency and subject of moral theology. From its loving motivation through its inclusiveness of the ordinary to its personification in the lives of saints, ascetical theology has offered moral theology a way of exploring a broadened and positive agenda for examining the ethical life.

AN INDEBTEDNESS TO ASCETICAL THEOLOGY

Though unacknowledged, the recent retrieval of virtue ethics[46] is certainly indebted to the work of ascetical theology. As Slater and others cited above noted, ascetical and not moral theology preserved and promoted the virtues as positive dispositions for growth in the past four centuries.[47] Though certainly none of the ascetical books treated the virtues with the systematic rigor that the scholastics like Thomas Aquinas provided, still the tradition of the virtues from the end of the sixteenth century until Vatican II was cultivated primarily in ascetical theology.

Not surprisingly, any return to the virtues would eventually prompt an historical turn to the ascetical theology that sustained them during these last four centuries. The moral theologian William Spohn is a perfect example of this. In three successive essays in *Theological Studies* he noted a renewed interest in the passions, then the virtues and finally spirituality.[48] Any retrieval of the virtues leads us back to spirituality.

In fact, when we see what ascetical theology was, we realize that the major reformers of Catholic moral theology in this century each turned to this field when they tried to *amplify* the task of moral theology which had the long-standing, singular purpose of knowing, describing and avoiding sin. They did this by culling some of the work of Aquinas and integrating it into the positive, relational concerns of ascetical theology. Odon Lottin, after working on his *Psychologie et morale aux XIIe et XIIIe siecles*, turned to the extraordinarily positive and goal-oriented text, *Morale Fondamentale*;[49] Gilleman turned explicitly to an ascetical theology of the heart to retrieve the virtue of charity;[50] Tillmann integrated a Scripturally-based ethics into a discipleship model that was rooted in ascetical theology;[51] Pieper retrieved the virtues from Thomas but described them in the language of ordinary life that one finds in ascetical theology;[52] Häring followed Tillmann and turned right to an *imitatio Christi* as a context for his discipleship ethics in his *Law of Christ*;[53] and, Fuchs followed Lottin in developing a positive goal oriented ethics.[54] Thus, unlike their predecessors who went from Aquinas to the manuals, these reformers went from Aquinas to a literature that broadened the scope of moral theology.

CONCLUSION

The more we understand history, the more we may understand, then, the significance of Rigali's claims as both challenging and promising. The challenge comes when we recognize the recurring tendency in moral theology to look only at the narrowly problematic; the promise comes when we recognize the dramatic influence of ascetical theology in the writings of the thirteenth century Thomas or in the writings of this century's wonderful innovators. When animated by spirituality, moral theology becomes broad enough to engage the human in her simplicity, her complexity, and in her destiny.

NOTES

1.   Rigali's essays are numerous; a few salient ones are, "The Unity of the Moral Order," *Chicago Studies* 8 (1969), 125–43; "Christian Ethics and Perfection," *Chicago Studies* 14 (1975), 227–40; "The Future of Christian Morality," *Chicago Studies* 20 (1981), 281–89; and, "The Unity of Moral and Pastoral Truth," *Chicago Studies* 25 (1986), 224–32.

2.   *Optatam Totius*, in Walter M. Abbot, ed., *The Documents of Vatican II* (New York: America Press, 1966), § 16.

3.   Thomas Slater, *A Manual of Moral Theology*, 2 vols. (New York: Benziger Brothers, 1908, 2nd ed.), I.6.

4.   At (I:36) as quoted in Henry McAdoo, *The Structure of Caroline Moral Theology* (London: Longmans, 1949), 10–11.

5.   Henry Davis, *Moral and Pastoral Theology* (London: Sheed and Ward, 1941), I, 4. Herbert Jone made the same point in his *Moral Theology* distinguishing his work from what "is concerned with the attainment of Christian perfection" (*Moral Theology* [Westminster, MD: Newman Press, 1959], 1).

6.   Quoted in Joseph de Guibert, *The Theology of the Spiritual Life* (New York: Sheed and Ward, 1953), 6. Like Rigali, de Guibert argued against the distinction.

7.   Adolphe Tanquerey, *The Spiritual Life: A Treatise on Ascetical and Mystical Theology*, Herman Branderis, trans. (Tournai: Desclee & Co., 1932, 2nd ed.), 3. See also Anne Patrick, "Ethics and Spirituality: The Social Justice Connection," *The Way Supplement: Spirituality and Social Issues* 63 (1988), 103–16.

8.   Reginald, Garrigou-Lagrange, *Christian Perfection and Contemplation,*

According to Thomas Aquinas and St. John of the Cross (St. Louis: Herder, 1937).

9. Bernard Häring, *In Pursuit of Holiness* (Liquori, MO: Liquori Publications, 1982); and, *Heart of Jesus: Symbol of Redeeming Love* (Liquori, MO: Liquori Publications, 1983).

10. Robert Persons, *The Christian Directory*, reprint of 1607 edition in *English Recusant Literature* series, vol. 41 (Menston, Yorkshire: Scholar Press, 1970); "The Allen-Parsons Cases," in Peter Holmes, ed., *Elizabethan Casuistry* (London: Catholic Record Society, 1981).

11. Thomas Tentler, *Sin and Confession on the Eve of the Reformation* (Princeton: Princeton University Press, 1977). On the issue of the social control of the confessional see Tentler's debate with Leonard Boyle: respectively, "The Summa for Confessors as an Instrument of Social Control," and "The Summa for Confessors as a Genre, and its Religious Intent," in Charles Trinkhaus and Heiko Oberman, eds., *The Pursuit of Holiness in Late Medieval and Renaissance Religion* (Leiden: E. J. Brill, 1974), 103–25, 126–30.

12. For these two tasks, the confessor was considered both physician and judge. See John O'Malley, *The First Jesuits* (Cambridge: Harvard University Press, 1993), 136–52.

13. Recently I have written on the role of the object in manualist thought and its import for medical ethics, "Moral Horizons in Health Care: Reproductive Technologies and Catholic Identity," in Kevin Wildes, ed., *Infertility: A Crossroad of Faith, Medicine and Technology* (Dordrecht: Kluwer Academics, 1997), 53–71.

14. On the overall impact of these manuals on moral theology see, John Mahoney, *The Making of Moral Theology* (Oxford: Oxford University Press, 1989), 1–36. On specifically the penitentials see John T. McNeill and Helen M. Gamer, eds., *Medieval Handbooks of Penance* (New York: Columbia UP, 1990); James Dallen, *The Reconciling Community* (New York: Pueblo Publishing Co., 1986); Bernard Poschman, *Penance and Anointing of the Sick* (New York: Herder and Herder, 1964). On the confessional manuals see Kilian McDonnell, "The *Summae Confessorum* on the Integrity of Confession as Prolegomena for Luther and Trent," *Theological Studies* 54 (1993), 405–26. On casuistry see Albert Jonsen and Stephen Toulmin, *The Abuse of Casuistry: A History of Moral Reasoning* (Berkeley: University of California Press, 1988); Edmund Leites, ed., *Conscience and Casuistry in Early Modern Europe* (New York: Cambridge University Press, 1988); and, James Keenan and Thomas Shannon, eds., *The Context of Casuistry* (Washington, DC: Georgetown University Press, 1995).

15. John Bossy, "Moral Arithmetic: Seven Sins into Ten Commandments," *Conscience and Casuistry in Early Modern Europe*, 214–34

16. Certainly more in the moral manuals than in the primitive penitential or

their later confessional manual.

17. All this being said, the manualists did not absolutely reject all development. See positive presentations on the more recent work of manualists in the essays by Thomas Kopfensteiner, Charles Curran, and John T. Noonan, Jr. in *The Context of Casuistry* as well as John Gallagher, *Time Past, Time Future: An Historical Study of Catholic Moral Theology* (New York: Paulist Press, 1990). More specifically, see the manualists as they worked in the United States in Charles Curran, *The Origins of Moral Theology in the United States: Three Different Approaches* (Washington, DC: Georgetown University Press, 1997).

18. Along with de Guibert, other important texts dealing with ascetical or devotional theology include Jean Leclercq, Francois Vandenbroucke, and Louis Bouyer, *History of Christian Spirituality* (London: Burns and Oates, 1968); Bernard McGinn and John Meyendorff, eds., *Christian Spirituality* (New York: Crossroad, 1985); Caroline Walker Bynum, *Jesus as Mother: Studies in the Spirituality of the High Middle Ages* (Berkeley: University of California Press, 1982). On English literature, see John Roberts, *A Critical Anthology of English Recusant Devotional Prose, 1558–1603* (Pittsburgh: Duquesne University Press, 1966); Martin Thornton, *English Spirituality: An Outline of Ascetical Theology According to the English Pastoral Tradition* (London: SPCK, 1963); Helen White, *English Devotional Literature: 1606–1640* (Madison: University of Wisconsin Press, 1951); *id.*, *The Tudor Books of Private Devotion* (Madison: University of Wisconsin Press, 1951); *id.*, *Tudor Books of Saints and Martyrs* (Madison: University of Wisconsin Press, 1963). More recently, Elizabeth Hudson, "English Protestants and the *imitatio Christi*, 1580–1620," *Sixteenth Century Journal* 19 (1988), 541–58; *id.*, "The Catholic Challenge to Puritan Piety, 1580–1620," *The Catholic Historical Review* 77 (1991), 1–20.

19. Bernard McGinn, "The Human Person as Image of God," in Bernard McGinn and John Meyendorff, eds., *Christian Spirituality*, 323. While the twelfth century marks the enormous systematic development of ascetical texts, a few appear earlier, e.g., Dhuoda's *Manual for My Son* (843) and Jonas of Orleans' treatise *Instruction of the Laity* (c. 828), see Jacques Fontaine, "The Practice of Christian Life: The Birth of the Laity," *ibid.*, 453–91.

20. Bynum, "Did the Twelfth Century Discover the Individual?" in *id.*, *Jesus as Mother*, 109.

21. *Ibid.*, 86.

22. Francois Vandenbroucke, "Lay Spirituality in the Twelfth Century," *History of Christian Spirituality*, 243–82.

23. Bynum, *Jesus as Mother*, 106.

24. Thomas Aquinas, *S.T.*, II–II, q. 184, a. 1. See ad 2, where Thomas states that perfection belongs to charity simply, the other virtues relatively.

25. *S.T.*, II–II, q. 186, a. 2c.

26. *S.T.*, II–II, q. 186, a. 1, ad 4.

27. *S.T.*, II–II, q. 186, a. 3c.

28. *S.T.*, II–II, q. 184, a. 4c.

29. Giles Constable, *Three Studies in Medieval Religious and Social Thought* (New York: Cambridge University Press, 1995), 218.

30. *Ibid.*, 239.

31. See O'Malley, *The First Jesuits*, 192–98.

32. Fritz Tillmann, *Der Idee der Nachfolge Christi* (Dusseldorf: Patmos, 1953); and, *id.*, *The Master Calls: A Handbook of Christian Living* (Baltimore: Helicon Press, 1960).

33. See the interest Aquinas had in the formation of young Dominicans in Leonard Boyle, *The Setting of the Summa Theologiae of Saint Thomas* (Toronto: University of Toronto Press, 1982); see also Simon Tugwell's lengthy introduction to Aquinas in *Albert and Thomas: Selected Writings* (New York: Paulist Press, 1988), 201–352.

34. de Guibert, *The Theology of the Spiritual Life*, 5.

35. See my discussion on the word "exercise" in Thomas' writings in *Goodness and Rightness in Thomas Aquinas' Summa Theologiae* (Washington, DC: Georgetown University Press, 1992), 50–52.

36. Besides my *Goodness and Rightness*, see Conrad van Ouwerkerk, *Caritas et Ratio: Etude sur le double principe de la vie morale chretienne d'apres S. Thomas d'Aquin* (Nijmegen: Drukkerij Gebr. Janssen, 1956).

37. See Constable, *Three Studies in Medieval Religious and Social Thought*, 146–49; Also Philip Sheldrake, *Images of Holiness: Explorations in Contemporary Spirituality* (London: Darton, Longman and Todd, 1987) who discusses the "spirituality of struggle." Also see Jean Leclerq's discussion of the "Christian Hero," in *History of Christian Spirituality*, 60–62.

38. See James Keating, "Listening to Christ's Heart: Moral Theology and Spirituality in Dialogue," *Milltown Studies* 39 (1997), 48–65; *id.*, "The Good Life," *Church* 11 (1995), 15–20; James Keenan, "Morality and Spirituality," *Church* 12 (1996), 40–42; Mark O'Keefe, *Becoming Good, Becoming Holy: On the Relationship of Christian Ethics and Spirituality* (Mahwah: Paulist Press, 1995).

39. See Mark O'Keefe's article in this collection.

40. In particular the ordinary was caught in domestic life, see Thornton, *English Spirituality*, 215–17.

41. Aquinas, *S.T.*, I–II, q. 1, a. 3c; see my discussion of this claim in "Ten Reasons Why Thomas Aquinas is Important for Ethics Today," *New Blackfriars* 75 (1994), 354–63.

42. Colin Atkinson and William Stoneman, "'These Griping Greefes and Pinching Pangs': Attitudes of Childbirth, in Thomas Bentley's *The Monument of Matrones* (1582)," *Sixteenth Century Journal* 21 (1990), 193–203.

43. See Constable, "The Interpretation of Martha and Mary," in *id.*, *Three*

Studies in Medieval Religious and Social Thought, 1–142.

44. Certainly ascetical theology is filled with lives of saints. See the discussion, for instance, in Vandenbroucke, "Lay Spirituality in the Twelfth Century," 254–257. Still, it is stunning to realize that though ascetical literature continuously offered to both genders a variety of models, the leadership in the Church was hardly inclusive in their canonization selections. Between 1000–1900 about 87% of those canonized were men! Philip Sheldrake "Spirituality in History: A Social Perspective," *The Way Supplement: Spirituality and Social Issues* 63 (1988), 45.

45. See Donna Orsuto, "The Saint as Moral Paradigm," in Dennis Billy and Donna Orsuto, eds., *Spirituality and Morality: Integrating Prayer and Action* (Mahwah: Paulist Press, 1996), 127–40.

46. See William Spohn, "The Return of Virtue Ethics," *Theological Studies* 53 (1992), 60–75; also my "Virtue Ethics," in Bernard Hoose, ed., *Basic Christian Ethics: An Introduction* (London: Geoffrey Chapman, 1997); and Joseph Kotva, *The Christian Case for Virtue Ethics* (Washington, DC: Georgetown University Press, 1996).

47. See my "Catholic Moral Theology, Ignatian Spirituality, and Virtue Ethics: Strange Bedfellows," *Supplement to the Way: Spirituality and Ethics* 88 (1997), 36–45. In the same issue, Jean Porter makes a very different claim than I do about the relationship between ascetical and moral theology, see "Virtue Ethics and Its Significance for Spirituality," 26–35.

48. William Spohn, "Passions and Principles," *Theological Studies* 52 (1991), 69–87; "The Return of Virtue Ethics," *Theological Studies* 53 (1992), 60–75; and "Spirituality and Ethics: Exploring the Connections," *Theological Studies* 58 (1997), 109–123.

49. Odon Lottin, *Psychologie et morale aux XIIe et XIIIe siecles*, 6 Tomes (Louvain: Abbaye du Mont Cesar, 1942–57); and *id.*, *Morale Fondamentale* (Tournai: Desclee, 1954). See Mary Jo Iozzio, *Self-Determination and the Moral Act: A Study of the Contributions of Odon Lottin, O.S.B.* (Leuven: Peeters, 1995).

50. Gerard Gilleman, *The Primacy of Charity* (Westminster, MD: Newman Press, 1959).

51. Fritz Tillmann, *The Master Calls: A Handbook of Christian Living* (Baltimore: Helicon Press, 1960).

52. Josef Pieper, *The Four Cardinal Virtues* (Notre Dame, IN: University of Notre Dame Press, 1966).

53. Bernard Häring, *The Law of Christ* (Westminster: Newman Press, 1961).

54. Josef Fuchs, *Human Values and Christian Morality* (Dublin: Gill and Macmillan, 1970).

God's Gifts and Our Moral Lives

Edward Collins Vacek, S.J.

Many theologians argue that God's gifts and our grateful response are at
the heart of the moral life.[1] As Timothy O'Connell puts it, moral theology attempts to answer the question, "How ought we, who have been
gifted by God, to live?"[2] But few theologians have seriously analyzed
both the meaning and the moral implications of God's gifts. The topic is
surprisingly complicated. I will examine three basic kinds of gift: God's
gift of self, the gift of our life, and the gift of material goods. I will explore some "oddities" that arise when we use the term "gift" for each of
these, and I will point out some mistaken ways that moral theologians
use the idea of gift. I will also indicate how these problems may be
avoided by re-imaging God.

In his provocative book, *God Without Being,* Jean-Luc Marion insists that we must rethink the Christian concept of God. He argues that
contemporary Christian life is better served by beginning with the Jo-
hannine idea that God is love, indeed, excessive love, rather than with
the more cosmological or metaphysical ideas that God is Ultimate Cause
or Being Itself.[3] Something similar might be said about imaging God as
the ground of being or as the unthematizable horizon of our self-
transcendence. These approaches tend to obscure the centrality of God's
covenant with us.[4] When, however, we image God as love, our own life
and the material goods that sustain us are more likely to be experienced
as gifts from God. Responding to God's goodness to us, we are also
more likely to feel drawn into a mutual love relationship or friendship
with God. In other words, God usually does not become the central devotion of our lives because we realize that God is pure Being but because we realize that God has first loved us (1 Jn 4:10).[5] As I have tried
to show elsewhere, this mutual love relationship lays down a radically
new foundation for moral theology.[6] I want to begin this essay with the
aboriginal gift that makes this friendship possible.

GOD'S GIFT OF SELF

When asked about God's gifts to them, few Christians spontaneously name the unfathomable gift that is God's gift of self. This "oversight" is not without reason. As practical animals and social creatures, all of us have the tendency to focus on the things about us and on the people who touch us. When we reflect prayerfully, we are inclined to be grateful to God for these creaturely blessings. A deeper and more pervasive gratitude, however, is possible when we become aware that God offers us not only creaturely goods but also God's own self. In this gift, as Rahner noted, "the giver in his own being is the gift."[7] Giving one's self is different from offering some assistance, donating one's possessions, sharing one's wit, or contributing one's insight. All these can be done without love.[8] A self-giving God is not the deist God who as a philanthropist brings the world into existence, establishes the goods of creation, and then disappears.[9] Nor is a self-giving God identical with an all-powerful Sovereign who establishes laws for our living, promises curses or blessings in accord with our fealty, helps or hinders us, but otherwise remains apart from and unaffected by our lives.

The deist creator God and the ruling sovereign God are not sufficient for Christian life. Just as for many people there was a moment when they realized that their human parents—the givers of their life and the source of most of the laws and practices by which they guide their lives—actually loved them, so there should be for us Christians a moment of major conversion when we realize that God loves us and has chosen to devote God's self to us and our community. We realize that God's gift of our life and God's ordering activity in our lives flow from God's prior love for us. More profoundly, we realize that who we are and how we live makes a difference to God's own affective life and that our fulfillment is a matter of importance to God. In other words, we realize that God has transcended divine aseity to enter into our lives and share in our deeds. Whether gradually or suddenly, we realize that God is committed to loving us and that it is important to God that we love God in return (Isa 41:8–10; Rom 8:14–17).

In brief, the Christian God gives not only life and law but also God's own self. A self-gift is a very odd gift because we do not lose the self when we give it away in love; rather we gain it (cf. Lk 9:24).[10] But how do we gain ourselves in giving ourselves? And what does it mean to give one's self? The self-gift involved in love has four aspects. It is out-going (self-transcending), in-coming (other-receiving), other-affirming, and self-realizing. First, when we give ourselves to people, we enter into their lives, unite with them, and thereby share their world. Second, when we give ourselves in love to people, we also, paradoxically, allow who they are, what they do, and the goodness of their existence to affect, inform, challenge, and enrich us. If we affirmed them, but did not allow ourselves to be modified or affected by them, we might be said to be beneficent, but not to have given ourselves. Third, when we give ourselves to people, we also commit ourselves to live for their advancement and the advancement of what they hold dear. Finally, when we give ourselves to people, we develop in ourselves capacities that without this loving activity would be felt only as restless longings. That is, to put it positively, when we give ourselves, our ability to love grows, our own distinctive identity develops, and we feel fulfilled.[11] Even when love requires us to sacrifice, as it sometimes does, we grow at least in our core freedom as lovers.[12]

I emphasize that love involves not only affirmation but also reception because this complexity is often implicitly denied when speaking of the love between God and ourselves. God's affirmation of us as free and intelligent beings is slighted by spiritual writers who in asserting God's lordship insist that our highest calling is that of blind obedience to God's commands.[13] God's receptivity is often denied by theologians who say that our lives can make no difference because God is immutably perfect. In the same vein, the tradition often imagined God as an absolute sovereign in whose eyes we are property duly bought and paid for (1 Cor 6:19–20), or mute clay to be molded (Is 45:9), or helpless objects, or unfree slaves (Rom 5:6–11, 18–19; 6:16; 7:20, 23). These images or models capture some part of the Christian experience of God, but they are insufficient.[14]

Once we experience God as loving and as desiring a mutual or covenantal love with us, it becomes clear that the images of God as either immutably perfect or as absolutely sovereign need to be corrected or transposed. If God loves us, then we make a difference in God's life. We are the creatures for whom God chooses to become creator. God cares about us, and God's own love, as John writes, is made perfect in the love that is manifested in our lives (1 Jn 4:12).[15] Again, if God loves us as persons, we are not rightly pictured as God's possessions or as slaves of God. Accordingly, we do not aspire to be unresisting clay in God's hands, nor is it our ideal to be blindly obedient to God. Such images not only violate our human dignity and human responsibility,[16] they are also not consistent with being persons beloved by God. Rather, we rightfully imagine ourselves as daughters and sons of God, as sisters and brothers of Christ (Rom 8:16; Gal 3:26; 4:6–7; 5:1; Heb 2:10–14).[17] The implication of both our personhood and our status as beloved is that God must await our free response. God cannot force the communion that God wants with us. We have the power either to frustrate or to fulfill God's plan of salvation for us.[18] In Rahner's words, "The history of God's offer of himself, offered by God in freedom and accepted or rejected by man in freedom, is the history of salvation or its opposite."[19] In order to achieve God's goal of communion with us, God can and does resist our resistances, expose our unfreedoms, and steadfastly invites us to be partners in salvation. But we must cooperate by accepting God in our lives.

What then does it mean for us to accept God's self-gift? When we accept God's love for us, we welcome God into our lives, wanting to consciously share with God our past, present, and future. We relish the way we are enriched by God's presence and involvement. We are touched that God should take notice of us. If we thought that we made no difference to God, but that we were only the objects of God's beneficence, we would sense that we were not truly loved. In accepting God's love for us, however, we become aware that God has made God's self vulnerable to us. God allows us to influence God's life in human history. We are glad that God has become for us our creator, redeemer, and sanctifier. We trust that God will not try to control us or to treat us as possessions because, if God were to do so, God would no longer be loving us. In consenting to God's love, we grow confident that God wants us to flourish as persons, and this means that God affirms our own quasi-independent intelligence and freedom.

The love relationship between God and ourselves is the meaning of grace and salvation. As I have argued elsewhere, salvation does not mean that God infuses into us a super-nature, nor does it mean that God chooses to look away from our sinfulness. Rather, salvation means a new mutual love between ourselves and God.[20] We cannot create this relationship on our own. But neither can God do so. No mutual love relationship can be created and sustained by only one member of the relationship. As Vincent Brümmer well writes, "each partner in a relationship of love is necessarily dependent on the freedom and responsibility of the other partner for establishing and for maintaining the relationship. It is logically impossible for either partner to establish or maintain the relationship by him or herself."[21] We are persons meant for relationship with God, not blackboards that can be wiped clean by a divine janitor. God's saving forgiveness, proceeding from God's abiding love for us, can be finally effective in our lives only when it is welcomed and cherished by us.

MORAL RESPONSE TO SELF-GIFT

Moral theologians usually do not begin ethics with God's love for us and they rarely give it a central place in their systematic reflections. One (admittedly incomplete) way to test the suitability of a theological image is to examine its implications for Christian living.[22] Using that test, how does God's self-gift affect Christian ethics? In a word, it gives moral theology a new foundation.[23] The foundation of our moral life is neither God's commandments nor natural law, but rather this mutual love relationship itself.[24]

Let me begin with an odd connection. Suppose a friend were to say, "I love you; therefore you must obey me." Most of us would reject such a connection. Doubtless, a link between love and obedience has historically been used of relationships between a sovereign lord and his vassals. Accordingly, when God has primarily been imaged as the Sovereign Lord, obedience to God and to God's laws in return for love (usually meaning election and then favors) has not seemed odd (Deut 10:12–14). As Old Testament scholars note, God elects Israel, and then the way God's people are to relate to God is through obedience.[25] God's continued love for them is contingent upon whether they do what God commands (Exod 19:5; Deut 4:37–40; Jer 11:4).

When, without denying the divine prerogative of sovereignty, we re-image God primarily as one who wants to form a mutual love relationship with us, the foundation of our moral life becomes startlingly different. Obedience to the will of God is not central. Rather, the response due to someone's self-gift of love is to love in return, that is, to be a friend. If love essentially required obedience, then, since God loves us more than we love God, God should be more required to obey us than we to obey God. We learn in Jesus that God wants to share our lot. We learn in Christ that God sees us more like partners, adult children, or friends than obedient servants (Jn 15:15; Phil 2:6).[26] As a consequence, it is misleading to say that we should give up our own desires and seek instead to obey God's will. Rather, our desires are part of what we contribute to our relationship with God. Thus, we must pay attention to our own desires not simply because they may be worthy in themselves but, more importantly, they may be part of what we add to our relationship with God. This does not mean that we should neglect God's will. If we love people, we want their will to be fulfilled. Hence we will want, wherever appropriate and in our power, to help God's will be done.

When we act within a mutual love relationship with God, our acts are ways of cooperating with God's will. This cooperation distinguishes our Christian moral life from the natural law morality that is available in the secular forum. An atheist and a Christian who take care of a sick person are not doing the same act, unless that act is narrowly conceived. Rather, the Christian is consciously engaged in a shared activity, namely, cooperating with God in the healing or comforting of the sick person. Atheists do not personally engage in this shared activity. Christian morality is fundamentally specific when and because our acts are forms of sharing life with God.[27] Christians consciously strive to live within their relationship with God, Jesus, and the Spirit.[28]

This love relationship with God should inform all of our actions. The final moral criterion, then, is not "Do good and avoid evil." As Thomas Aquinas argued, right reason is only the proximate norm for our decisions. The ultimate norm of our moral life, he says, is charity or friendship with God.[29] As we have just seen, our friends do not ask us to obey them. Friends also do not ask from us that impartial reasonableness that characterizes relationships between strangers. Rather, friends affirm us and set us free to become who we are. But friends do not ask us just to "become who we are." Instead, friends desire that who they are will influence who we are and they desire to share in our lives. They desire, not submission or obedience, not neutral reasonableness, not simply that we fulfill ourselves, but also that their friendship be an important part of our lives. Similarly, God wants our love relationship with God to be the ultimate criterion for how we act in the world.

We have seen that our primary response to God's self-gift should not be obedience. Even gratitude is not the most fundamental response. Rather, since we have a natural tendency to love those who love us, our primary response to being loved by God is to love God in return. We will, of course, be grateful for God's love. But that gratitude itself depends on already being involved in and affected by this love relationship with God. We must first welcome God's self-gift and respond to it, entrusting ourselves to the mutual relationship God wants with us. Otherwise God's self-gift will be treated as some external good. Indeed, with intimates, expressions of gratitude are not always necessary. At times they are signs of distance, since explicit recollections of our debts of gratitude to a beloved may indicate that the spontaneous give-and-take of mutual love is waning.[30] To be sure, God must never become a comfortable, taken-for-granted friend. God is the absolute and incomprehensible mystery who will always be a "stranger" to us.[31] Nevertheless, this transcendent God is at the same time the God revealed in Jesus Christ, the God-with-us who wants us to be friends. Accordingly, our first and fundamental moral task is not to offer sacrifices and other gifts of gratitude but rather, in endlessly varying ways, to live and grow in cooperative union with our God. As Augustine preached, "God wants you much more than your gift."[32]

This return love to God is not morally optional. Though many would disagree with him, Pope John Paul II rightly observed that forgetfulness, exclusion, and atheistic denial of God are in fact objectively sinful.[33] Furthermore, love of neighbor is not an adequate substitute for an explicit love for God.[34] Rather, the central affection of our lives, an affection that can crystallize and organize all other affections, should growingly be our love for God. The process of bringing all our affections within this one great passion is, of course, not automatic. We cannot presume that those who strive to keep the first great commandment will readily and properly love God's creation. There are other distinct moral obligations, chiefly, the obligations to love our neighbors and ourselves. Still, moral theology properly begins with our friendship with God, and from there to all the loves and hates of our lives.

THE GIFT OF LIFE

God could not give us God's own self if we did not exist. So, in order to be able to love us, God creates us.[35] This act of bringing us into being is itself an act of love, that is, an affirmation of ourselves in the direction of our own fullest reality. Further, God could not communicate God's personal self to us if we were not also spiritually alive. Thus, through the mediation of multitudinous creatures, God gives us our own particular physical, biological, psychological, cultural, and spiritual life, that is, those characteristics that make us the alive, alert, social, religious beings we are.[36] In brief, God has fashioned us out of the clay of the earth, and God has attuned our minds and hearts through the stories and songs of many traditions.

But is our biological-cultural life really a gift? Before answering "Yes" to that question, I want to note three oddities that make this life different from most other gifts. First, the gift of life is not expressive of an actual relationship; rather, it creates the basis for a relationship. Before each of us existed, there was no one to whom God could give the gift of life. Furthermore, our life is not something that God first has and then gives to us.[37] We are not other than our life. Thus, we speak in an odd fashion when we say that God gives us the gift of life. Something analogous is true of our cultural gifts. These gifts form our minds and hearts; without them we are not ourselves. Thus, they create their recipient

The second oddity is that we are usually free to accept or decline a gift, but we had no choice about the gift of life or about the various socio-cultural gifts we received early in our lives. The gift of life and the gift of our many traditions are like the gift of grace: each creates the possibility of its own free acceptance or rejection. We have to be alive before we can reject life; and we must become sufficiently educated before we can freely accept or reject the education that has already become part of our very identity. To the extent that these goods are life-giving, we can and should say "Amen" to them, lest they be experienced only as our fate. Accepting them as gifts, however, means accepting who we are as good. If our life is not good, it is not a gift. Thus, we have to be grateful for ourselves. Unfortunately, some strands of the Christian tradition have encouraged Christians to view themselves simply as wretched sinners. These strands often denounce self-love. To be consistent, such Christians should *refuse* to be grateful to God for their own biological, cultural, and even religious lives.[38]

The third oddity is that the gift of life follows a pattern that is contrary to most tangible forms of gift-giving. When we think of gifts, we usually think of some good that is first the possession of one person but then becomes the possession of another. But in giving us existence, God does not lose something. Neither is culture diminished in being handed on to us.[39] In fact, these forms of life take on new existence in our flesh, and they are thereby increased rather than diminished by being given.[40] The further oddity is that, when we receive these gifts and they then belong to us, we ourselves at the same time come to belong to their respective realms of existence, nature, society, and religion beyond ourselves. Thus, when we appropriate the various gifts of life, we achieve self-possession, but we also come to participate in realms of life that are greater than ourselves.

MORAL RESPONSE TO THE GIFT OF LIFE

Part of the usual obligation of gratitude is to use a gift in accord with the intentions of the donor. Does gratitude to God require us to set aside our own desires, intentions, and choices in matters of life and death or in matters of culture and religion? Out of gratitude, should we conform our lives to God's designs for us? Suppose a parent were to exclaim, "I have given you life and education; therefore throughout your life you must pursue my goals for you." The inference seems odd because parents, we think, should not dictate how their children should live, at least not after the children have achieved maturity. A similar inference, however, has been part of the Catholic tradition in two ways. First, theologians have claimed that since God has given us life, out of gratitude we should live in accord with God's plan for us. Aquinas remarks that in this sense every sin is a form of ingratitude.[41] Second, the tradition has often invoked God's sovereignty in decisions concerning the beginning and end of life.[42] This is the God who announces: "there is no god besides me. I kill and I make alive" (Deut 32:39; cf. Wis 16:13). The fundamental oddity here is the standard argument that life is a gift from God and *therefore* outside human dominion. Usually, when someone gives us a gift, it then comes under our dominion. Here, however, it is said that, because life is God's gift, we have no right to exercise choice either by interfering in the natural processes of a life's beginning or by directly intending to end a human life.[43]

The image of God that supports these two claims is, again, the image of God as sovereign ruler. This God creates according to a plan that we must conform to. This God forbids alterations of natural structures.[44] This God must open the womb or else there shall be no life. This God is behind the deaths that happen to people, including the innocent (Gen 30:1–2; Isa 45:7; Amos 3:6; Prov 16:4; Mk 14:21; Jn 9:1–3; Acts 4:28).[45] But, if, as I have suggested, we ground Christian ethics more fundamentally in a mutual love relationship between God and ourselves, these implications appear inconclusive or even mistaken.

First, if God loves us, then God does not want us simply to discover and closely follow some pregiven plan embedded in nature. Rather, God wants us to use our freedom and our intellect to develop our personhood in unique, unpredictable ways and to make a creative contribution to history. We are, as Karl Barth noted,[46] "partners" of God in Christ (Heb 3:14). We do not accept our role as partners if we refuse to creatively shape areas of personal and social life such as marriage and to exercise a proper, creative dominion over the world. Similarly, we do not use well our freedom and intelligence if we are passive towards the many traditions, including the Christian tradition, that we participate in. Put more positively, when our lives are experienced as gifts from a God who loves us, we realize that we have some responsibility for deciding our own life patterns and history.[47] Put paradoxically, we are not faithful to God's love for us if we do not exercise our quasi-independence from God. We must do our part in shaping our own moral selves and our moral deeds in the world; God cannot do this for us.[48] Otherwise, there is no mutuality in our love relationship with God.

Second, must we consign all decisions about life and death to God's sovereign decision? Human existence is, to be sure, a gift from God. And to see something as a gift from God is to see it as related to God and thus as important not just in itself but also as part of our relationship with God. But this derivation of our life from God does not mean that we have no say or choice about how to dispose of this gift. Everything, not just our life, is a gift from God. The fact that something is a gift from God does not tell us what we should do with the gift.[49] We properly consume some gifts, wear out still others, and kill even others. Thus, it does not follow that, because human life is a gift from God, we have no leeway when it comes to its beginning or end. Indeed, from the fact that God "gives" us life, it more follows that we have considerable control and responsibility over our lives. Otherwise God does not really give us a gift.[50] Suicide and murder are not wrong because we are destroying a gift from God. Nor are they wrong because our lives belong to God alone. Rather, suicide and murder are wrong to the degree that these actions are inconsistent with the mutual love relationship that God wants to have with human beings and to the degree that they are inconsistent with the good that God wants to achieve through us. These highly formal criteria demand great discernment, and ordinarily they require the careful preservation of our lives.

Similarly, we should not argue that, because human life is a gift from God, we cannot intervene in the natural processes of its creation. When God enters into a mutual love relationship with us, God calls us to be cooperators with God. God shares God's life-giving power with us. Thus, as partners of God, we can and should be active as co-creators with God. In the area of life-giving, we can be procreators in bringing forth new life (Gen 4:1).[51] Once again, the formal criterion for whether we do this well or badly is whether this act befits our friendship with the God who is still creatively active in the world.

Must we take other persons into account in how we use the gifts of our bodily life and our inculturation? Since we did not ask to be born or to have our present culture, do we owe anything to the human beings who have given us birth and who have socialized us, particularly when they may not have chosen to give us life or to impart culture to us? After all, our unique biological conception is something of an accident, and culture is more caught than taught. Indeed, the web of human life is made up of "mostly anonymous giving and receiving."[52] Thus, do we have any responsibilities to others that flow from the gift of our birth and our inculturation?

To begin, we should relish and foster the gifts we have been given. We should love and cherish our own lives, taking care of our physical, mental, and religious health. We should treasure the way our social and religious traditions live in us and the way they enable us to appreciate and contribute to the world. Of course, as we love these gifts, we should also love those who gave them to us. Thus, we should gratefully acknowledge how dependent we are on God and on innumerable people living and dead. Self-sufficiency is an illusion. Furthermore, we should humbly admit that we will rarely have a chance to make an adequate return to those who have benefited us. We cannot give existence to God; we cannot give biological life or parental love to our parents; and we can give relatively little to our culture. Nevertheless, in spite of our insufficiency, we should be grateful for all the "unearned benefits" that have made us who we are.

Furthermore, out of gratitude, we can and should, where possible and fitting, carry on and contribute to the various persons and communities that have given us life.[53] We can, for example, have our own children, involve ourselves in the intellectual life, create music, or promote faith. Our actions are our offering to the family-stock that gave us life, to the society that formed our minds and hearts, or to the Church that baptized us into the faith.

More fundamentally, all these gifts are given by God in view of developing a mutual love relationship with us. Hence, we have an obligation to use these gifts in a way that is consistent with this love relationship. That means we have an obligation to support God's interests. Since God has an interest in the sustenance, redemption, and progress of history, we should devote ourselves to furthering that interest. This point may be put even more strongly: if, as Rahner argued, God has made human history God's own,[54] then the positive contributions we make to history are also contributions made to God's activity in the world. Indeed they are thereby contributions to God. As Daniel Day Williams wrote, "What happens in this world makes a difference to God. He responds concretely to every new event by taking it as a datum into a new phase of his own life."[55]

GIFTS OF CREATION

A third basic type of gift from God is the material world, e.g., delicious food, gorgeous sunsets, warm housing, and tail-wagging dogs. Obviously, since even atheists are grateful for these goods, it is not self-evident that they are gifts from God. Even for Christians, there are at least three oddities that may be put in the form of objections.

First, some might argue that, once God decides to create us, God has a duty to provide us with a supportive environment. We hold human parents to at least that much. Hence, one might argue that the goods of the world should be considered our due rather than gifts from God. In response, it has traditionally been argued that the absolutely sovereign God never owes anyone anything. But I think it better to say that, even if it is true that God owes us some of the world's goods, these goods are still gifts, that is, unearned benefits graciously given to us by God. Unlike the situation of a contract where both parties freely give in order to get, our existence is freely given by God for our sakes. We do not earn this blessing, and it has never been owed to us. The worldly goods that God subsequently gives us partake in that original liberality. Whenever people freely assume a personal relationship and then happily discharge the duties of that relationship, the subsequent goods they offer share in the generosity that initiated and continue the personal relationship. Thus, even if God has a duty to provide us with material goods, we should still receive them as gifts, since God provides these goods out of God's original desire to carry on a mutual love relationship with us.[56]

Second, some might argue that nearly every good in our lives comes to us through the mediation of human beings. Clothes, houses, cars, even the flowers and trees about us are usually there because human beings have exerted themselves. So some may say that these goods are not *God's* gifts. Further, since we often have to exert ourselves to gain these goods, it may seem better to say that we have earned them, and so they don't seem to be gifts at all. In response, let me observe that even the material goods we ourselves produce or earn through our own labor have much of the quality of being gifts to us. We could not earn them if countless others had not prepared for our labor. We depend on others for materials, tools, organizational and productive systems, ideas, and so forth. In other words, even the "works of our own hands" are for the most part materially, socially, and historically given to us. More fundamentally, all human beings who mediate the world's goods to us are themselves ultimately dependent on God primordially for their existence and more immediately for the energy and creativity they inject into this world. Put in terms of classical metaphysics: as secondary causes we depend on God as the primary cause of every creaturely activity. Thus, we can and should look upon material goods as gifts not only from others but also from God. As Aquinas wrote in describing the working of God's providence, these goods are wholly from God and wholly from creatures.[57]

A third and more important oddity involves the question of whether we can really say these gifts are ours. Christian authors commonly claim that God gives us the world's goods not as our possessions but *so that* we can help others to flourish (1 Cor 12:7; 2 Cor 9:7–11; 1 Pet 4:10). In response, some might conclude that, if God gives *us* gifts only to pass them on, then God does not really give us gifts. When people give us a gift, they want to benefit us. They want us to use or enjoy their gift. If they have specially chosen the gift for us, it can even be an abuse to give it away to others. Thus, some might argue, if God expects that we will pass our goods onto others, we are not recipients of gifts but only distribution centers that God uses.

In order to reply to this oddity, we should reexamine the stewardship theology that leads to it. Most forms of stewardship theology deny that we actually own the gifts that God gives us. Along with many others,

James and Evelyn Whitehead assert: "We are stewards of gifts received, not owners."[58] According to this theology, God only permits us to use some of the world's goods, but always without owning them, always with an eye to helping others, and always provisionally.[59] According to this theology, we are all aliens, tenants, and stewards, but none of us are owners (Lev 25:23; Ps 24:1–2; 1 Chron 29:11–12). We are dependent daughters and sons of God who can enjoy but should not want to own any material goods.[60]

Christians urge this stewardship theology because it serves important Christian purposes. It counters the human tendency to deny our duty to share our possessions with others. It also counters our tendency to think we can arbitrarily or wantonly do whatever we want with our worldly goods. Further, it counters both our tendency to become overly anxious about our things (1 Cor 7:28–35) and our tendency to try endlessly to accumulate goods. It delegitimates such tendencies by claiming that the rights and cares of ownership should not concern us because this world belongs exclusively to God.

Though this theology of stewardship helpfully corrects certain errant human tendencies, it comes at a high cost. To begin with, the logic of a gift is that, if people give us a present, they really give it to us, and so we really own it. Thus, if God alone has ownership of the world's goods, God never really gives us these goods as gifts. Indeed, stewardship theology renders otiose God's commandment against stealing since, if people do not own their goods, no one can really steal from them. Similarly, since people ought not give away what they do not own, stewardship theology makes it wrong for us to generously give our goods to others. There is no generosity in passing on to others various goods that we do not own. Further, we would rightly be able to pass on to others these goods only if we have some prior assurance that God wants some particular alternative distribution. Otherwise, we would be deciding on our own how to give away another's property. Indeed, contrary to its intention, this theology has historically encouraged some people to conclude that the rich are rich and the poor are poor by God's decree.[61]

Stewardship theology also tends to alienate us from the world. Again, contrary to its intention, it makes it harder to see the world as God's gift to us. We human beings are essentially relational. Although we chiefly define ourselves by the ways that we relate to God and other human beings, we also rightly define our identity by the way we relate to the material goods of the world. We are body persons who not only exercise but also need to exercise responsible dominion over at least some things (Gen 1:26). We develop a mature identity when we invest ourselves in caring for some small portion of this world.[62] Without to some degree investing ourselves in this world, we shrivel as embodied persons. Though this world is not our lasting home, God wants us to inhabit this world and grow to maturity here. To do that, we must develop certain special relationships with various material goods of this world. The world is a gift offered by God, but it does not become fully a gift until we take ownership of it.

The main mistake of stewardship theology is to picture God and ourselves as competitors struggling for ownership of the world.[63] As I shall next try to show, something can be both God's and ours, though in different ways. A second mistake is to think that if ownership were allowed we would have no moral responsibilities either to the goods we own or to others who need them. To the contrary, it is frequently ownership that induces proper care for the world's goods, and it is our ownership of things that enables us to give to others in need.

I want to propose an alternative view that will achieve many of the aims of stewardship theology, but without such difficulties. Above, I suggested that the starting point of our reflection on God's gifts should be God's offer of God's self. When God is imaged as involved with us in a mutual love relationship, then this world is, in different ways, "our world," where the "our" includes God, the human race, and each human being. That is, humanity has with God a common though metaphysically differentiated ownership and responsibility for this world. Thus, it is a mistake to think that either God or we exclusively own the world. A Catholic 'both/and' should replace this misleading 'either/or.' Similarly, each of us has with other human beings a common though socially differentiated ownership and responsibility for this world. John Noonan once wrote that "The gift once given is wholly the donee's and no one else's."[64] While his point may be true in law, it is not straightforwardly true in personal relationships, particularly in our relationship with God. Rather, a gift symbolizes the unity-in-difference of the giver and the recipient. Thus, the gift "belongs" to both, though in different ways.[65]

When we claim ownership, we do not claim the right to wantonly do as we will with the gifts of creation. Such a claim betrays a lingering image of absolute sovereignty, an image that is finally appropriate neither to the Christian God nor to human beings. Rather, when we claim ownership, we claim that some worldly things are specially related to us, that we have responsibility for caring for them, and that we can at times freely, though respectfully, dispose of them. We do not claim that we own, use, or enjoy these goods apart from our relationship to God or others. Rather, as sharers in divine life we are co-responsible with God for creation, and as fellow human beings we are co-responsible to one another for some parts of this world.[66]

MORAL RESPONSE TO GIFTS OF CREATION

If the goods of this world are gifts from God to humanity, can we refuse these goods? We can and often must. Unfortunately, but realistically, ethical decision-making often requires us to say "No" to one good when we say "Yes" to another. Thus, we must regularly say "No" to most of what God offers to humanity as not really for us (1 Cor 6:12). In this finite world, two goods may potentially be God's gift to us, yet we can choose only one. As Rahner noted, while one potential good may be seen "as a special providence of God, as his intervention, as his favorable hearing, as a special grace," its opposite may also be seen as the same.[67] Accordingly, we must discern whether the goods that God offers to humanity are really good for us individually. For this decision we need the help of the tradition, of the saints, of the present Church, of the Bible, of natural law thinking, and so forth.

Again, even when we are confident that something is God's gift to us, that awareness does not determine *how* we should treat it. To be sure, we should not abuse God's gift. But the fact that something is a gift from God does not of itself tell us what is an abuse and what is not. Thus, the argument is flawed that says we have no right, for example, to kill animals or to cut down forests or to throw away food or to pollute rivers because these are gifts from God. Rather, such decisions must be made on the basis of the intrinsic value of the gift itself and its actual bearing on others, ourselves, and God as well as on our various relationships. Because a gift continues both to represent the giver and to express the relationship between the giver and receiver, "grateful use" is required. Thus, it is usually wrong to use a gift in a way the donor would not approve.[68] Recipients cannot treat it simply as they please. Rather, recipients should use the gift in accord with the "intentions of the donor."

This obligation of "grateful use," however, should ordinarily not be strictly specified by the donor. The individuality and freedom of the recipient, the unpredictable process of history, and the liberality involved in giving gifts imply that recipients should have considerable latitude in using gifts. If someone gives us money for a new coat, we are not free, other things being equal, to give the money to the poor, even though the latter might do more good. But we are free within limits to pick out any coat we like. And, faced with our own starvation, we reasonably judge that the donor would want us to use the money for food, since the primary function of the gift is to foster our life and our on-going relationship with the donor. Needless to say, a huge casuistry could and should be developed around this point of grateful use.

How do we respect the "intentions of the donor" when that donor is God? The answer depends on our image of God. On the one extreme, the God of deism does not care how we use the world. On the other extreme, an absolutely sovereign God would want to alone decide how we use the world. But when God has become our partner in an on-going, historical relationship of mutual trust, then we have considerable discretion in the use of these gifts. In any interpersonal relationship, gifts are given to express and strengthen a relationship.[69] Gifts are also given to enhance the well-being of the recipient, and some latitude in deciding how they are used is essential to human well-being. Hence, the giver ordinarily does not demand that the gift be used in one particular way, as long as it is used in a way that respects the love that it represents. Thus, when God gives us the goods of the world, we may freely and creatively dispose of these gifts as long as our use honors God, ourselves, our neighbors, our relationships as well as the material goods themselves.[70]

Though God's gifts are intended for the whole human race (Rom 5:12–17; Tit 2:11),[71] each of us, as I have argued and as most people take for granted, "own" some of the world's goods. Our cloak is really *our* cloak. But if some people are without a cloak, they of course deserve to have one. Still, their need does not imply, as some have argued, that we then no longer own our own cloaks.[72] We would have no obligation to generously give them our cloak if our ownership ceased in the face of their need. Rather, we have an obligation to see that they obtain a cloak, whether from ourselves, from others, or through their own efforts. God is the God of our sisters and brothers, and we must, out of love for God as well as love for them, help them satisfy their needs and promote their well-being. Because of our friendship with God, we want to cooperate with God's desire to give material goods to them. All of us together are called to a community of life with one another and with God; and one vital way we express and realize this communion is by sharing with one another.

In sum, theologians have often failed to develop how God's gifts contribute to our understanding of the moral life. When God is understood as wanting to share in a mutual love relationship with us, then God's gift of self, of our life, and of the goods of this world become both freshly intelligible and existentially demanding. Accepting this offer of friendship, we Christians want gratefully and whole-heartedly to love God, ourselves, and our world.[73] Our moral life in the world follows: we value our own life and the material goods of creation because—and insofar as—these gifts share in and contribute to our mutual love relationship with God.

> "O give thanks to the Lord, for the Lord is good, for the
> Lord's steadfast love endures forever" (Ps 136:1).

NOTES

1. Brian Childs, "Gratitude," in Rodney Hunter, ed., *Dictionary of Pastoral Care and Counselling* (Nashville: Abingdon, 1990), 470–71; John Koenig, "The Heartbeat of Praise and Thanksgiving," *Weavings* 7 (November/December 1992), 15; Richard Gula, S.S., *Reason Informed by Faith* (New York: Paulist, 1989), 52; Edna McDonagh, *Gift and Call* (Dublin: Gill and Macmillan, 1975), 86.

2. Timothy O'Connell, *Principles for a Catholic Morality* (San Francisco, Harper & Row, 1990, rev. ed.), 7.

3. Jean-Luc Marion, *God Without Being*, Thomas Carlson, trans. (Chicago: University of Chicago, 1991), 47–48, 63–64.

4. For a fuller presentation of this revision, see Edward Vacek, S.J., *Love, Human and Divine* (Washington, DC: Georgetown University Press, 1994), 22–24, 87–106, 117–50.

5. Marion, *God Without Being*, 75–76.

6. "Divine-Command, Natural-Law, and Mutual-Love Ethics," *Theological Studies* 57 (1996), 633–53.

7. Karl Rahner, S.J., *Foundations of Christian Faith* (New York: Seabury, 1978), 120.

8. Jules Toner, *The Experience of Love* (Washington, DC: Corpus, 1968), 125.

9. Rahner, *Foundations of Christian Faith*, 222.

10. Evelyn Eaton Whitehead and James Whitehead, *A Sense of Sexuality* (London: Doubleday, 1989), 305.

11. Vacek, *Love, Human and Divine*, 23, 44–54.

12. McDonagh, *Gift and Call*, 35.

13. Andrew Lustig, "Natural Law, Property, and Justice," *Journal of Religious Ethics* 19 (1991), 135, 138; Courtney Campbell, "Body, Self, and the Property Paradigm," *Hastings Center Report* 22 (September–October 1992), 38.

14. Vincent Brümmer, *The Model of God* (New York: Cambridge University, 1993), 19–29.

15. Raymond Brown, *The Epistles of John* (Garden City: Doubleday, 1982), 555.

16. Sallie McFague, *Models of God* (Philadelphia: Fortress, 1987), 29.

17. For a study of this tension in the Bible, see D. A. Carson, *Divine Sovereignty and Human Responsibility* (Atlanta: John Knox, 1981), 201–05.

18. Vincent Brümmer, *Speaking of a Personal God* (New York: Cambridge, 1992), 143.

19. Rahner, *Foundations of Christian Faith*, 143.

20. Vacek, *Love, Human and Divine*, 320–25.

21. Brümmer, *The Model of Love*, 160; and *id.*, *Speaking of a Personal God*, 76–77, 143.

22. See my essay, "Divine-Command, Natural-Law, and Mutual-Love Ethics," 634, 637, 641; and Brümmer, *Model of Love*, 26–29.

23. See Norbert Rigali, S.J., "Morality as an Encounter with God," *Cross and Crown: A Spiritual Quarterly* 26 (1974), 262–68.

24. See my essay, "Divine-Command, Natural-Law, and Mutual-Love Ethics," 633–53.

25. Walther Eichrodt, *Theology of the Old Testament*, 2 vols. (London: SCM Press, 1967), 2:299; William Spohn, S.J., *What Are They Saying About Scripture and Ethics?* (New York: Paulist, 1984), 6; Walter Brueggemann, *The Creative Word* (Philadelphia: Fortress, 1982), 101, 104; cf. John Milbank, "Can a Gift Be Given?" *Modern Theology* 11 (1995), 128–31.

26. Terrance McConnell, *Gratitude* (Philadelphia: Temple University Press, 1993), 206; Mary Rose D'Angelo, "Re-membering Jesus," *Horizons* 19 (1992), 217.

27. Vacek, *Love, Human and Divine*, 116–56.

28. Richard McCormick, S.J., *Corrective Vision* (Kansas City: Sheed & Ward, 1994), 136–37; and Khaled Anatolios, "Christian Ethics and Christian Faith," *Communio* 22 (1955), 250–51.

29. Thomas Aquinas, *S.T.*, II–II, q. 17, a. 1; q. 23, a. 3; q., 23, a. 6; q. 27, a. 6.

30. McConnell, *Gratitude*, 11, 221, 229.

31. Karl Rahner, S.J., "Thomas Aquinas on the Incomprehensibility of God," *The Journal of Religion* 58 (Supplement 1978), S 122.

32. Augustine, "Sermon 82," *Sermons* in John E. Rotelle, ed., *Works of Saint Augustine* (New York: New City Press, 1991), III/3, 371.

33. John Paul II, *Reconciliatio et paenitentia*, "On Reconciliation and Penance," (Boston: St. Paul Editions, n.d.), § 14.

34. See Edward Vacek, S.J., "The Love of God—Is It Obligatory?" *Annual of the Society of Christian Ethics* (1996), 221–47.

35. Michael Himes, "Catholicism as Integral Humanism," in F. Clark Power and Daniel Lapsley, eds., *Challenge of Pluralism* (Notre Dame, IN: University of Notre Dame Press, 1992), 123; and Rahner, *Foundations of Christian Faith*, 222.

36. Aquinas, *S.T.*, II–II, q. 101, a. 1; Stanley Hauerwas, *The Peaceable Kingdom* (Notre Dame, IN: University of Notre Dame Press, 1983), 27; and Douglas John Hall, *Imaging God: Dominion as Stewardship* (Grand Rapids: Eerdmans, 1986), 134–35.

37. Paul Camenisch, "Gift and Gratitude in Ethics," *Journal of Religious Ethics* 9 (1981), 28; and Kenneth Schmitz, *The Gift: Creation* (Milwaukee: Marquette University Press, 1982), 33–34.

38. Oliver O'Donovan, *Resurrection and Moral Order* (Grand Rapids: Eerdmans, 1986), 252; and Vacek, *Love, Human and Divine*, 198–201.

39. See Norbert Rigali, S.J., "Christian Morality and Universal Morality: The One and the Many," *Louvain Studies* (1994), 18–33.

40. Schmitz, *The Gift*, 18.

41. Aquinas, *S.T.*, II–II, q. 107, a. 3.

42. John Paul II, *Reconciliatio et paenitentia*, § 14.

43. Aquinas, *S.T.*, II–II, q. 64, a. 5; Janet Smith, *Humanae vitae* (Washington, DC: Catholic University of America, 1991), 21–22, 256; United States Catholic Bishops, "Ethical and Religious Directives for Catholic Health Care Services," *Origins* 24 (December 15, 1994), Part 5, Introduction, 458; Paul Johnson, "Selective Nontreatment of Defective Newborns," in Stephen Lammers and Allen Verhey, eds., *On Moral Medicine* (Grand Rapids: Eerdmans, 1987), 495–96; Richard Gula, *Euthanasia* (New York: Paulist, 1994), 7–14; and Congregation for the Doctrine of the Faith, "Instruction on Respect for Human Life in Its Origin and on the Dignity of Procreation," *Origins* 16 (March 19, 1987), 699, 708, 711.

44. Aquinas, *S.T.*, II–II, q. 66, a. 1. The debate continues: Mark Sagoff, "Animals as Inventions," *Report from the Institute for Philosophy and Public*

Policy 16 (1996), 15–19; and Campbell, "Body, Self, and the Property Paradigm," 38.

45. Carson, *Divine Sovereignty and Human Responsibility*, 128–32; Jon Levenson, *The Death and Resurrection of the Beloved Son: The Transformation of Child Sacrifice in Judaism and Christianity* (New Haven: Yale University 1993), 5–7.

46. Karl Barth, *Church Dogmatics: Volume III: The Doctrine of Creation*, G.W. Bromiley and T.F. Torrance, eds. (Edinburgh: T. & T. Clark, 1961), III/4:474, 482–83, 520–21.

47. Toner, *The Experience of Love*, 76.

48. Vacek, *Love, Human and Divine*, 102–06.

49. Cf. Gareth Moore, O.P., *The Body in Context* (London: SCM Press, 1992), 87–91.

50. Let me be clear: I am concerned here only with the arguments that are too often uncritically put forward. I am not trying here to make a case for euthanasia or reproductive technology.

51. The term "Co-creator" is consistent with the thinking of Pope John Paul II, though its use in most reproductive technologies would not be. See Edward Vacek, S.J., "John Paul II and Cooperation with God," *The Annual of the Society of Christian Ethics* (1990), 81–108; and *id.*, "Moral Notes: Vatican Instruction on Reproductive Technology," *Theological Studies* 49 (1988), 110–31.

52. Schmitz, *The Gift*, 56.

53. Lawrence Becker, *Reciprocity* (New York: Routledge & Kegan Paul, 1986), 113–15, 231–49; and McConnell, *Gratitude*, 77.

54. Karl Rahner, S.J., "Man (Anthropology)," *Sacramentum Mundi*, 6 vols. (New York: Herder and Herder, 1969), 3:366; and *id.*, *Foundations of Christian Faith*, 221–22.

55. Daniel Day Williams, *Spirit and Forms of Love* (New York: Harper & Row, 1968), 109.

56. Fred Berger, "Gratitude," *Ethics* 85 (1975), 300.

57. Thomas Aquinas, *Summa contra gentiles*, 3 vols., Vernon Bourke, trans. (Notre Dame, IN: University of Notre Dame Press, 1975), 3:70.

58. Whitehead and Whitehead, *Sense of Sexuality*, 305.

59. Aquinas, *S.T.*, II–II, q. 66, a. 7; George Monsma, "Biblical Principles Important for Economic Theory and Practice," and Leland Ryken, "Work as Stewardship," in Max Stackhouse, *et al.*, eds., *On Moral Business* (Grand Rapids: Eerdmans, 1955), 38–42, 80–86.

60. Marion, *God Without Being*, 95–100, makes this mistake in analyzing the parable of the prodigal son. He is right, however, that filiation is the central issue.

61. Lewis Smedes, *Mere Morality* (Grand Rapids: Eerdmans, 1983), 39.

62. *Ibid.*, 186–91.

63. John Mahoney, S.J., *The Making of Moral Theology* (Oxford: Clarendon, 1987), 247.

64. John Noonan, Jr., *Bribes* (New York: Macmillan, 1984), 695.

65. Aquinas, *S.T.*, I, q. 38, a. 1.

66. John Paul II, *Evangelium vitae*, in *Origins* 24 (April 6, 1995), §§ 42–43.

67. Rahner, *Foundations of Christian Faith*, 89.

68. Thomas Murray, "Gifts of the Body and the Needs of Strangers," *Hastings Center Report* 17 (1987), 32; David Holley, "Voluntary Death, Property Rights, and the Gift of Life," *Journal of Religious Ethics* 17 (1989), 108–13; and James Childress, "The Art of Technology Assessment," in Stephen Lammers and Allen Verhey, eds., *On Moral Medicine*, 239.

69. Alan Schrift, "Rethinking Exchange: Logics of the Gift in Cixous and Nietzsche," *Philosophy Today* 40 (1996), 201.

70. Camenisch, "Gift and Gratitude in Ethics," 9–10.

71. John Paul II, *On Human Work* (Washington, DC: United States Catholic Conference, 1981), § 14.

72. See Aquinas, *S.T.*, II–II, q. 66, a. 7. Thomas confusedly holds that, in the face of another's need, people both possess and do not possess their goods.

73. I am grateful to Dan Harrington, John Kselman, Meg Causey, and Maureen Donohue for their helpful comments on earlier drafts of this essay.

The Ecclesial Context of Moral Theology

Charles E. Curran

Catholic moral theology in the past has paid little or no explicit attention to the church and its influence on the discipline.[1] The manuals of moral theology, which practically became identified with the whole discipline of moral theology during their existence from the sixteenth century to the Second Vatican Council (1962-1965), aimed at preparing confessors (and indirectly penitents) for the sacrament of penance. Sins, according to the Council of Trent (1545), had to be confessed according to number and species, and all the faithful were obliged to confess their mortal sins at least once a year. These very practical manuals dealt with the narrow questions raised by the practice of the sacrament of penance of what constituted sinful acts and the degree of sinfulness. Such manuals presumed but never explicitly developed the broader context of the church for the moral life and moral theology.[2]

The second and more theoretical strand of Catholic moral theology became identified with the approach of Thomas Aquinas (d. 1274) whose *Summa theologiae* became the textbook for theology in the sixteenth century. Pope Leo XIII's imposition of Thomism in the late nineteenth century as the Catholic philosophy and theology insured the hegemony of the Thomistic method and approach until Vatican II. Both the religious culture of the time in which Aquinas wrote and his philosophical bent called for a universal ethic, and he gave no explicit attention to the church.[3]

However, since moral theology deals with the systematic study of the moral life and actions within the Christian community, this discipline must recognize the primary context of the church community.

WHAT IS THE CHURCH?

What is the church in the Catholic understanding? The church community is the reality within which the triune God comes to people, and God's people respond to God's gracious gift.[4] Vatican II describes the church as the sign and instrument of communion with God and of unity among all humankind. The church today continues in time and space, through the Spirit, the salvific work of the risen Jesus and the one he called Abba. The response of the people of God, the church, is to give praise and thanks for the triune God's salvific work and to live out their new life as children of God, brothers and sisters of Jesus. The church community is called to be the light of the world and the salt of the earth.[5] An early name for the community of the disciples of Jesus was "The Way."[6]

The members of the church are truly the community of the disciples of Jesus called to live out the reality of their Christian lives. Discipleship has often been used as a way of describing the life of the members of the church. The *Dogmatic Constitution on the Church* of Vatican II insists that all members of the church are called to holiness. Jesus called each and every one of the disciples to be perfect even as the heavenly Father is perfect. All Christians in whatever state or walk of life are called to the fullness of Christian life and to the perfection of love.[7] The Christian moral life thus arises within the context of the church community which is called to nurture and foster the life of discipleship.

The ecclesial or church dimension of the Christian moral life has not been explicitly developed in the two main approaches found in Catholic moral theology. This moral dimension of the church has also been ignored in systematic treatments of the church in Catholic theology. The modern theologies of the church grew up in the light of the controversies following the Reformation and tended to stress the aspects which differed from Protestant approaches such as the Petrine office in the church and the structural elements in Roman Catholicism. Subsequent developments especially in the context of the dialogue of Vatican II put these into a wider and broader framework. But even contemporary and reforming theologies of the church do not develop the moral life of the disciples of Jesus.[8]

The present situation is quite paradoxical. Catholic theology has stressed the importance of the visible community of the church, but existing systematic theologies of the moral life and the church fail to develop the ecclesial context of the moral life. At best, the teaching role of the church is emphasized in the discussion of various acts in moral theology (e.g. birth control, distributive justice issues) where church teaching authority has taken a position.

The ecclesial aspect of the Catholic moral life needs to be developed in depth. God wills to make human beings holy and to save them not as isolated individuals without any bond or link among themselves, but rather to make them into a people to acknowledge and serve God in holiness. God chose the Israelites as his own people. The church is the new Israel with which God has made a new covenant, but contemporary Catholic theology still recognizes the enduring reality of the first covenant. The messianic people of God, the church, are "a chosen race, a royal priesthood, a holy nation...who in times past were not a people, but now are the People of God (1 Pet 2:9-10)."[9]

Most Americans tend to think of the church as a voluntary society in which like-minded individuals come together to sustain, nurture, and develop their spiritual lives. But this understanding is not the Catholic understanding and betrays individualistic presuppositions. We are not saved as individuals and then come together to deepen our spiritual life within the community of the church. The saving love of God comes to us in and through the church. The church is the way in which God has chosen to come to us with God's saving love. We are saved by belonging to the people of God. Since this is the way Catholics believe God comes to us, we find God's saving love in and through belonging to the people of God.[10]

One good illustration of this understanding of the church as the community in which God wants to encounter human beings comes form the continued practice of infant baptism. Many pastoral and practical problems arise with the practice of infant baptism, but this practice reminds us that we are not first saved by God as individuals in the depths of our own hearts and then form a community with like-minded individuals. The church is not a voluntary society like the Elks or the Lions. One does not belong to the church because one likes the pastor or the preacher or the choir or the people. One belongs to the church, the community of disciples, because this is the way that God has chosen to enter into saving love with us.

At times the Catholic tradition so stressed the communitarian aspect that it did not give enough importance to the individual and the individual's experience of God's saving gift. The Protestant Reformation put more emphasis on the individual's relationship to God and downplayed the role of the church. Over time the Catholic Church has attempted to recognize the greater importance and role of the individual person within the community, but even today Catholics often criticize their church for not giving enough importance to the needs and rights of individuals.[11] However, a truly Catholic understanding can never reduce the church to a voluntary society in the sense that individuals join the group if they want to nurture and sustain their Christian life. The church is the way God has chosen for us not the means we voluntarily embrace to help ourselves as individuals.

CATHOLICITY OF THE CHURCH

The theory and practice of the church will thus greatly affect and shape the moral life of its members. The Roman Catholic Church calls itself catholic. This very word helps to elucidate the reality of the church. Catholic (with a small c) means universal and all-inclusive. In my judgment, the Catholic Church is Catholic with a large C and catholic with a small c. Large C Catholic Church refers to the totality of its Catholicity including what is unique to the Roman Catholic Church and how it differs from other churches. Catholic with a small c refers to a broader sense of catholic which the Roman Catholic Church shares with many other churches. The Nicene-Constantinopolitan Creed professes belief in the church as one, holy, catholic, and apostolic. Ecumenical discussions within the World Council of Churches (to which the Roman Catholic Church does not belong) have emphasized the need for the church to be catholic in this sense.[12]

The catholicity (small c) of the church involves four important characteristics for our understanding of the church and how it shapes the moral life of its members. In all these four areas, the Roman Catholic Church is not necessarily unique or different from other churches which claim to be catholic. This can thus serve as the basis for an ecumenical discussion among the churches.[13] All these characteristics spell out the basic catholic reality of universality and all-inclusiveness.

First, the Catholic Church is an inclusive community open to all and appealing to all. In the early church, the openness to gentiles was a very significant development (Acts, 10). The ideal of catholicity is well spelled out in Galatians 3:28—there is neither Jew nor Greek, slave nor free, male nor female in Christ Jesus. The church catholic goes beyond ethnic, racial, gender, political, and economic differences. The church catholic thus differs from so many other communities which are based on human bonds of various kinds that unite specific groups of people.

The church catholic is big in the sense of being all-embracing. Some religious groups restrict membership to the spiritually elite and perfect. But the church catholic recognizes that its members are also sinners. The Catholic tradition has distinguished two kinds of sin—mortal and venial sin. Mortal sin, from the Latin word for death, involves spiritual death and separation from God thus meriting eternal punishment. Venial sin comes from the Latin word for pardon and refers to light sin which does not destroy our relationship to God and can be more readily pardoned and forgiven. No one in the world is perfect; venial sin exists in all. But the Catholic tradition also recognizes that people in mortal sin still belong to the church. Yes, there are boundaries on the church catholic, but it tends to be inclusive recognizing all its members are sinful and some have even broken their relationship with God.[14]

If the church were the home of only the perfect, it would have a different moral ethos and a very different moral tone. One of the perennial problems in the church catholic comes precisely from the tension between inclusivism involving sinners and the call to follow Jesus. Before Vatican II, Catholics generally accepted a two-tiered division in the church between the ordinary Catholic who lived in the world and obeyed the basic ten commandments and those who wanted to be perfect and followed what was called the evangelical counsels. In this interpretation, if you want to be perfect, you must leave this world and go into the religious life based on the evangelical counsels of poverty, chastity, and obedience. Vatican II insisted that all Christians are called to holiness. The tension, however, remains between the call to holiness and the recognition that sinners of various kinds belong to the church. The danger also remains that the church catholic will fail to be the light of the world and the salt of the earth. This inclusive characteristic of being open to all, including sinners, is intimately linked to the catholic understanding of the church as the way in which God offers salvation to human persons.[15]

A second characteristic of the church catholic is that its faith and its moral life are inclusive and touch all aspects of reality in the world. The church catholic does not withdraw from the world but lives in the world and is directly involved with it. The *Pastoral Constitution on the Church in the Modern World* of Vatican II makes the point very clearly from its opening words: "The joy and hope, the grief and anguish of the [people] of our time, especially of those who are poor or afflicted in any way, are the joy and hope, the grief and anguish of the followers of Christ as well. Nothing that is genuinely human fails to find an echo in their hearts."[16]

Thus, the church catholic has traditionally been distinguished from the sect. In his classical discussion of different models, Ernst Troeltsch distinguishes between the sect and the church. The sect proposes a radical and perfectionist ethic, tends to have a small and limited membership, and does not directly become involved in the world but tends to withdraw from the world. Many traditional Christian sects insist on the literal interpretation of the sayings of Jesus as found in the Sermon on the Mount. For example, they will take no oaths. Living in the world makes it impossible to live out this radical ethic of Jesus, so consequently the sectarians have to withdraw from the world. In Troeltsch's understanding, one sees clearly the difference between the church and the sect model and how the different characteristics cohere with a systematic understanding of each model.[17] The Catholic Church, according to Troeltsch and many others, has been the best illustration of the church model although mainstream Protestant churches belong to the same church model.[18]

The church catholic also differs from the understanding of the church and the Christian community proposed today by John Howard Yoder and Stanley Hauerwas. In general, they are not strict sectarians. However, in their approach, the church is primarily concerned with its own internal moral life and not directly and immediately concerned with the world. The church, however, by its witness and example, can and should have some effect on the world.[19] Hauerwas starts from the consideration that there cannot and should not be a universal ethic for all. Moral identity is tradition dependent. Consequently, his moral theology is directed at the church community itself.[20] Such an approach has some appealing aspects but it is not the approach of the church catholic. The United States Catholic bishops in the 1986 pastoral letter on the economy well illustrate the catholic approach by the fact that their letter addresses two different audiences—church members and the broader public. The bishops specifically want to add their voice to the public debate about the directions in which the United States economy is going. Church members and all other human beings are called to work for a more just economic life.[21]

A third characteristic of the church catholic with its universality and all-inclusiveness recognizes that church members belong to many other different communities, institutions, and groupings. In the past, there has been a tendency for the Catholic Church to absorb these other institutions into a subordinate relationship to itself. Think, for example, of the relationship between church and state. In the post-Constantinian era, the church recognized the state as a separate reality with its own ends and means, but the state had to serve the higher reality of the church. One sees here the danger and temptation of the universal and all-inclusive approach especially when joined to a hierarchical ordering.

The development in the twentieth century of the understanding of the relationship between church and state illustrates how in contemporary times the Catholic Church has come to recognize the proper domain of other institutions and not make them directly subordinate to the church. The *Declaration on Religious Liberty* of Vatican II clearly sets out the proper relationship of the church and state recognizing the legitimate and independent role of each but also avoiding a total separation between the two that would call for the privatization of the church and religion. The church, through its members who are both Christians and citizens, can and should work for justice in society and the state.[22] In addition, the *Pastoral Constitution on the Church in the Modern World* devotes a section to the rightful autonomy of earthly affairs "if by the autonomy of earthly affairs is meant the gradual discovery, exploitation, and ordering of the laws and values of matter and society, then the demand for autonomy is perfectly in order: it is at once the claim of modern [humans] and the desire of the creator."[23] The last sentence is fascinating. This emphasis on rightful autonomy has obviously come to the fore with modernity, which recognizes that it has not always been so. But this autonomy also expresses the desire of the creator.

The *Pastoral Constitution* goes on to say that methodological research in all branches of knowledge, provided it is carried out in a truly scientific manner and does not override moral laws, can never conflict with faith because the things of this world and the things of faith both derive from the same God. The footnote to this section refers to a book on Galileo. It is the only footnote in the long constitution that does not come from scripture, a father or doctor of the church, a recognized theologian in the church, or a document of the hierarchical magisterium.[24] The claim that faith and reason cannot contradict one another has been emphasized in the Catholic tradition since the time of scholasticism in the Middle Ages although in practice the Catholic Church has not always lived up to that axiom.

The individual Christian is a member of the church but also lives in the world with familial, friendly, and social relationships in the midst of cultural, political, and economic institutions. Whereas Christian faith should permeate life in all these spheres, relationships, and institutions, such institutions have their own structures and meanings that are not derived directly from faith. The Christian thus belongs to many institutions and groupings that have a rightful autonomy from the church. Once again, the catholic nature of the church differs from a sectarianism which sees the world as evil and opposed to the church and the gospel. The church catholic recognizes that it exists in the world among many other institutions and must be in dialogue with these realities and can even learn from them.

This understanding of catholicity also says something about the nature and role of theology in general and of moral theology in particular. Catholic theology serves three different publics—the church, the academy, and the world at large. Different emphases can be given to these three different audiences, but Catholic theology is related to all. Theology learns from and is in contact with other academic disciplines. Likewise, theology is in dialogue with the world as well illustrated in the *Pastoral Constitution on the Church in the Modern World* of Vatican II. The church catholic and its theology are not isolated from the academy and the world.

A sharply debated question has arisen within Roman Catholicism in the last decades that is ultimately connected with the notion of Catholicity: Is there a unique moral content for the Christian that differs from the content for other persons living in this world? The disputed question does not concern individual vocations or functions in the church but life in the world. All admit that Christian intentionality and motivation are quite different. Many non-Christians love enemies, forgive others, and work for social justice just as Christians are called to do. All recognize that the older Catholic natural law approach claims no unique status for its teaching which was based on human nature and human reason which are common to all humankind. Ever since *Pacem in terris* in 1963, papal social encyclicals are addressed not only to Catholics but to all men (sic) of good will. Thus, all would have to admit that the moral obligations of Christians and of all others in the world have much in common. I defend the thesis that there is no unique content to Christian morality for the

Christian living in the world, but this discussion lies beyond the purpose of this essay.[25]

A fourth characteristic of the church catholic with its emphasis on universality and inclusiveness concerns the various embodiments of the church. The church catholic is obviously universal, but it also is very much local as well.

Without doubt, the Roman Catholic Church until the recent past has overemphasized the universal aspect of the church at the expense of the local church. Vatican II tried to overcome this one-sided emphasis on the church universal. The growing importance of the role of the papacy in the church, abetted by the First Vatican Council's definition of papal infallibility and discussion limited only to the papal role in the church, continued until Vatican II. This council tried to overcome the one-sided development of the papacy and the universal church by spelling out the role of the college of bishops and of the local or residential bishop. All the bishops with the bishop of Rome as their head form the college of bishops which "have supreme and full authority over the universal church."[26] The local bishop is not merely a delegate of the pope but has what is called proper, ordinary, and immediate power over his diocese.[27] Vatican II also recognized that the local church is not simply a portion or branch office of the church, but the ecclesial body of Christ is truly present in each local Eucharistic community.[28] The term "local community" remains somewhat ambiguous and can be referred to the church in a particular nation, a particular diocese, or even a particular parish. Today the Catholic Church recognizes the church existing on the universal, regional, national, diocesan, and local levels, but much greater emphasis is given to the local Eucharistic community. [29]

Although Vatican II gave a more well-rounded understanding of the different levels of church, the new code of canon law has failed to give enough importance and independence to regional and national churches. Catholic ecclesiology should incorporate into its understanding of the church the principle of subsidiarity which plays an important role in Catholic social ethics. According to this principle, the higher level should help the lower level to do all it can and only take over whatever cannot be done properly on the lower level.[30]

The present discussions about inculturation call for the church to be more truly incarnated in the local culture. Too often in the past, a false universalism too readily identified the church with Western culture.[31]

This process of inculturation will also have significant ramifications for moral theology.

MEDIATION AND HIERARCHICAL STRUCTURE

The Roman Catholic Church shares the above four characteristics with all churches that accept the mark of catholicity. For our purposes, there are two important characteristics which tend to be distinctive of Roman Catholicism—the emphasis on mediation and the hierarchical structure and organization of the church.

The Roman Catholic emphasis on mediation is somewhat connected with catholicity, but it constitutes the most distinctive aspect of Roman Catholic theology and self-understanding. Sometimes the words sacramentality[32] or analogical imagination[33] are used to describe the same basic reality. Mediation refers to the fact that the divine is mediated in and through the human and the natural. All of creation shows forth the work of the creator and gives us a glimpse of the creator. In this understanding, the created, the natural, and the human are not evil but basically good and even contain within themselves a reflection of the creator.

The Catholic understanding of the church well illustrates the reality of mediation through the human. Just as in Jesus, the divine became incarnated in the human, so, too, in the church the divine element works in and through the human. The church is not primarily an invisible reality involving a relationship between God and the saved. Nor is the external aspect of the church merely a coat or a garment to cover over the divine element. The divine aspect and the human, the invisible and the visible, are united. The church is a visible community with visible structures which mediate God's loving presence in our world. Many other churches do not give that great a significance to the human or to the visible and structural aspects of the church. However, as will be mentioned later, the problem in the Catholic tradition has been to identify the human church too closely with Jesus.

The church carries out its mission and function primarily through the sacraments which again illustrate the reality of mediation. The liturgy is the summit toward which the activity of the church is directed; it is also the fount from which all her power flows.[34] The Eucharist is the heart and center of the liturgy and the place where the church most fully expresses its true reality.[35] But the Eucharist is primarily a meal. The solemn or celebratory meal is the primary way in which human families and friends gather to celebrate their love and make themselves present to one another. They share food, converse, remember the past, tell stories, and sustain one another in love and friendship. So the liturgy takes this fundamental human way of family and friends coming together in love to remember, to sustain, and to nurture one another and makes it the sign of the reality of God's presence to her people. Jesus is present to us in and through the celebratory meal recalling the many meals he shared with his own disciples and the final meal which has now come to be known as the Last Supper. The other sacraments also illustrate how the divine is mediated through the natural and the created. Baptism is conferred with water with the entire natural significance and meaning of water (life-sustaining, refreshing, cleansing) and the historical and salvific meaning (Noah's Ark saved in the water, the Israelites passing through the Red Sea). Oil is used in the sacraments to anoint certain ministers in the church and to symbolize the healing love of Jesus for the sick.

The Catholic tradition in its Thomistic philosophy insisted that reason could prove the existence of God by going from the natural and the created to the divine. Analogy or mediation formed the basis for claiming that from the order of the universe one could reason back to the all-knowing orderer whom we call God. The shadow of God is present in all creation and we can see something of God in all that is. God not only tells us something about creation and the human but creation and the human tell us something about God.[36] Catholicism in the past gave great importance to natural theology or theodicy which was an understanding of God based totally on human reason. Today some people question this emphasis on proving the existence of God strictly from reason, but its existence and role in the Catholic tradition well exemplify the Catholic insistence on mediation.[37]

Karl Barth once claimed that his major problem with Roman Catholicism was its *and*. Catholics believed in scripture *and* tradition, faith *and* reason, grace *and* works, Jesus *and* the church, and Mary *and* the saints. I disagree with Barth, but he is correct in pointing to the distinctive Catholic emphasis on mediation as exemplified in the *and* in all these pairs. [38]

This emphasis on mediation has important ramifications for the moral life and for moral theology. A very important manifestation of mediation is the Catholic acceptance of grace and works. Some Protestants have spoken about grace alone, but the Catholic tradition has recognized the important role of the human response. This response serves as the whole basis for the importance of the moral life and for theoretical and systematic reflections on it. [39]

The Catholic tradition recognizes the role of the church and the disciples of Jesus in carrying on the mission and work of the risen Jesus in time and space. This work involves not only the internal life of the church but also activity in the broader human community. According to the 1971 international synod of bishops, action on behalf of justice and the transformation of the world are a constitutive dimension of the preaching of the gospel or of the church's mission for the redemption of the human race and its liberation from every oppressive situation.[40] Thus, the Christian and the church continue through their actions and works the redeeming work of Jesus.

The importance of works and the human response are also illustrated in the sacrament of reconciliation. By our sins we offend God and need the mercy and forgiveness of the loving parent and the community. The sacrament of reconciliation thus shows the great importance and significance of human actions but now more from their negative side.

The Roman Catholic insistence on mediation strongly grounds the basic goodness of the natural, the human, and human reason and experience. Whatever is created is good and can even tell us something about God. One example of the Catholic *and* is the insistence on both faith and reason and the assertion that there can be no conflict between the two.[41] Thus, human reason and all that is created constitute important sources of moral wisdom and knowledge for the Christian. Catholic moral theology is not sectarian; it shares much with all other human approaches to ethics.

Andrew M. Greeley maintains, on the basis of his sociological studies, that Catholics have a distinctive imagination different from the Protestant imagination. This perduring Catholic imagination is grounded in what he calls the "analogical imagination" and what I have called "mediation." Greeley has designed surveys that prove the existence and importance of this Catholic imagination with its emphasis on the sacramental presence of God in all things and on a more communitarian understanding of the human person. This Catholic imagination explains why Catholics like being Catholic and remain in the Catholic Church despite their problems with the church leadership and disagreements

with some official church teachings. Thus, Greeley's sociological findings support the distinctive Catholic emphasis on mediation developed
here.[42]

The Catholic emphasis on mediation with its acceptance of the
goodness of the human also brings with it dangers that have not always
been avoided in the past. The primary danger comes from the tendency
to identify the divine with the human. This has occurred especially in
ecclesiology. Too often, the church was seen as only divine or as the
Kingdom of God. Vatican II recognized what was called the danger of
triumphalism, which was a practical illustration of this identifying the
total church with the divine. The church was thought to be perfect, holy,
and without spot. This council emphasized the pilgrim nature of the
church which sees the church as continually needing to grow and develop and also to overcome its own sinfulness.[43] The church in Catholic
theology today is no longer identified with the Kingdom of God but is
seen as a sign or sacrament of the Reign of God. The problem of too
closely relating the church to Jesus also comes from seeing the church
primarily in the light of Christology and not giving enough importance
to the role of the Holy Spirit's assistance in guiding the church over
time.[44]

A related danger or problem comes from a poor understanding of
mediation which tends to absolutize or give too much importance to the
second element or the aspect after the *and*. Thus, in the understanding of
Jesus and the church, the church at times came to have a greater importance than Jesus. Likewise in the understanding of scripture and tradition, tradition seemed to have an independent value apart from scripture.
In the area of morality, Catholics emphasize human works at the expense of grace. The danger for Catholic morality has always been that of
Pelagianism or semi-Pelagianism—the heresy that claims we save ourselves by our own works and not by the grace of God. Invariably, even
today, Protestants and Catholics in practice give different answers to the
question of how the Christian is saved. Protestants inevitably respond by
saying we are saved by faith, while Catholics see salvation as coming
from obeying God's law or keeping the commandments. This popular
testimony thus shows how, at times, the Catholic tradition has overstressed works at the expense of grace.

A second unique characteristic of Roman Catholicism involves the
hierarchical nature of the church. The Roman Catholic Church includes
the roles of pope and bishops in the church. As mentioned, Vatican II

has tried to overcome the one-sided emphasis on the papacy in the pre-Vatican II church by insisting on the collegiality of bishops with the pope in governing the whole church and the role of the bishop as a proper and immediate shepherd in his own diocese. The hierarchical nature of the church also has significant ramifications for moral theology because of the authoritative nature of church teaching. Catholic teaching recognizes the role of the magisterium (more accurately, the hierarchical magisterium) or teaching office of pope and bishops. The teaching authority and role of pope and bishops is usually described as referring to matters of both faith and morals.[45] The papal magisterium has issued authoritative teachings in many areas of personal and social morality. A 1962 textbook in medical ethics, for example, refers to the authoritative teaching of Pope Pius XII on almost forty different issues.[46]

However, within the church, one cannot limit the teaching and formation function only to those who hold hierarchical offices within the church. Vatican II has insisted that the church is primarily the total people of God. Through baptism all Christians share in the three-fold office of Jesus as priest, teacher, and ruler.[47] Thus, through baptismal commitment everyone in the church has a calling to teach and share the good news of faith and its implications for life with others. Such an understanding affects the way in which the whole church goes about its moral teaching and learning. In a pre-Vatican II understanding, the distinction was often made between the teaching church and the learning church. The teaching church was the hierarchical magisterium and the learning church was the rest. Truth trickled down from the teaching church to the learning church. However, this distinction can no longer be maintained.[48] In addition, the Catholic Church has always recognized the role that theologians play in the church. Perhaps the most heated discussions within the Catholic Church in the last two decades have centered about the exact relationship between the hierarchical teaching office, the experience of the people of God, and the role of theologians. These discussions lie beyond the focus of this essay.

CATHOLIC PRACTICE

This essay has shown in theory that the Roman Catholic Church is truly catholic in the sense of being universal, inclusive, and in dialogue with all others. In practice, the Catholic Church well illustrates this approach.

The Catholic Church borrowed some of its structural aspects from the institutions of the Roman Empire.[49] The theology of Thomas Aquinas (d. 1274), the greatest figure in the history of Catholic theology, borrowed heavily from the work of Aristotle.[50] Look at how the Catholic Church in the United States structures its own social mission. Education, social service, and care for the sick have always formed a very important aspect of the church's mission. However, in the United States today, Catholic higher education, health care, and social services are institutionalized in a way that is truly catholic. These institutions include in their governing bodies, their employees, and their clients both Catholics and non-Catholics. In addition, such institutions could not survive in their present form without money from the government. Catholic Charities, for example, receives about two-thirds of its budget from government tax money.[51]

Since Vatican II, the Catholic Church in the United States has structured its social mission in another way which also shows the catholic influence. The *Campaign for Human Development* started by the United States Catholic bishops over twenty-five years ago recognizes that social change involves more than just providing services for those in need. Structural change is absolutely necessary. This campaign aims to finance and support community action programs in which the members of the local, pluralistic community themselves come together, determine their needs, and work together for the structural changes that will fulfill these basic needs. Here the church supports broad-based community groups comprising people of all religions or none which enable people to help themselves. The direction and action of the group comes from the people themselves and not from the church.[52] In practice, the Catholic Church strives to be inclusive and universal in its dialogue with others in theory and in its working with all people of good will to obtain a greater justice in our world.

DANGERS IN THE CATHOLIC APPROACH

The Catholic Church has many strengths in its theory and practice, but as in all realities there are also dangers. The primary danger arises from the temptation for the church to conform itself too much to the *zeitgeist* or to the world around it. Historically, the Roman Catholic Church has not always avoided this danger. Too often, the church became too closely aligned with those in power and people of affluence and influence. Many have pointed out the failure of the Roman Catholic Church to condemn the Holocaust because of the harm it might have caused the church.[53] In the United States, the fear has always been that the church might too readily accommodate itself to the American ethos and culture.

The basis for this danger and temptation comes from the Catholic understanding that whatever God made is good. The church catholic must be in dialogue with all reality, even being able to learn about God, to say nothing about human actions, from all that exists in our world. The danger is that an inclusive church open to embracing all will lose the dynamism and commitment that should mark the body of the disciples of Jesus. Specifically, the church might become too conformed to the world and forget that while the goodness of God is present in our world, so too are human finitude, sinfulness, and the lack of the fullness of the reign of God.

An old axiom of the spiritual life counsels the individual to act against the predominant vice or fault. In an analogous way, the church catholic must try to confront the dangers inherent in catholicity. A number of important steps can help to alleviate such dangers.

First, the universal call of all to holiness and the fullness of the Christian life, which was so clearly taught at Vatican II, must become more central in the teaching and life of the church. This serves as the primary antidote to the danger of an inclusive church which can too easily lose the flavor of its salt. All are called to be perfect even as the gracious God is perfect. Perfection or holiness does not mean that one has to leave the world and one's many obligations in the world, but faith should permeate all our relations and actions in our daily lives.

Second, and intimately connected with a call to holiness, is the call of continual conversion. No one has fully responded to the gift of God; we all fall short. No one who meditates seriously on the Sermon on the Mount can ever say: "All these things I have kept since my youth." The call to continual conversion means that the individual Christian and the church must always be self-critical. We must continually be on the lookout for the danger that we have too easily bought into the *zeitgeist*. The Roman Catholic Church has perennially had a difficulty in recognizing and acknowledging its own sin and failings. Recall the tendency to readily identify the church totally with the divine. However, the recent emphasis on the pilgrim church underscores the need for the church to be constantly self-critical and always willing to confess its sins and ask for forgiveness.

A third important antidote for the church catholic is to recognize and foster the prophetic voice in the church. Prophecy has always played an important role in the Judeo-Christian tradition. The prophets of the Hebrew Bible constantly upbraided the people of God for their infidelity. These prophets especially inveighed against the failure of the people to hear the cry of the poor and the oppressed. The prophetic voice is always disturbing. Prophets are not the easiest people to live with, but the church must always encourage the prophetic voice no matter how disturbing it might be. Without the prophet's voice and witness, the church will never be able to hear the calls to holiness and continual conversion. However, just as there are dangers and temptations for the church catholic, there are also dangers and temptations for prophets. The prophet, too, must always be self-critical and recognize the primary temptations of delusion and self-righteousness. But the church catholic is always willing to encourage and listen to the prophetic voice no matter how painful or difficult it might be.

Fourth, the recognition of different vocations and callings within the church is clearly associated with the prophetic function. The church catholic has traditionally recognized that in this imperfect world justice and peace do not always lie down together. Sometimes violence might be the only way to insure that some measure of justice is achieved. Nations in this world cannot be pacifists. However, individuals within the church can and (thanks be to God) are called to be pacifists.[54] How can both pacifism and just war (or the equivalent) be acceptable positions within the church? Yes, there is some overlap between them in the sense that even the just war theory operates with a presumption against violence. But ultimately from a moral perspective, the two positions are contradictory.[55]

However, from an ecclesial perspective, the church catholic can and should recognize both positions as exemplified in hierarchical teachings. Nations cannot be pacifists today. Many individuals will accept some use of violence, but there are also pacifists in the church. Peace is a very important value in human existence which too often is forgotten about or discarded. Vocational pacifists are called by God to bear witness to this very significant value.

The church catholic recognizes many important moral values but also realizes that these values are not absolute but exist in relationship with many other values. However, certain values are so important that individuals are called to bear witness to these values for the sake of the whole church and the whole world. In my judgment this explains the tradition of religious life as we have known it until now. The three vows of poverty, chastity, and obedience do not make monks or religious better Christians than those that do not take these vows. Monks and religious are not called to a higher state of life or holiness but choose to bear witness to these very important values.

Many people, especially in the Protestant tradition, have often understood monasticism as a flight from the world with many similarities to sects.[56] However, such is not the case. From a very practical perspective, why is it that some of the best liqueurs in the world are named after monks? Thomas Cahill has recently pointed out how historically the Irish monks saved civilization.[57] In contemporary times, Thomas Merton has shown that monasticism is not a flight from the world.[58] Monks and religious strive to bear witness to the significant values of poverty, chastity, and obedience and not necessarily flee the world.

Today this calling or vocation to bear witness to particular virtues must be extended to all Christians. A significant number of Christians bear witness to voluntary poverty. The whole church cannot embrace such poverty. But the danger for the church as a whole and Christians living in the world is to be entrapped by the allure of wealth. Today other Christians voluntarily make themselves one with the oppressed and powerless—a magnificent witness that serves the church and the world. We in the church must recognize and support this vocational witness that is not a flight from the world but an important witness for the world. The church catholic must make room for and encourage such witness which contributes to the good of the whole church and the world and serves as an antidote against the danger of the church catholic's becoming too conformed to the world around us.

SOCIAL LOCATION AND POSTMODERNISM

The morality of the Catholic Church is an inclusive and universal morality affecting the whole world. The Catholic Church is concerned about what happens to all peoples all over the globe and not just about what goes on only within the church. Many reasons justify this catholic or universal social ethics. The belief in creation reminds us we are brothers and sisters of all other human beings since we recognize God as the mother and father of us all. In Genesis, the name given to the first human being is Adam which means man or, for us today, human being. The first human being is not identified as belonging to a tribe or clan or race but simply as a human being. The church's emphasis on love and justice insists the object of such love and justice includes all humankind.

Universalism and inclusivism in morality and ethics have been strongly challenged in recent years. In theory, postmodernism has attacked modernity with its emphasis on autonomous, objective, value-free, neutral knowledge. In practice, struggles for justice and equality by groups that have been marginalized and oppressed have also argued against the dangers of universalism and essentialism.

Postmodernism has disagreed with modernism's acceptance of the rational, objective, neutral, value-free, universalist perspective of the ideal knower. This understanding is intimately connected with the Enlightenment approach and has been the major and perhaps the only way of approaching knowledge and education in the western world. The ideal scientist is the person who has these characteristics and then can better understand and judge more objectively what is occurring.

On both the theoretical and practical levels, liberation theology in all its ramifications (e.g. South American, African-American, feminist) has challenged the understanding of the ideal knower. There is no such thing as a neutral, objective, value-free, universalist perspective. Everyone comes to the scene with one's own background, commitments, and history. We have often been reminded lately that history is not the objective science we once thought it was. History has always been written by the winners. If the Native Americans were still the predominant group in this country, we would not accept as an historical fact that Columbus discovered America.

The universalism and essentialism connected with the Enlightenment have had disastrous effects on the needs and concerns of the poor, the marginalized, and the oppressed. These people have either been forgotten or totally absorbed by the dominant ideology. Liberation in Latin America begins with the experience of the oppressed and the marginalized in society. But such an approach also recognizes that the Christian God is not just a neutral, value-free observer. God is prejudiced. In our culture, and often for good reasons, prejudice is usually seen as a pejorative term. However, the root meaning of the word is simply a "prejudgment." The Judeo-Christian tradition recognizes that God is defi-

nitely on the side of the poor. Although many others will oppress the
poor, God will be their defender and supporter. The psalmist reminds us
that God hears the cry of the poor. The prophetic books of the Hebrew
bible strongly support such an understanding of God's prejudice. Our
God has a special love and concern for the poor and is not neutral or
value-free.[59]

Feminist theology and ethics, especially as it has developed in this
country, show how a universal and essentialist approach has so distorted
reality. The claim to be a universally valid, neutral, and objective approach to the role of women in society (and the church) was in reality
the imposition of patriarchy by the dominant group in society. Women
were assigned a subordinate, private, and generally passive role. Patriarchy has seriously affected the Catholic Church and its tradition. Feminist
ethics begins with the experience and particularity of women. Most
feminists in the beginning of this movement were white, middle- and
upper-class American women. Some African-American women pointed
out that their experience was quite different, and womanist theology and
ethics emerged from this experience.[60] Then Hispanic women recognized that their experience was different from both the middle class
white women and African-American women and began developing a
mujerista theology and ethics.[61] To their credit, most feminist theologians and ethicists recognize the need for these other approaches. Feminist
theology and ethics in themselves are still too universal and have to be
broken down into the experiences of particular women in diverse cultures and situations.

In theory and in conjunction with feminism and other defenders of
the marginalized, postmodernism has insisted on the particular and diverse not the universal and the all-inclusive. Modernism's emphasis on
the universal has provided a means to further subordinate and even
eradicate the "other" who is not like us. Postmodernism deconstructs the
self and glories in emphasizing the particular and the different.[62] But as a
result, postmodernism often has no place for the universal and even denies the possibility of a universal ethics or morality.

Where does and should Catholic ethics stand with regard to these
developments? Catholic moral theology in its own way has also been
opposed to the Enlightenment especially with regard to the latter's stress
on individualism, autonomy, and freedom.[63] However, the Catholic tradition, in its own way, stressed universalism and essentialism. The essential nature of human beings could be known by reflecting on this na-

ture which is the same all over the world. From this universal nature, reason can deduce how human beings should act. Manuals of moral theology stress this very essentialist, universalist, and deductive approach to moral theology which has recently been described as classicism. Classicism emphasizes the universal, the immutable, and the unchanging, while employing a deductive methodology well illustrated in the syllogism. The syllogism contains a major premise (all humans are rational); a minor premise (Mary is a human); and a conclusion (therefore, Mary is rational). The conclusion is just as certain as the premise if the logic is correct. Certitude was thus the goal of a deductive methodology.[64]

Many commentators following Bernard Lonergan have pointed out that the most significant change which occurred at Vatican II was the shift from classicism to historical consciousness. Vatican II brought about important changes in the Catholic Church and in Catholic self-understanding, but the church still had the same scripture and the same tradition it always had. What changed was the way in which we looked at reality. Historical consciousness gives more importance to the particular, the individual, and the contingent. In addition, historical consciousness pays greater importance to human subjectivity. Such an understanding tends to employ a more inductive methodology which recognizes that one is searching for the best hypothesis and is not necessarily seeking absolute certitude. An historically conscious approach avoids the extreme dangers of classicism on the one hand and sheer existentialism on the other. Sheer existentialism sees the particular human person with no real connection to the past and future and with no binding relationships to other human beings and to the world.[65]

Within Roman Catholic moral theology, the *Pastoral Constitution on the Church in the Modern World* well illustrates a more historically conscious methodology. In discussing specific areas, this constitution does not begin with definitions that are always and everywhere true but with the signs of the times—the current historical and cultural realities that are characterizing the present.[66] The clearest example of historical consciousness and an inductive approach in the official documents of the post-Vatican II church is found in Pope Paul VI's apostolic letter *Octogesima adveniens*:

> In the face of such widely varying situations, it is difficult for us to utter a unified message and to put forward a solution which has universal validity. Such is not our

ambition, nor is it our mission. It is up to the Christian communities to analyze with objectivity the situation which is proper to their own country, to shed on it the light of the Gospel's unalterable words and to draw principles of reflection, norms of judgment, and directives for action from the social teaching of the church.[67]

Post-Vatican II historical consciousness wants to give more importance to the particular, the individual, and the historical, but it does not want to give up or deny some aspects of universality. Postmodernism at times denies the universal in the name of protecting the particular and the diverse which appear to be threatened by the recognition of the universal. Catholics have addressed the issue of the challenge of postmodernism especially in the area of liberation theology and feminist theology. Most Catholic thinkers in these areas recognize the great failure to give enough importance to the particular, the other, and the diverse in the past, but they do not want to deny some universalism today.

Liberation theology, especially in the Roman Catholic tradition, holds on to both particularity and diversity and also the universal by its insisting on a preferential option for the poor, not an exclusive option. God loves all people, but God has a preferential option for the poor.[68]

The Christology and soteriology of liberation theology also stress the particular and the concrete. The pre-Vatican II manuals of dogmatic theology neglected the soteriology of Christology and stressed rather the metaphysical and ontological aspects of Christ (one person—two natures) rather than the saving work of Jesus. Liberation theology emphasizes the soteriological aspect of Christology. Jesus is Savior and Liberator. In the process, liberation theology develops a Christology from below as differentiated from the older Christology from above. Christology from above begins with the pre-existing *Logos* who is consubstantial with the Father. The *Logos* later takes on a human nature and saves us by dying and rising for all. Liberation theology emphasizes the Christology from below without denying the divinity of Jesus or the fact that salvation is open to all. The liberation approach gives more importance to the humanity of Jesus and to the historical circumstances surrounding his life and death. Salvation and redemption thus become more particular and concrete. Jesus was a victim who was unjustly put to death and stands in solidarity with all those who are victims of oppression and injustice. Jesus sides with the poor, the outcasts, and the oppressed. Redemption is thus both particular and concrete and not just abstract and with no particular differentiations.[69]

Feminist ethicists in the United States have been dealing with the problem of the particular and the universal for the last few years. Attention to diversity, otherness, and difference is the essential methodological concern of contemporary feminist theologies. This calls for attention to women's experiences, differences in the analysis of subjectivity and language, and the need for a hermeneutic of suspicion with regard to past traditions since they have been so deeply affected by patriarchy.[70] Feminists are very aware of the social construction of moral norms, the grave inadequacy of past views of women's nature, and the need to appreciate diversity and particularity, though most feminists also realize the need to avoid total relativism. Margaret Farley is very conscious of the problems that have resulted from an essentialism and abstract universalism that all too readily ignore particularity and the diversity of persons in their concrete context. Farley tries to develop a feminist version of respect for persons that is the same for all persons, male or female, whatever their diversity and particularity. This author proposes a revised understanding of autonomy and of relationality as obligating features of persons. An obligation to respect persons requires that we honor their freedom and respond to their needs, that we value difference as well as sameness, and that we attend to the concrete realities of our own and others' lives.[71]

Anne E. Patrick appreciates many of the chief points of postmodernism with its attention to discourse, its recognition of plurality and ambiguity, and its acknowledgment of the moral significance of language forms and the politics of discourse. Epistemology can never again claim the abstract certainty and stability so often aimed at in the past but must strive for relatively adequate knowledge in our given historical circumstances. In discussing the moral self, attention must be paid to a critical analysis of social, historical, political, psychological, and economic factors. For Patrick, however, feminist ethics can never become relativistic.[72]

Lisa Sowle Cahill, in her presidential address to the Catholic Theological Society of America, insisted that feminist theology is thoroughly particular, historical, and concrete, but is also committed to equal personal dignity, equal mutual respect, and equal social power for women and for men. Some feminists often rely on postmodern understandings (her view of postmodernism is more negative than Patrick's precisely because she feels many postmodernists seem to deny any possibility of the universal) by either retreating romantically into tradition bound and limited approaches which do not allow for any intercultural comparison or evaluation or buying no-holds- barred deconstruction of all social reality so that any communality is lost. Cahill wants to retain the need and importance of objectivity and some universality while rejecting the Enlightenment ideal of abstract reason and ahistorical universalism. Cahill develops and revises somewhat the Roman Catholic natural law tradition with its acceptance of an objective moral order knowable by reasonable reflection on human experience, especially on the basic goods that constitute human flourishing. Like Patrick, Cahill appeals to the approach of Roman Catholic systematic theologian David Tracy who expresses the reliability and generalizability of truth judgments in ethics in terms of analogy. In such an approach, we can understand and evaluate justice and injustice in different cultures by virtue of their resemblance to our own experience. The author wants to combine the historical consciousness of postmodernism with the inductive ethical approach of the Aristotelian-Thomistic tradition. Truth claims, especially through praxis and prudence, can be grounded in the culturally mediated but reliable stratum of common human experience. Cahill wants to move away from the manualistic natural law approach often associated with Catholic moral theology before Vatican II with its emphasis on abstract essentialism, *a priori* reasoning, and deduction to a renewal of ethics in an objective moral order discovered through experience, praxis, and classical reason in an intercultural context.[73]

The signs of the times point to the imperative of recognizing particularity and diversity but at the same time being able to maintain some universality and unity. On the political scene, countries today are being torn apart because of religious and tribal differences. In our own country, the divisions among races and cultures are becoming more acute as we see what is happening in so many of our large cities. Likewise the economic gap between the wealthiest and the poor is ever growing in our country. In the midst of all these differences and divisions, it is becoming harder to maintain some universality and unity. Can people with all their differences live together in peace and harmony in a particular country, in a hemisphere, and in the globe? This practical question is facing all of society today but is obviously more acute in some countries than in others. On the economic scene, we are now experiencing a global economy, but we desperately need a global ethic to bring about greater justice in our world. We have been conscious for so long of the great economic gap between the first world and the two-thirds world, but we have done little or nothing to close that gap. In the light of the needs of the times with the greater emphasis on the global aspect of all human realities, the *World Parliament of Religions* in Chicago in 1993 tried to develop a global ethic in the light of these pressing needs of our time.[74] International organizations have begun to stress the importance of universal human rights which must be applicable to all people in all places, but one also recognizes the great difficulty in agreeing on what these rights are.[75] Thus both theoretically and practically the challenge for all humanity today, as well as for the church catholic, is to be able to hold on to particularity and diversity while still claiming some universality and unity.

In the past, there can be no doubt that the Roman Catholic Church, in both its ecclesiology and in its ethics, gave too much emphasis to the essential and the universal and not enough to the particular, the individual, and the contingent. Now the challenge is for us as church to recognize the greater particularity and diversity existing but also to maintain some universality and unity. The shift to historical consciousness and the dialogue with postmodernism as illustrated in Catholic feminist thought also recognize fewer certainties and greater ambiguities than were found in the older Catholic approaches.

This essay has considered the ecclesial context for Catholic moral theology. The Roman Catholic understanding of the church provides very significant direction and parameters both for Catholic moral practice and for moral theology.

NOTES

1.   There is no definitive history of moral theology. Louis Vereecke is the recognized authority in the field, but he has not published books as such or a general history. He has published four volumes of printed notes for his students at the *Accademia Alfonsiana* in Rome. Entitled *Storia della teologia morale moderna*, these volumes have been widely diffused and cited, and they are for public sale. They cover the period from 1300 to 1789—*Storia della teologia morale dal XIV° al XVI° secolo: da Guglielmo di Ockham a Martin Lutero (1300–1520); Storia della teologia morale in spagna nel XVI° secolo e origine delle "Institutiones Morales" (1520–1600); Storia della teologia morale nel XVII° secolo: la crisi della teologia morale (1600–1700);* and *Storia della*

teologia morale nel XVIII° secolo: Concina e S. Alfonso de' Liguori, l'Aufklarung (1700–1789). Summaries of his research on the history of moral theology have appeared—L. Vereecke, "Moral Theology, History of (700 to Vatican Council I)," *New Catholic Encyclopedia* (New York: McGraw-Hill, 1967), IX, 1119–22; L. Vereecke, "Storia della teologia morale," *Nuovo dizionario di teologia morale* (Milano: Paoline, 1990), 1314–38. A very helpful collection of his essays has been published—Louis Vereecke, *De Guillaume d'Ockham à Saint Alphonse de Liguori: Etudes d'histoire de la théologie morale moderne 1300–1787* (Rome: Collegium S. Alfonsi de Urbe, 1986). The best available one volume history of moral theology is Guiseppe Angelini and Ambrogio Valsecchi, *Disegno storico della teologia morale* (Bologna: Dehoniane, 1972).

2. For my discussion of the development and approach of the manuals, see Charles E. Curran, *The Origins of Moral Theology in the United States: Three Different Approaches* (Washington, DC: Georgetown University Press, 1997), 12–167.

3. For a classic view of Aquinas as a philosopher, see Etienne Gilson, *The Christian Philosophy of St. Thomas Aquinas* (New York: Random House, 1956); for a contemporary theological perspective, see Thomas F. O'Meara, *Thomas Aquinas Theologian* (Notre Dame, IN: University of Notre Dame Press, 1997).

4. See Edward Vacek's, S.J., article in this collection.

5. "Dogmatic Constitution on the Church," in Austin Flannery, ed., *Vatican Council II: The Conciliar and Post Conciliar Documents* (Collegeville, MN: Liturgical Press, 1992, rev. ed.), §§ 1–17; for a summary of Vatican II's teaching on the church, see Michael A. Fahey, "Church," in Francis Schüssler Fiorenza and John P. Galvin, eds., *Systematic Theology: Roman Catholic Perspectives* (Minneapolis, MN: Fortress, 1991), II, 33–43.

6. Acts 9:2; 18:25–26; 19:9, 22:4, 23; 24:14, 22.

7. "Dogmatic Constitution on the Church," §§ 39–42.

8. Hans Küng, *The Church* (New York: Sheed & Ward, 1968); and Fahey, "Church," II, 3–74.

9. "Dogmatic Constitution on the Church," § 9.

10. For this reason Catholicism had to deal with the question of the possibility of salvation outside the church. Today all recognize that God's salvific call is addressed to all. See Francis A. Sullivan, *Salvation Outside the Church? Tracing the History of the Catholic Response* (New York: Paulist, 1992).

11. Hans Küng and Leonard Swidler, eds., *The Church in Anguish: Has the Vatican Betrayed Vatican II?* (San Francisco: Harper & Row, 1987).

12. Norman Goodall, ed., *The Upsala Report* (Geneva: World Council of Churches, 1968), 11–18. See also *Catholicity and Apostolicity*, a special issue of *One in Christ* 4 (1970), and Patrick W. Fuerth, *The Concept of Catholicity in the*

Documents of the World Council of Churches (Rome: Anselmiana, 1973).

13. Basilio Petrà, "Il dialogo etico interconfessionale: Considerazioni e prospettive," *Studia Moralia* 34 (1996), 295–321.

14. Marcellinus Zalba, *Theologiae moralis summa* (Madrid: Biblioteca de autores cristianos, 1952–1958), I, 609–32, 708–13.

15. Sociological studies confirm the theological understanding of the Roman Catholic Church as embracing people with different levels of commitment. See William V. D'Antonio, James D. Davidson, Dean R. Hoge, and Ruth A. Wallace, *Laity, American and Catholic: Transforming the Church* (Kansas City, MO: Sheed & Ward, 1996), 131–44.

16. "Pastoral Constitution on the Church in the Modern World," in Flannery, ed., *Vatican Council II*, § 1.

17. Ernst Troeltsch, *The Social Teaching of the Christian Churches* (New York: Harper Torchbooks, 1960), II, 691–729.

18. *Ibid.*, 461–65.

19. For an analysis of Yoder's approach from a Catholic perspective, see Kenneth P. Hallahan, *The Social Ethics of Non-Resistance: The Writings of Mennonite Theologian John Howard Yoder Analyzed from a Roman Catholic Perspective* (Ph.D. Diss., The Catholic University of America, 1997).

20. For his most systematic work, see Stanley Hauerwas, *The Peaceable Kingdom: A Primer in Christian Ethics* (Notre Dame, IN: University of Notre Dame Press, 1983); also *id.*, *Where Resident Aliens Live: Exercises for Christian Practice* (Nashville, TN: Abingdon, 1996).

21. National Conference of Catholic Bishops, *Economic Justice for All: Pastoral Letter on Catholic Social Teaching and the U.S. Economy* (Washington: National Conference of Catholic Bishops, 1986), § 27.

22. "Declaration on Religious Liberty," in Flannery, ed., *Vatican Council II*, 799–812.

23. "Pastoral Constitution on the Church in the Modern World," § 36.

24. *Ibid.*

25. Charles E. Curran and Richard A. McCormick, S.J., eds., *Readings in Moral Theology No. 2: The Distinctiveness of Christian Ethics* (New York: Paulist, 1980); Vincent MacNamara, *Faith and Ethics: Recent Roman Catholicism* (Washington, DC: Georgetown University Press, 1985). On this issue, I have been in academic discussion and disagreement with Norbert Rigali. Our exchange serves as a model of the way in which people can disagree but retain their mutual respect and even friendship. For Rigali's latest article on the subject, see Norbert Rigali, "Christian Morality and Universal Morality: The One and the Many," *Louvain Studies* 19 (Spring 1994), 18–33.

26. "Dogmatic Constitution on the Church," § 22.

27. *Ibid.*, § 27.

28. *Ibid.*, § 26.

29. Fahey, "Church," II, 39.

30. John Mahoney, "Subsidiarity in the Church," *Month* 21 (1988), 968–74.

31. S. Iniobong Udoidem, *Pope John Paul II on Inculturation: Theory and Practice* (Lanham, MD: University Press of America, 1996); and Eugene Hillman, *Toward an African Christianity: Inculturation Applied* (New York: Paulist, 1993).

32. Richard P. McBrien, *Catholicism* (San Francisco: Harper, 1994, rev. ed.), 9–12.

33. David Tracy, *The Analogical Imagination: Christian Theology and the Culture of Pluralism* (New York: Crossroad, 1981).

34. "Constitution on the Sacred Liturgy," in Flannery, ed., *Vatican Council II*, § 10.

35. *Ibid.*, §§ 47–58.

36. Thomas Aquinas, *S.T.*, I, q. 2, a. 3.

37. McBrien, *Catholicism*, 209–23.

38. From a Catholic perspective see Hans Urs von Balthasar, *The Theology of Karl Barth* (New York: Holt, Rinehart, and Winston, 1971), 40–41.

39. Joseph P. Wawrykow, *God's Grace and Human Action: "Merit" in the Theology of Thomas Aquinas* (Notre Dame, IN: University of Notre Dame Press, 1995).

40. Synod of Bishops, 1971, *Justita in mundo*, in David J. O'Brien and Thomas A. Shannon, eds., *Catholic Social Thought: The Documentary Heritage* (Maryknoll, NY: Orbis, 1992), 289.

41. Robert Sokolowski, *The God of Faith and Reason: Foundations of Christian Theology* (Washington, DC: Catholic University of America Press, 1995).

42. Andrew M. Greeley, *The Catholic Myth: The Behavior and Beliefs of American Catholics* (New York: Charles Scribner's Sons, 1990), especially 34–64.

43. "Dogmatic Constitution on the Church," §§ 48–51.

44. *Ibid.*, § 3.

45. *Ibid.*, §§ 18–29.

46. John P. Kenny, *Principles of Medical Ethics* (Westminster, MD: Newman, 1962, 2nd ed.), 272.

47. "Dogmatic Constitution on the Church," §§ 9–12.

48. Fahey, "Church," II, 49–50.

49. James A. Coriden, *An Introduction to Canon Law* (New York: Paulist, 1991), 65–99.

50. See, for example, Dennis J. Billy and Terence Kennedy, eds., *Some Philosophical Issues in Moral Matters: The Collected Ethical Writings of Joseph Owens* (Rome: Editiones Academiae Alphonsianae, 1996); and Daniel

Westberg, *Right Practical Reason: Aristotle, Action, and Prudence in Aquinas* (New York: Oxford University Press, 1994).

51. Charles E. Curran, "The Catholic Identity of Catholic Institutions," *Theological Studies* 58 (1997), 90–108.

52. Cardinal Joseph Bernardin, "The Campaign for Human Development at Age 25," *Origins* 25 (1995), 196–99; and William T. Poole, *The Campain for Human Development: Christian Charity or Political Activism?* (Washington, DC: Capital Research Center, 1988).

53. Robert G. Weisbord, *The Chief Rabbi, the Pope, and the Holocaust: An Era in Vatican-Jewish Relations* (New Brunswick, NJ: Transaction Publishers, 1992).

54. National Conference of Catholic Bishops, "The Challenge of Peace: God's Promise and Our Response," in O'Brien and Shannon, eds., *Catholic Social Thought*, §§ 56–121.

55. Kenneth R. Himes, "Pacifisim and the Just War Tradition in Roman Catholic Social Teaching," in John A. Coleman, ed., *One Hundred Years of Catholic Social Thought: Celebration and Challenge* (Maryknoll, NY: Orbis, 1991), 329–44.

56. E.g., H. Richard Niebuhr, *Christ and Culture* (New York: Harper Torchbook, 1956), 56.

57. Thomas Cahill, *How the Irish Saved Civilization: The Untold Story of Ireland's Heroic Role from the Fall of Rome to the Rise of Medieval Europe* (New York: Doubleday, 1995).

58. William H. Shannon, *Silent Lamp: The Thomas Merton Story* (New York: Crossroad, 1992).

59. For the thought of the father of liberation theology in South America, see Gustavo Gutierrez, *Essential Writings* (Minneapolis, MN: Fortress, 1996).

60. Diana L. Hayes, *Hagar's Daughters: Womanist Ways of Being in the World* (New York: Paulist, 1995).

61. Ada Maria Isasi-Diaz, *Mujerista Theology: A Theology for the Twenty-First Century* (Maryknoll, NY: Orbis, 1996).

62. Zygmunt Bauman, *Life in Fragments: Essays in Postmodern Morality* (Oxford: Blackwell, 1995).

63. R. Bruce Douglass and David Hollenbach, eds., *Catholicism and Liberalism: Contributions to American Public Philosophy* (New York: Cambridge University Press, 1994).

64. Richard M. Gula, *Reason Informed by Faith: Foundations of Catholic Morality* (New York: Paulist, 1989), 30–39.

65. For my development of historical consciousness, see *Directions in Fundamental Moral Theology* (Notre Dame, IN: University of Notre Dame Press, 1985), 137–55.

66. "Pastoral Constitution on the Church in the Modern World," §§ 47,54,

63, 73, and 77. See also, Charles Moeller, "Preface and Introductory Statement," in Herbert Vorgrimler, ed., *Commentary and Documents of Vatican II*, V *Pastoral Constitution on the Church in the Modern World* (New York: Herder & Herder, 1969), 94.

67. Pope Paul VI, *Octogesima Adveniens*, in O'Brien and Shannon, eds., *Catholic Social Thought*, § 4.

68. Steven J. Pope, "Proper and Improper Partiality and the Preferential Option for the Poor," *Theological Studies* 54 (1993), 242–71.

69. Jon Sobrino, *Jesus the Liberator: A Historical-Theological Reading of Jesus of Nazareth* (Maryknoll, NY: Orbis, 1993).

70. Susan A. Ross, "Feminist Theology: A Review of the Literature," *Theological Studies* 56 (1995), 327–30.

71. Margaret A. Farley, "A Feminist Version of Respect for Persons," in Charles E. Curran, Margaret A. Farley, and Richard A. McCormick, S.J., eds., *Readings in Moral Theology No. 9: Feminist Ethics and the Catholic Tradition* (New York: Paulist, 1996), 164–83; and Farley, "Feminism and Universal Morality," in Gene Outka and John P. Reeder, Jr., eds., *Prospects for a Common Morality* (Princeton, N.J.: Princeton University Press, 1993), 170–90.

72. Anne E. Patrick, *Liberating Conscience: Feminist Explorations in Catholic Moral Theology* (New York: Continuum, 1996), 40–71.

73. Lisa Sowle Cahill, "Feminist Ethics, Differences and Common Ground: A Catholic Perspective," in Curran, Farley, and McCormick, eds., *Readings in Moral Theology No. 9*, 184–204; and Cahill, *Sex, Gender, and Christian Ethics* (New York: Cambridge University Press, 1996), 14–72.

74. Hans Küng and Karl-Josef Kuschei, eds., *A Global Ethic: The Declaration of the Parliament of the World's Religions* (New York: Continuum, 1993).

75. A. H. Robertson, *Human Rights in the World: An Introduction to the Study of the International Protection of Human Rights* (New York: St. Martin's, 1996, 4th ed.).

THE SPECIFICITY OF
CHRISTIAN ETHICS AND/OR
MORALITY

The Question of the Uniqueness of Christian Morality: An Historical and Critical Analysis of the Debate in Roman Catholic Ethics

James J. Walter

For more than three decades there has been an ongoing debate about whether or not there is anything unique about Christian morality. The participants in this discussion have been principally Roman Catholic, though a few Protestant scholars have entered the fray from time to time.[1] Not surprisingly, all the Catholic discussants until recently have assumed that there exists a universal or common morality, called the natural law, that all people of goodwill, in principle, can know independently of explicit faith and revelation. Acknowledging the existence of this universal morality, they then asked whether the realities of explicit faith and revelation might add anything to this morality.

However, in recent years this debate and its assumption about a common morality have been influenced by another longstanding debate that has been raging within the disciplines of both philosophy and theology. This latter debate, frequently referred to as the debate about non-foundationalism,[2] is concerned with whether or not any morality, including Christian morality, can have a universal foundation or ground such that one could claim the existence and/or knowledge of a common morality for all. Because nonfoundationalists argue that all knowledge and morality are dependent on a specific culture, tradition, or some other particular reality, they affirm not only that there are plural moralities but that each morality is necessarily unique. Consequently, many of these proponents reject the existence, and even the possibility, of a universal common morality that could be shared by all independent of their unique culture, tradition, etc.

Recently some Catholic ethicists[3] have joined together these two debates in that the answer they give to the first question about whether there can be any uniqueness to Christian morality is strongly influenced, in part, by the assumptions and terms of the second debate. To say the least, the joining of these debates has made the discussion about the uniqueness of Christian morality even more complex in the Catholic tradition because now it may no longer be taken for granted that all the participants accept the possibility of a universal moral order.

This chapter has three purposes. The first is to chart the historical and theological contexts within which the debate about the uniqueness of Christian morality arose in Roman Catholic ethics over the past thirty years. The second purpose is to analyze the debate by reference to several confusions and false dichotomies that became part of the discussion almost from the very beginning. Finally, I will return to the topic of how this debate about the uniqueness of Christian morality has been incorporated within the broader philosophical and theological discussion of nonfoundationalism. To this end, I will focus on the writings of one of the key Catholic participants in both debates, Norbert J. Rigali, S.J., in order to analyze two of the crucial issues that need attention if this debate is to progress in any satisfactory way.

HISTORICAL AND THEOLOGICAL CONTEXTS

When the Second Vatican Council formally convened on October 11, 1962, the reigning type of moral theology in Roman Catholicism was manualist in style and neo-Scholastic in character. Like their predecessors originating from the end of the sixteenth century, these manuals were written to train ordained clerics to hear confessions, and their focus was practical in nature, sin-oriented, individualistic, minimalist and legalistic. Probably the most significant characteristic of these handbooks, however, was the near separation of the moral life from the great Biblical themes of scripture, e.g., conversion and discipleship, and from the important treatises of both dogmatic and ascetical theology, e.g., grace and soteriology. Because the dominant metaphor for understanding morality was law, manualist moral theology focused much attention on the natural law. Not only did these manualists accept the existence of a common morality grounded on universal human nature (natural law), they agreed with Thomas Aquinas' position that in general Christian faith did not add any new content to the moral life that went beyond the natural law.[4]

It is fair to say that these neo-Scholastic authors did not fashion a close relation between Christian faith and morality. To be sure, God was necessary to morality as the source of moral obligation, and the origin of morality was generally viewed as God laying a precept (obligation) on persons to seek their final end, i.e., union with God.[5] Though these two assertions were clearly used to deny the existence of a completely autonomous morality like the one articulated and proclaimed by Immanuel Kant, they could hardly be considered adequate grounding for a morality seeking to be deeply nourished by the Christian faith.

A renewal had been underway in Catholic moral theology since the 1940s to establish a closer relation between the realities of Christian faith and morality.[6] Some of the basic tenets of this movement found their way into three of the important documents at Vatican II. In the opening paragraph of Part I of the *Pastoral Constitution on the Church in the Modern World* (*Gaudium et Spes*) the Council proclaimed, "For faith throws a *new light on everything*, manifests God's design for man's total vocation, and thus directs the mind to solutions which are fully human" (§11).[7] In the *Dogmatic Constitution on Divine Revelation* (*Dei Verbum*) it was claimed that,

> Sacred theology rests on the written word of God, together with sacred tradition, as its primary and perpetual foundation... For the sacred Scriptures contain the word of God and, since they are inspired, really are the words of God; and so the study of the sacred page is, as it were, the soul of sacred theology. (§24)[8]

In the *Decree on Priestly Formation* (*Optatam Totius*) the Council addressed the issue of theological renewal and stated that,

> Special attention needs to be given to the development of moral theology. Its scientific exposition should be more thoroughly nourished by scriptural teaching. It should show the nobility of the Christian vocation of the faithful, and their obligation to bring forth fruit in charity for the life of the world. (§16)[9]

What is clear in all these texts is the concerted effort at the Council to nourish the moral life of the Christian by the scriptures and by faith in Jesus Christ. In turn this effort gave rise to two important and interrelated methodological issues: on the one hand, the use of scripture in moral theology and moral argument and, on the other hand, the relationship between Christian faith and morality. It is only the latter issue that will occupy our attention here.[10]

In the post-conciliar era the discussion of the general relationship between faith and morality[11] has concentrated principally on the narrower issue of the uniqueness of Christian morality, i.e., on whether the realities of explicit Christian faith or revelation add any new normative content to the moral life. No doubt the Council's claim that faith throws a new light on everything was partially responsible for focusing the discussion on this particular issue. I will limit my analysis to this narrower issue as it has evolved over the past three decades since Vatican II. After briefly describing the nature of the debate, I will outline the lineaments of the two basic positions that have emerged—the *Glaubensethik* position and the autonomy position.

Much has been at stake in the debate over the uniqueness of Christian morality. Vincent MacNamara has claimed that the central issue is a debate about the very identity of Christian ethics.[12] Lucien Richard has argued that the question of the uniqueness of Christian morality is one of the most difficult questions that Christian theology must answer at both the theoretical and practical levels.[13] The issues that underlie and orient one's position on this question range over almost the entire theological map. For example, how God is thought to relate to moral obligation and the moral life, and how one construes the relation of the moral life to salvation are certainly pertinent issues.[14] What the nature of scriptural revelation is and whether that revelation reveals a new morality or more basically reveals who we are in relation to the divine and to one another are other important questions involved in this debate. Does Christian ethics as a discipline have a different methodology from philosophical ethics? What are the sources of Christian ethics, and can one really distinguish or maybe even separate moral and religious experiences and their respective interpretations? Is there a ground or foundation for a universal, common morality that is, in principle, open to all people of goodwill? These and many more issues are at stake in determining one's position on this question.

As indicated above, almost from the beginning the debate has been carried on principally within Roman Catholic theological circles. There are three key contexts that focused the Catholic character of this debate. The first context was the early renewal movement of the 1940s and 1950s that had sought to articulate a theme or paradigm, e.g., grace or charity, other than natural law for understanding Catholic morality. As this movement began to take shape and mature in the post Vatican II era[15] an affirmative answer to the question of the uniqueness of Christian morality brought into view the specifically Christian character of morality that had been grossly overlooked in the moral theology of the neo-

Scholastic manuals.[16] The second context—an ecclesial one—concerned the issues of magisterial authority over the proper interpretation of natural law morality[17] and the possibility of dissent from the magisterium's authoritative but noninfallible teachings. For example, in the opening lines of Josef Fuchs' important 1968 lecture in Zurich titled *"Gibt es eine spezifisch christliche Moral?,"*[18] he asked whether it was Paul VI's intention in *Humanae Vitae* to offer a specifically Catholic or Christian solution to the issue of birth control. Finally, the debate over the uniqueness of Christian morality had its cultural and intellectual origins in Europe, especially in Germany, as part of the discussion of the possibility of communicating with secularists and Marxists over moral issues.[19] If Christian morality were truly unique in normative content because it was judged to be explicitly revealed, then Catholic theologians surmised that a dialog with humanists on important moral issues would be impossible.[20]

In general, two basic positions have been developed in the debate over the uniqueness of Christian morality. The first, or so-called *Glaubensethik*, position,[21] which had its origins in the pre-Vatican II renewal movement of moral theology, has suggested that a portion of Christian morality is not only revealed but also unique and therefore closed to all unbelievers.[22] Though the proponents of this position all accepted the existence of a universal moral order in the natural law, they argued that there is a portion of Christian morality that is considered unique, and it is found only in the Bible. Thus, according to this position, one is not really doing *Christian* ethics if one does not recognize the revealed character of this morality. Consequently, some proponents of this position have asserted that natural law morality is not sufficient for Christians, and so they have sought to supplement this natural morality with a supernatural morality based upon faith and grace. They have argued that if faith throws a new light on everything, as *Gaudium et Spes* had claimed, and if as a result we are new creatures in Christ, then the Scholastic axiom *agere sequitur esse* requires that a new and unique morality must exist that corresponds to this new being.

The second—or so-called "autonomy"—position[23] has vigorously argued that the general content of Christian morality is the same for Christians and non-Christians alike. Not only is the basic normative content of morality the same for all, but these proponents argue that, in principle, all people of goodwill can arrive at the general demands of the moral life, including self-sacrificing love. Because these authors claimed that explicit revelation does not contain any new normative moral content, they have argued that there is no unique morality for Christians that only believers can know through explicit revelation. Furthermore, these proponents have claimed the authority of Vatican II for their position by citing the passage in *Gaudium et Spes* (§36) about the rightful autonomy of earthly affairs that enjoy their own laws and values.[24] Thus, this position, which reclaimed but also thoroughly revised the Catholic approach to natural law morality, has argued for the relative autonomy of faith and moral experiences and their respective interpretations. If the general demands of the moral life are not logically or even epistemically dependent on Christian faith, then the human person, apart from explicit faith and revelation, can arrive at these demands through a careful reflection on human experience.[25]

CRITICAL ANALYSIS OF THE DEBATE

Almost from the beginning this debate over the uniqueness of Christian morality has been beleaguered by conceptual and linguistic confusions and by a general lack of proper distinctions to guide the discussion. At many crucial points it has even been difficult to decipher what the precise terms of the debate were. Norbert Rigali, who has been a regular contributor to this debate but who has also consistently criticized the way the discussion has been carried on, has claimed that,

> In short, then, the debate is not about Christian ethics; not about the distinctiveness of Christian morality; not about Biblical fundamentalism nor even about Biblical morality or ethics; not about ecclesiastical authoritarianism nor even about ecclesiastical authority; not about whether morality should be autonomous rather than heteronomous; not about whether morality should be theonomous rather than autonomous; not about whether morality should be rooted in reason or in Christian faith; not about whether reason is too weak to achieve certainty with regard to moral norms; and not about preserving, in crusade-like or other fashion, a Christian character of morality. The debate is about whether Christian faith makes any difference with regard to the material content of moral life.[26]

Though somewhat overstated, Rigali's characterization of the debate is basically accurate. The discussion got side-tracked and confused at certain key points because the proponents on both sides did not make proper distinctions and because dichotomies were set up such that one could argue for the possible existence of two different moralities, one natural and the other Christian. I will briefly analyze some of these dichotomies and confusions as they developed within the debate.

Several dichotomies were established early in the debate that inappropriately set up two terms and then compared them. The consequences of this procedure have been confusion and misunderstanding among the participants in the discussion. Sometimes a dichotomy was set up between the human (*humanum*) and the Christian (*Christianum*).[27] In this case the human was understood as the abstract nature of persons apart from Christian reality. Once Christian reality, e.g., grace, was sharply distinguished from human reality, then it was viewed as extrinsic to the latter and able to add to it.[28] In some cases a similar dichotomy was set up between absolute, metaphysical nature and historical nature.[29] Whereas absolute nature (*natura pura* or *natura absoluta*) was understood as proper to the human as such and not yet introduced into the supernatural order, historical nature was understood as the human existentially situated in the supernatural order. Consequently, historical nature could add something new or different to absolute nature because the latter had now been introduced into the new supernatural order. Furthermore, in the early renewal movement of moral theology in the 1940s and 1950s some authors wrongly compared abstract human nature with supernature or the life of grace.[30] This comparison made several erroneous assumptions. First, it wrongly assumed that these two realities could be clearly distinguished and separated from one another in the historical order. Second, such a comparison gave the impression that absolute or pure human nature was indeed a real entity rather than a remainder concept (*Restbegriff*), and thus many wrongly assumed that it was possible to grasp and to define the exact moral content of this postulated pure nature by itself.[31] Finally, and a consequence of the above, it wrongly assumed that supernature could add another new morality on top of "natural" morality. Thus, the proponents reasoned that, if the life of grace created an entire new mode of living, then the Scholastic axiom of *agere sequitur esse* required a new morality.

A similar dichotomy was established between a morality based on creation and a morality based on redemption. Some authors in the early renewal movement argued this point to establish a unique Christian morality,[32] but others in the post-Vatican II era sought to establish the opposite position based on this dichotomy. For example, John Macquarrie argued for a link between Christian and non-Christian moral striving "not on the ground of a doctrine of redemption but on the ground of a doctrine of creation."[33] The problem with this type of comparison is once again to make a wrong assumption that the realities of creation and redemption can be clearly distinguished, or even separated, in the concrete historical order.

Other inappropriate comparisons were set up that created further confusion in the debate over the uniqueness of Christian morality. J. M. Aubert has noted that sometimes a comparison was made between fallen human nature and redeemed nature. Such a comparison not only idealized redeemed nature but it obviously attempted to establish a new morality that surpassed what fallen nature could achieve.[34] Furthermore, some authors sought to establish the validity of a new and unique Christian morality based on the comparison between the natural law and the evangelical law. René Coste has argued that the evangelical law of love is from a whole other essence than the demand to love in the natural law and thus charity is an "astronomical distance" from the natural law.[35] Another false comparison that has been made is the one between human history and salvation history. Though in general he denied that there is any new content to Christian morality, René Simon has argued that there is a Christian morality in the sense that faith has integrated human morality into the economy of salvation.[36] Once again, this comparison wrongly assumed that it is possible to distinguish neatly between these two histories such that one could clearly know what belonged integrally and uniquely to each history.

Confusion and misunderstandings have also been created in this debate because the participants have failed to make proper distinctions. Many of these distinctions are basic to any discussion of either Christian or philosophical ethics. Thus, when these distinctions are not made or attended to, it is obvious why the debate appears at times as if the authors were not even addressing the same issue.

Rigali has introduced several important distinctions into this debate. He has argued[37] that when we speak of Christian *morality*[38] we should distinguish four levels: 1) essential morality, which is that aspect of morality incumbent on all persons as members of the human race; 2) existential morality, which originates in the individuality of the person; 3) Christian essential morality, which originates in membership in the Christian community; and 4) Christian existential morality, which is derived from a person's individuality within the Christian community. Rigali has maintained that Christian morality cannot be identified with any one of these levels but must be understood as consisting of all four. Thus, he has consistently argued that, if the discussion of the uniqueness of Christian morality (not ethics) is to bear any fruit, we must pose the question of the debate properly. He is correct to state that the real issue is whether Christian identity can add any new normative content to the level of *essential morality*. To pose the question in other terms is either to confuse the levels that constitute Christian morality or to reduce all Christian morality to one or other of the various levels. Thus, Rigali rightly argued that the comparison between "human" morality and "Christian" morality already confused the whole issue by identifying the "human" with only the essential level of morality.

Second, it is necessary to distinguish properly between the terms morality and ethics. Frequently in this debate, however, these two terms have been used interchangeably. For example, early in the post-Vatican II era Abbé Jean-Jacques Latour argued that the term Christian morality (*morale chrétienne*) is well founded because of an infusion of a "second sense" by faith into ethics (*l'éthique*).[39] Properly distinguished, ethics is the thematic and systematic approach to morality, and morality is concerned with the actual normative content of the moral life. By distinguishing ethics from morality one could argue that there might be a uniqueness to Christian *ethics* but that the normative content of Christian *morality* might be the same for all at what Rigali has called the essential level of morality.

Another distinction that was introduced into this debate is the one between the terms "specificity" and "distinctiveness."[40] Unfortunately, all too often these two terms were used synonymously. For example, in addressing this debate Timothy O'Connell has formulated his own position in the following way: "Thus our conclusion is that there is, in fact, no specifically, uniquely, distinctively Christian ethic."[41] When properly distinguished, however, the term "specificity" should refer to something that is peculiar or unique to a reality, while the term "distinctive" should refer to something that is characteristic of a reality but not unique to it. Thus, that which is specific is exclusive to the reality under discussion, and that which is distinctive is only regularly found in a reality but could also be found elsewhere. When this distinction is applied to the question under debate, one could claim specificity or uniqueness at one level of the discussion, e.g., at the level of *ethics* or at the level of *existential* morality, but only claim a distinctiveness at another level, e.g., at the level of what Rigali has called *essential* morality.

Another distinction that may have avoided confusion and misunderstanding is the one between a moral ideal and a moral obligation. The neo-Scholastic moral tradition had made a similar distinction between a moral obligation and a moral counsel, and this tradition argued that a moral counsel did not strictly belong to morality. Vincent MacNamara has rightly pointed out that Christian ethics does not regard ideals in the same way that philosophical ethics regards them. In other words, ideals have a different status in each system. Thus, MacNamara has reasoned that the Biblical ideals of *agape*, humility before God and before others, and an attitude of suffering are not matters of choice—and thus they are obligatory—within Christianity in the way that they would be considered heroic for the philosopher.[42]

In addition, it is important in this debate to make sure that one places these Christian ideals in the proper area of experience, i.e., within the area of moral experience or within the area of faith experience. Mac-Namara has claimed that some authors may have possibly shifted some Christian ideals from the area of morality into the area of faith and then argued that in Christianity there are no new normative demands in the moral life.[43] If such shifting of categories has indeed occurred in order to accommodate a desired conclusion on this issue, then both the accuracy and the adequacy of the conclusion itself may be questionable.

Bruno Schüller sought to offer a distinction into the discussion by distinguishing between parenetic and normative discourse. He argued that, when the requirements of morality are brought up either in connection with the gospel and future judgment or in terms of the virtues or vices in the Old and New Testaments, we have exhortation and not normative discourse. In these instances the Biblical witness is not deciding the rightness and wrongness of actions (normative discourse) but exhorting or admonishing the hearer (parenesis) to do or to avoid what he or she already knows.[44] Thus, Schüller has argued that, whereas there is no new normative content to Christian morality, there is a specifically Christian parenesis, i.e., a parenesis that stands or falls with belief in Jesus.[45] This distinction was helpful in some respects, and it did clarify some confusion within the debate. However, in the end some authors had serious disagreements with the way Schüller had applied it,[46] and even some proponents of the autonomy position have argued that the scriptures can be used to provide some general normative content in social ethics.[47]

CRUCIAL ISSUES YET TO BE RESOLVED

The Council members at Vatican II sought to renew moral theology by calling for a closer relation between the realities of Christian faith and the moral life than what the dominant neo-Scholastic theology had been able to accomplish. They claimed that faith should both inform human reason and direct the mind to truly human solutions. Furthermore, they argued that the scriptures should nourish Christian morality and become the very soul of moral reflection. Moral theologians in the mid-1960s quickly took up these challenges, but unfortunately the early discussion that ensued was unfocused and even confused. Two sides formed in the debate—the *Glaubensethik* position and the autonomy position—and the central issue that emerged only gradually was whether there was anything specific or unique to Christian morality, i.e., whether Christianity could add any new normative content to what Rigali has called the essential level of morality.

It is possible that, even when the question in this debate is properly formulated, in the end the entire issue may be misplaced. Rigali has proposed that the question about whether there is a specifically Christian morality is at root a classicist question.[48] In other words, he believes such a question presupposes that there is a single, undifferentiated human morality that is based on a universal human nature and then wonders what the realities of Christian faith might add to it. On the other hand, Rigali has claimed that historically conscious moral theology has an entirely different starting point and thus asks an altogether different question. It begins with the historical fact of moral pluralism and then discovers a unique Christian morality as a given. Then it inquires how this unique morality should be shaped in the contemporary world.[49] Because historical consciousness centers its reflection not on some abstract, ahistorical nature or on individual actions but on human persons in history[50] and on the plurality of ways in which persons realize themselves in historical communities, not only is there *a* unique Christian morality but indeed there are many unique Christian moralit*ies*. In fact, for Rigali every morality has its source in a community's story, and thus a particular Christian morality can be unique to the extent that its community's story is unique.[51] In Rigali's view, then, for a moral theology that has adopted historical consciousness the entire debate over the uniqueness of Christian morality, which has spanned over thirty years, "is resolved by being dissolved."[52]

Rigali's position raises a number of important questions, the answers to which could take the future of Catholic moral theology into either a new stage of development or into more culs-de-sac. I will briefly address only two of these questions.

One crucial question certainly is this: is it possible to be committed both to historical consciousness and to a universal morality? Rigali himself does not believe that a commitment to historical consciousness must necessarily entail a denial of the natural law of morality. This "natural law" of morality or the moral law, though, is the natural norm deep within every human soul that contains "a historical coefficient of relativity."[53] Historical consciousness, however, must deny both a universal ethic and the existence of a universal normative morality. "For historical consciousness, natural law neither is nor results in a universal morality and an unconditioned ethics."[54]

On the face of it, Rigali's statements appear quite nonfoundationalist in content, if not in intent, because they seem to deny the possibility of being committed both to historical consciousness and to some universal element in morality. Should we understand his claims to be nonfoundationalist without remainder? I think not. In various places Rigali clearly claims that there is a universal basis or foundation for morality. He argues there is a "natural orientation of human beings to specific goods that constitute these goods, collectively, as a realm of objective moral values and as a universal basis of morality."[55] Though these moral values are always inculturated for Rigali, nonetheless they constitute "the universality-in-particularity that is the universality of morality."[56] These shared goods or values, though, are not necessarily comprehended the same way in each time or culture. They are more of a "remainder" or abstract universal stratum of morality and ethics that represent "points of contact" between different ethics, including Christian ethics and other forms of ethics.[57]

Charles Curran has recently responded to Rigali's criticisms of his position as essentially classicist. Curran has argued that his own view is committed both to a universal morality and to historical consciousness. He believes that the issue of universality properly belongs at the level of morality, but the discussion of classicism and historical consciousness properly belongs at the level of ethics, which for him is defined as a second-order discipline that reflects on morality in a thematic, systematic and reflexive way. Thus, Curran has claimed that one could hold to "a general and an 'in-principled' universality on the level of morality without necessarily embracing classicism on the level of ethics."[58] The universality to which Curran refers is not the "remainder" concept that Rigali uses to describe the "points of contact" between various unique types of moralities. Rather, for Curran this universality is comprised of actual normative content that, in principle, is or ought to be shared among all people of goodwill.

The question here is whether Curran has adequately differentiated the various levels of *morality* that Rigali had proposed. It might be recalled that Rigali had offered a quadripartite division of Christian morality in which only one level related to an essential (universal) morality incumbent on every person *qua* person; the other three referred to levels of morality that are non-essential and thus not shared by persons *qua* persons. For Curran not to distinguish the level of essential morality from the other levels implies that for him there is only one morality (moral order), which, for Rigali, is a classicist presupposition. On the other hand, though, it seems Curran is correct to note that historical consciousness is a presupposition of ethics, not of morality. Thus, I believe that one could argue in the area of morality for the possibility of some actual normative content that is common to all people at the level of essential morality and still claim that historical consciousness in the area of ethics requires some normative content to be unique, and thus variable, in the other three levels of morality, e.g., at the existential level. In my position, then, the existence of commonly-shared goods or values constitutes at least one of the universal foundations for the possibility of shared normative content at the level of what Rigali has called essential morality.[59]

The second important question concerns whether one can remain committed to historical consciousness and at the same time avoid both a sectarianism and a moral relativism. Curran has argued that Rigali's position necessarily entails moral relativism because it admits of many Christian moralities and, by implication, many non-Christian moralities. In addition, Curran has contended that Rigali's position is sectarian in nature because it ascribes such a uniqueness to Christian morality that Christians and non-Christians are not able to cooperate with one another on important moral issues that confront society.[60] These are clearly important issues, and a full treatment of them would require more space than is available here. Briefly though, I would argue that it is possible to be committed to historical consciousness in the area of ethics and not adopt either moral relativism or sectarianism. To claim that there are several *levels* of morality does not at all imply that there are plural *moralities*. The factual reality that plural moralities exist in the human community does not and should not lead us to the claim that these moralities do or should possess moral standing or validity. Moral relativism, it seems to me, leaves open the possibility of a relative equality of moral standing and validity for each of the unique moralities.[61]

On the other hand, one could reasonably affirm that there is unique normative content at the levels of existential morality, Christian essential morality, and Christian existential morality without adopting a form of moral relativism. These are distinct *levels* of morality that exist in addition to the essential level; these levels do not constitute different moralities. This position is neither relativist nor sectarian because it clearly accepts that there is the possibility of establishing some universal normative content that is common to all persons as such. In addition, one could also affirm that there are different ethics, i.e., systematic ways of reflecting on the normative content of morality. Such an affirmation that there are many different Christian ethics, e.g., Catholic Neo-Scholastic, Calvinist Protestant, etc., and many different non-Christian ethics, e.g., humanist, Buddhist, etc., does not necessarily result in a form of moral relativism. That different ways of systematically understanding and arriving at the normative content of morality at its various levels, including the essential level, can legitimately exist is one of the insights of historical consciousness. Similarities between and among these various ethics certainly can and do exist. For example, all Christian ethics share a uniqueness about their general vision or stance, their starting point and their connection to the historical person of Jesus Christ. However, a claim about the existence of many ethics, Christian and non-Christian, does not require, nor does it entail, that the actual content of normative morality *at all its various levels* must also be unique. There are different ways to arrive at the same reality.

I would contend that explicit Christian faith and revelation do not add any new normative moral content to the essential level of morality. However, that does not at all imply that the resources of these explicit Christian realities are either peripheral or extraneous to Christian morality. The unique influence and the many effects of faith on the moral life are principally found elsewhere at the two Christian levels of morality, in the ways we come to know the normative content of morality, and in the area of ethics.

This debate has been important, and many issues have been sorted out in the process. In the end, however, it may be the case that this debate has run its due course. Now we need to turn our attention straightforwardly to the challenge that Vatican II gave us to clarify how the resources of explicit faith and the scriptures can inform our moral lives. There are clear signs that we have already begun to move in this direction.[62]

NOTES

1. For example, see James M. Gustafson, *Can Ethics Be Christian?* (Chicago, IL: The University of Chicago Press, 1975) and Stanley Hauerwas, *The Peaceable Kingdom: A Primer in Christian Ethics* (Notre Dame, IN: University of Notre Dame Press, 1983).

2. Though there is no particular founder of this critical approach to knowledge and morality, most often the philosophers Willard Quine and Rich-

ard Rorty and the theologians George Lindbeck and Ronald Thiemann are associated with the approach. What all these proponents share is a deep suspicion about any theory that assumes there is a universal ground of knowledge and morality. Many theologians have adopted this stance because they judge any foundation other than Christian belief and practice as problematic. Whatever this foundation may be, they assert, it is granted primacy over the Christian context of meaning. The literature on nonfoundationalism is enormous; however, two books that could serve as helpful guides to both the philosophical and theological issues are John E. Thiel's *Nonfoundationalism* (Minneapolis, MN: Fortress Press, 1994) and Stanley Hauerwas, Nancey Murphy and Mark Nation, *Theology Without Foundations: Religious Practice & the Future of Theological Truth* (Nashville: Abingdon Press, 1994).

3. In addition to the writings of Norbert Rigali, S.J., which I will discuss in part three, one might mention the recent attempts by Kevin Wildes, S.J., to articulate a non-ecumenical Christian bioethics. For Wildes, "A non-ecumenical Christian bioethics is skeptical about the extent to which there can be a bioethics that appeals to our common humanity." See Kevin Wm. Wildes, S.J., "The Ecumenical and Non-Ecumenical Dialectic of Christian Bioethics," *Christian Bioethics: Non-Ecumenical Studies in Medical Morality* 1 (September 1995), 123. For a Catholic author who has recently taken a much different tack in the area of bioethics and who has argued that we need a foundation for medical morality that would serve as a corrective to the current moral pluralism, see David C. Thomasma, "Antifoundationalism and the Possibility of a Moral Philosophy of Medicine," *Theoretical Medicine* 18 (1997), 127–43.

4. "...lex nova, quae praeter praecepta legis naturae, paucissima superaddit in doctrina Christi et Apostolorum...." *S.T.*, I–II, q. 107, a. 4. The "paucissima" to which Aquinas refers are the sacraments (q. 108, a. 2) and the evangelical counsels (q. 108, a. 4).

5. Vincent MacNamara, *Faith & Ethics: Recent Roman Catholicism* (Washington, DC: Georgetown University Press, 1985), 13–14.

6. Some of the influential authors in the early renewal movement were: Gustave Thils, *Tendances Actuelles en Théologie Morale* (Paris: Gembloux, 1940); Gérard Gilleman, *Le Primat de la Charité en Théologie Morale: Essai Méthodologique* (Louvain, Belgium: E. Nauwelaerts, 1952); and Philip Delhaye, "La Théologie Morale d'hier et d'aujourd'hui," *Revue des Sciences Religieuses* 27 (1953), 112–30.

7. Walter M. Abbott, S.J., ed., *The Documents of Vatican II* (New York: America Press, 1966), 209. Emphasis added. Fifteen years later this same theme was taken up again by the *Declaration on Euthanasia*: "The considerations set forth in the present document concern in the first place all those who place their faith and hope in Christ, who through his life, death and resurrection, has given *new meaning to existence* and, especially to the death of the Christian...." *Origins* 10 (August 14, 1980), 155. Emphasis added.

8. Walter M. Abbott, S.J., ed., *The Documents of Vatican II*, 127.

9. *Ibid.*, 452.

10. For a spectrum of positions on the relationship between Christian faith and morality, see James J. Walter, "The Relation Between Faith and Morality: Sources for Christian Ethics," *Horizons: The Journal of the College Theology Society* 9 (1982), 251–70.

11. John Paul II has recently addressed the issue of the relationship between Christian faith and morality in his encyclical *Veritatis Splendor* (Vatican City: Libreria Editrice Vaticana, 1993), §§ 4, 6, 26, 85, 88, 89, 90, and 98. His position could be generally characterized as a relationship of "correlation" because he argues that we ask the question about morality and Christ gives us the answer, i.e., there is a correlation between our question and Christ's answer. See especially chapter 1 of his encyclical. John Paul II's position is reminiscent of the Protestant theologian Paul Tillich's general position on the task of theology in which he correlates the "questions" expressed in the "situation" with the "answers" provided by the Christian message. On Tillich's theological method, see David Tracy, *Blessed Rage for Order: The New Pluralism in Theology* (New York: The Seabury Press, 1975), 45–46.

12. MacNamara, *Faith & Ethics*, 113.

13. Lucien Richard, O.M.I., *Is There A Christian Ethics?* (New York: Paulist Press, 1988), 96.

14. MacNamara, *Faith & Ethics*, 179.

15. The earliest discussion of the uniqueness of Christian morality that occurs after the close of Vatican II was the XXVIII Week of French Catholic Intellectuals (March 2–8, 1966). The results of this meeting were published in *Recherches et Débats* 55 (1966).

16. Norbert Rigali, "The Uniqueness and the Distinctiveness of Christian Morality and Ethics," in Charles E. Curran, ed., *Moral Theology: Challenges for the Future* (New York: Paulist Press, 1990), 80.

17. For Pius XII's statements about the magisterium's competence to interpret the natural law, see his two allocutions: *Si Diligis* and *Magnificate Dominum Mecum* in *The Pope Speaks* 1 (1954), 153–58 and 375–85.

18. This lecture was published two years later in *Stimmen der Zeit* 185 (1970), 99–112. In addition, one of the contexts of Alfons Auer's early book on this topic *Autonome Moral und christlicher Glaube* (Düsseldorf: Patmos, 1971) was the magisterium's claims to a special competence in matters of the natural law.

19. Interestingly, the comparison was not between the Christian morality and another religious morality, e.g., Islam. In the early renewal movement, however, the comparison was between the Christian and the unbaptized person, who bore only the natural image of God and who could be expected to live not by the supernatural elements of the Christian but by the natural law alone. See MacNamara, *Faith & Ethics*, 21.

20. See Dionigi Tettamanzi, "Is There a Christian Ethics?" in Charles E. Curran and Richard A. McCormick, eds., *Readings in Moral Theology No. 2:*

The Distinctiveness of Christian Ethics (New York: Paulist Press, 1980), 20. Also, see Charles E. Curran's first discussion of this question in the United States, "Is There a Distinctively Christian Social Ethic?," in Philip D. Morris, ed., *Metropolis: Christian Presence and Responsibility* (Notre Dame, IN: Fides Publishers, 1970), 92–120.

21. Joseph Ratzinger and Philip Delhaye have been two of the leading proponents of this position.

22. MacNamara, *Faith & Ethics*, 69.

23. Alfons Auer, Josef Fuchs, and Bruno Schüller have been the most avid proponents of this position in Europe, and in the U.S. Charles Curran and Richard McCormick have been the most prominent supporters.

24. "If by the autonomy of earthly affairs we mean that created things and societies themselves enjoy their own laws and values which must be gradually deciphered, put to use, and regulated by men, then it is entirely right to demand that autonomy. Such is not merely required by modern man, but harmonizes also with the will of the Creator. For by the very circumstance of their having been created, all things are endowed with their own stability, truth, goodness, proper laws, and order." Abbott, *The Documents of Vatican II*, 233–34.

25. For an analysis of the various ways in which Christian morality can be understood to be dependent on faith, see James J. Walter, "The Dependence of Christian Morality on Faith: A Critical Assessment," *Église et Théologie* 12 (1981), 237–77.

26. Rigali, "The Uniqueness and the Distinctiveness of Christian Morality and Ethics," 80. Richard McCormick has also remarked about how the discussants seem to disagree because often they are not even discussing the same question. See Richard A. McCormick, *Corrective Vision: Explorations in Moral Theology* (Kansas City, MO: Sheed & Ward, 1994), 137.

27. Josef Fuchs, "Is There a Specifically Christian Morality?" in Curran and McCormick, eds., *Readings in Moral Theology No. 2*, 15.

28. Rigali, "Christian Morality and Universal Morality: The One and the Many," *Louvain Studies* 19 (1994), 23.

29. See Tettamanzi, "Is There a Christian Ethics?" 44–45, 52, and 56.

30. Namara, *Faith & Ethics*, 18–24.

31. See Karl Rahner, S.J., "Concerning the Relationship Between Nature and Grace," in *id.*, *Theological Investigations*, Vol. 1, trans. by Cornelius Ernst, O.P. (Baltimore: Helicon Press, 1961), 297–317, especially at 313–15.

32. J.P. Audet and Philip Delhaye were proponents of this position. See MacNamara, *Faith & Ethics*, 15. In the post-Vatican II era the Protestant theologian N.H.G. Robinson argued his position on the uniqueness of Christian morality by reference to the doctrine of redemption. See N.H.G. Robinson, *The Groundwork of Christian Ethics* (Grand Rapids, MI: William B. Eerdmans Publishing Co., 1972), esp. chapter 6.

33. John Macquarrie, *Three Issues in Ethics* (London: SCM Press, 1970), 88.

34. J.-M. Aubert, "La spécificité de la morale chrétienne selon Saint Thomas," *Supplément* 92 (1970), 67.

35. René Coste, "Loi naturelle et loi évangélique," *Nouvelle Revue Théologique* 92 (1970), 84–85.

36. René Simon, "Spécificité de l'éthique chrétienne," *Supplément* 23 (1970), 81.

37. Rigali, "On Christian Ethics," *Chicago Studies* 10 (1971), 227–47.

38. Interestingly, Rigali consistently uses the term "ethics" when he originally develops his quadripartite division of Christian "morality." In a later article on this topic, though, he clearly makes the distinction between ethics and morality, and in a footnote he refers back to his original article and states, ". . . for the terms ethics (*ethic*) and *ethical* should be substituted *morality* and *moral*, respectively." See Rigali, "Christian Morality and Universal Morality," 19, n. 5. Emphasis in the original.

39. Abbé Jean-Jacques Latour, "Morale, métaphysique et religion," *Recherches et Débats* 55 (1966), 125. He uses both of these terms without properly distinguishing their content. Also see A. Jousten, "Morale humaine ou morale chrétienne?" *La Foi et Le Temps* 1 (1968), 428.

40. I first proposed this distinction in James J. Walter, "Christian Ethics: Distinctive and Specific?" in Curran and McCormick, eds., *Readings in Moral Theology No. 2*, 90–110. I also applied it to the discussion of whether there is a unique professional ethics. See *id.*, "The Foundations of the Professions and of Professional Ethics: A Critical and Constructive Study," *Horizons: Journal of the College Theology Society* 12 (1985), 91–115.

41. Timothy O'Connell, "The Search for Christian Moral Norms," *Chicago Studies* 11 (1972), 93. In addition, when Fuchs' 1968 Zurich lecture ("Gibt es eine spezifisch christliche Moral?") was translated into English, one translation used "specifically" ("Is There a Specifically Christian Morality?" in Curran and McCormick, eds., *Readings in Moral Theology No. 2*) and another translation used "distinctively" ("Is There a Distinctively Christian Morality?" in Josef Fuchs, *Personal Responsibility: Christian Morality* [Washington, DC: Georgetown University Press, 1983]).

42. MacNamara, *Faith & Ethics*, 171.

43. *Ibid.*, 172.

44. Bruno Schüller, "The Debate on the Specific Character of Christian Ethics: Some Remarks," in Curran and McCormick, eds., *Readings in Moral Theology No. 2*, 207–33.

45. *Id.*, "Christianity and the New Man: The Moral Dimension—Specificity of Christian Ethics," in William J. Kelly, S.J., ed., *Theology and Discovery: Essays in Honor of Karl Rahner, S.J.* (Milwaukee: Marquette University Press, 1980), 321.

46. See James Gaffney, "On Parenesis and Fundamental Moral Theology," *Journal of Religious Ethics* 11 (1983), 23–34.

47. For example, see Charles E. Curran, *The Living Tradition of Catholic*

Moral Theology (Notre Dame, IN: University of Notre Dame Press, 1992), 179.

48. Rigali, "Morality and Historical Consciousness," *Chicago Studies* 18 (1979), 161–68, especially 162–64.

49. *Id.*, "The Uniqueness and the Distinctiveness of Christian Morality and Ethics," 90.

50. *Id.*, "Christ and Morality," in Curran and McCormick, eds., *Readings in Moral Theology No. 2*, 112–13.

51. *Id.*, "Moral Pluralism and Christian Ethics," *Louvain Studies* 13 (1988), 315.

52. *Id.*, "The Uniqueness and the Distinctiveness of Christian Morality and Ethics," 90.

53. *Id.*, "Moral Pluralism and Christian Ethics," 314. Rigali borrows the concept of a "norm deep within every human soul" and the phrase "a certain coefficient of relativity" from Louis Monden. See Monden's *Sin, Liberty and Law*, Joseph Donceel trans. (New York: Sheed and Ward, 1965).

54. Rigali, "Moral Pluralism and Christian Ethics," 318.

55. *Id.*, "Christian Morality and Universal Morality," 32. Rigali also makes the claim to a commonality among all moralities and ethics in his "The Story of Christian Morality," *Chicago Studies* 27 (1988), 175. Other Catholic authors have recently argued that the existence of shared objective goods or values can serve as a foundation for morality. For example, see Stephen Happel and James J. Walter, *Conversion and Discipleship: A Christian Foundation for Ethics and Doctrine* (Philadelphia: Fortress Press, 1986), 31–42, especially 40–42; and Lisa Sowle Cahill, *Sex, Gender & Christian Ethics* (New York: Cambridge University Press, 1996), 12 and 46–72.

56. Rigali, "Christian Morality and Universal Morality," 33.

57. *Id.*, "Moral Pluralism and Christian Ethics," 318. He borrows the phrase "points of contact" from Stanley Hauerwas in the *Peaceable Kingdom*, 59–61. Recently, John Reeder has adopted a neopragmatist moral epistemology that denies the claim that moralities are conceptual schemes that are mutually untranslatable. He argues that there are "points of contact" between moralities at the level of both issues and judgments, even though his position is nonfoundationalist and denies the existence of a universal morality. See John P. Reeder, Jr., "Foundations without Foundationalism," in Gene Outka and John P. Reeder, Jr., eds., *Prospects for a Common Morality* (Princeton, NJ: Princeton University Press, 1993), 191–214.

58. Curran, *The Living Tradition of Catholic Moral Theology*, 178.

59. Stephen Happel and I have argued in *Conversion and Discipleship* that the invariant and normative pattern of operations of intentional consciousness as described by Bernard Lonergan also constitutes a universal ground for moral experience and the possibility of a common morality at the essential level.

60. Curran, *The Living Tradition of Catholic Moral Theology*, 178.

61. Most theologians who subscribe to nonfoundationalism do not accept this claim of moral relativism that each unique morality in fact possesses a rela-

tively equal moral standing and validity. On the contrary, most of these theologians would strive to overcome the "moralities of culture" by the Christian morality. For example, see George Lindbeck's notion of "intratextuality" in which the Christian text absorbs the world rather than the world absorbing the Christian text. George Lindbeck, *The Nature of Doctrine: Religion and Theology in a Postliberal Age* (Philadelphia: Westminster Press, 1984).

62. An earlier version of this chapter was presented as a paper in Leuven, Belgium at a conference celebrating the thirtieth anniversary of the close of Vatican II and will be published as part of those proceedings.

Specificity, Christian Ethics, and Levels of Ethical Inquiry

Todd A. Salzman

Since Vatican II there has been a concentrated effort among moral theologians in the reconstruction of Catholic moral theology. In particular, there are two issues which have attracted a great deal of attention and have been cause for some acrimonious debates between different schools of thought. The first issue entails a reconstruction in ethical method that fundamentally shifts the reasoning utilized within the moral manuals. These manuals were used to prepare and guide confessors in administering the sacrament of penance and were not concerned with developing a solid method or ethical theory. Consequently, much of the focus in the renewal movement has been to formulate a coherent ethical method that was absent in the manuals and draw out its logical implications for Christian ethics. Two of the main movements in developing this methodical reconstruction are so-called traditionalists and revisionists. While method is frequently cited as the area of renewal in Catholic moral theology, however, method itself is rarely defined. What are the parameters of ethical method? Is it concerned primarily with normative ethics, meta-ethics, or moral behavior? How or does Christian ethical method differ from philosophical ethical method?

This latter question raises the distinct but intimately related issue in the renewal of Catholic moral theology. Namely, is there a specifically Christian ethic and/or morality?[1] What is at stake in the response to this question is whether or not Christian ethics is sectarian, and, therefore, either unable or at least limited in its ability to dialogue with non-Christian ethics.[2] And further, whether divine revelation contributes anything specific to ethical or moral discourse which one could not find in non-Christian ethics? There are basically two schools of thought on this issue, the 'autonomous-ethic' and *Glaubensethik* ('faith-ethic') schools. The former, led by Alfons Auer,[3] asserts that ethics is rationally autonomous and, therefore, revelation offers no new content to morality so that Christian and non-Christian alike can arrive at the same moral content and ethical truth.[4] The latter, led by Bernard Stöckle[5] and Konrad Hilpert,[6] argue that there is a specific Christian morality accessible through revelation alone. Certainly both schools of thought would agree on two fundamental aspects. First, for individual Christians and the moral decisions that they make, faith has an impact on their perception of reality, moral issues, and how they respond to those issues, regardless of whether or not non-Christians could arrive at the same moral judgments in and through reason alone. Second, for the Christian ethicist, the tools of philosophical reasoning and reflection are *necessary* for doing moral theology, though they may not be *sufficient*, as in the case of the *Glaubensethik* school. For example, even this school must minimally rely upon the basic logical principle of non-contradiction in formulating its ethic/morality. The question between these two schools then, may not be whether or not there is a specifically Christian ethic and/or morality, but rather, in what way, to what extent, and on what level of ethical discourse are Christian ethics and/or morality specific?

It is in response to this question that the first and second issues of renewal in Catholic moral theology merge. The specificity of Christian ethics and/or morality has been posited on different levels. For example, norms, moral judgments, motives, character, dispositions and sources for justification have all been cited as realms of this specificity. Interspersed throughout this discussion is an allusion to, description and definition of, various 'methods' that will facilitate clarity and renewal in moral theology. A frequently cited frustration of those who participate in the discussion on the specificity of Christian ethics and/or morality is that it is difficult to do so effectively given the terminological and conceptual ambiguity; the terms, concepts and issues of the discussion are not always clearly defined and are, therefore, conceptually ambiguous.[7] Much of the published material on this topic has turned to distinctions and definitions seeking clarity of the parameters of the discussion itself.[8] What is being debated is not necessarily *whether* Christian ethics and/or morality are specific, but *how* they are specific. Defining the different realms of ethical discourse and seeing where method fits into this discourse and how it is to be defined may clarify an aspect of the debate on the specificity of Christian ethics and/or morality.

This chapter will first investigate two different levels of ethical inquiry utilized by Norbert Rigali and Charles Curran, frequent participants in both the ongoing methodical reconstruction of moral theology and the question of the specificity of Christian morality. It will then consider an alternative division of levels of ethical inquiry borrowing, in part, from philosophical ethicists. Finally, on the basis of the presentation of various levels of ethical inquiry, it will probe the significance of this division first, on the exchange between Curran and Rigali; second, for the methodical reconstruction of moral theology; and finally, for the exchange between the *Glaubensethik* and autonomy ethic schools on the specific nature of Christian ethics and/or morality.

THEOLOGICAL DIVISION: ETHICS AND MORALITY

In 1971, evolving out of his critical analysis of Rahner's "supernatural existential" and in response to Curran's denial of a specifically Christian ethic, Rigali developed his quadripartite division of morality: essential, existential, Christian essential, and Christian existential.[9] Before explaining these four realms of morality, I will explain the parameters of the discussion, i.e., what Curran is asserting, what Rigali is responding to, and the limits of that exchange. First, Rigali is responding to an earlier proposition of Curran's that "the Christian and the explicitly non-Christian can and do arrive at the same [moral] conclusions and can and do share the same general [moral] attitudes, dispositions and goals." This proposition means "there is not a strict dichotomy between Christian [morality] and non-Christian [morality],"[10] or, simply, that there is no specific Christian morality.

Second, after positing his fourfold division of 'ethics' as an initial response to Curran, Rigali subsequently clarifies the parameters of their exchange. What Rigali asserts and Curran affirms[11] is that the fourfold division pertains to the realm of morality, not ethics. "Morality is a normative ordering, in terms of perceived meanings, values, purposes and goals of human existence, of the lives of human persons with regard to the ways in which they can choose to relate themselves to reality," whereas ethics is "the scientific study of such normative order."[12] Rigali makes two further assertions regarding Christian ethics. First, if there is a specifically Christian morality it is self-evident that there is a specifically Christian ethic. Second, even theologians who deny a specifically Christian morality recognize that moral theology uses specifically Christian sources. Thus, no theologian denies that there is a specifically Christian ethic; whether or not there is a specifically Christian morality is being debated.[13]

Rigali presents the following quadripartite division of Christian morality:

(1) essential morality, incumbent on a person as a mem-

> ber of a human race; (2) existential morality, originating
> in the individuality of the human person; (3) Christian
> essential morality, entailed in membership in the Chris-
> tian community; and (4) Christian existential morality,
> derived from a person's status as an individual in the
> Christian fellowship.[14]

According to Rigali, and Curran concurs with this assessment, "there is a
specifically Christian morality...and Christian and non-Christian can
reach the same moral decision only within the sphere of essential morality."[15]

In this division it is important to point out some distinguishing characteristics. Rigali's division is directed towards individuals making
moral choices and the particular *existential context* of those choices,
otherwise (2) and (4) would be redundant for the Christian. Also, the
decisions that correspond to each division are strictly contextualized
within the community to which one belongs, whether it is the universal
human community, the Christian community in general, or a specific
Christian community. For example, an 'essentialist' duty may entail
showing benevolence to one's benefactor. Or a 'Christian essentialist'
duty may entail a moral responsibility incumbent on a person who belongs to a specific Christian community such as "the duty to witness to
Christ." Or again, 'Christian existentialist' decisions would entail moral
responsibilities a person has as a member of the Christian community
such as

> decisions...to become a Roman Catholic priest, to join
> the Order of Preachers, to participate in a eucharistic lit-
> urgy, to receive the sacrament of penance, to pray with
> others in the name of Jesus, if they are authentic, are se-
> rious ethical decisions which arise within the context of
> a Christian community's self-understanding but not out-
> side of it.[16]

These examples demonstrate that for Rigali, whereas the two types of
essential morality pertain to *duties* or *norms* "incumbent on" a person,
the two types of existential morality pertain to the concrete *decisions* of
a person. From an existentialist perspective, specific morality is a mani-

festation of the person's individuality shaped by culture, history, community and relationships.

Reflecting on Rigali's earlier works, Curran affirms that he finds Rigali's fourfold division of morality helpful in clarifying the question of specificity and yet, wonders why he has abandoned that position.[17] Rigali's response is that the question of a specific Christian morality is a misplaced question based on a classicist worldview. The question

> presupposes that there is a single "human morality," based on human nature, and wonders what Christian faith adds to it. Historically conscious moral theology, however, has an altogether different point of departure and, hence, an altogether different question. Starting from the historical fact of moral pluralism, it finds specifically Christian morality—indeed moralities—as a given and wonders how it should be shaped in the contemporary world. For historical consciousness, therefore, the debate question is resolved by being dissolved.[18]

Indeed, Rigali's fourfold division of morality has been helpful in clarifying the specificity of Christian morality and has been endorsed by various moral theologians on several occasions.[19] Yet something more remains to be said on the relationship between ethics and morality. First, for both Rigali and Curran morality entails the decisions or moral judgments of the agent *and* moral norms or the reflection on those moral judgments by the moral theologian or ethicist. Philosophical ethicists, however, typically distinguish between moral judgments and normative ethics, where the latter is the scientific reflection on the former and belongs to the realm of ethics. A question for Rigali and Curran is, given the ongoing shift from classicism to historical consciousness, does this methodical shift require a shift in the division between ethics and morality as well that could facilitate clarity in the discussion of the specificity of Christian ethics and/or morality and also facilitate the ongoing reconstruction of moral theology?

Second, recall that Rigali maintains that insofar as there is a Christian morality it is self-evident that there will be a specifically Christian ethic. As the scientific reflection on morality, of what does Christian ethics consist? Third, Rigali points out that Curran's thesis that Christian ethics are universal is classicist; i.e., it posits a uniform moral order based on a universal human nature.[20] Curran, however, admits that while his position is no doubt universalist, it does not necessarily mean that it is classicist. Universality belongs to the moral realm whereas the distinction between classicism and historical consciousness belongs to the ethical realm, according to Curran. Consequently, one could logically hold to "a general and an 'in-principled' universality on the level of morality without necessarily embracing classicism on the level of ethics."[21] While Rigali responds to Curran's challenge on the question of universality,[22] he does not respond to the question on the relationship between method (historical consciousness), morality and ethics. Curran's insight is an astute observation and raises the issue of the role, nature, function and purpose of method and has implications for the overall discussion of a specifically Christian ethic and/or morality. Where does method lie in the realm of ethical inquiry? Is it limited to ethics or morality, or does it permeate both spheres? Is the division between ethics and morality, itself, adequate to account for the various realms of ethical inquiry? If so, where does method fit into this division and what are its implications on the specificity of Christian ethics and/or morality? The community of Catholic moral theologians is indebted to Rigali and his extensive work on many methodical dimensions of Christian ethics and morality. In fact, his scholarly contributions are frequently devoted to a critique and reconstruction of the manualist approach to moral theology with contemporary methodical developments. He relies especially upon historical consciousness and utilizes this method in developing an adequate view of the moral order, epistemology, anthropology, and understanding the human act.[23] To better understand both a specifically Christian morality and ethic, it may be helpful to see where and how method functions in relation to these two realms. Indeed, method is the central area of renewal in moral theology and defining its scope and place in ethical inquiry could be helpful in not only clarifying Curran's challenge to Rigali on mixing the moral and ethical realms, but could also facilitate the renewal movement in general.

Curran and Rigali's distinction between ethics and morality differs in various ways from the distinction in philosophical ethics between moral judgments, meta-ethics and normative ethics, though the place of ethical method in this division is somewhat ambiguous as well. The following will investigate a philosophical division of ethics and attempt to locate method within this division. Subsequently, I will explore the impact of this fourfold division on Curran and Rigali's division between ethics and morality in particular, the specificity of Christian ethics and/or morality in general, and its use in facilitating the reconstruction of moral theology.

PHILOSOPHICAL DIVISION OF ETHICS

H.J. McCloskey, a philosophical ethicist, notes that ethics can be divided into three realms: morality or moral judgments, normative ethics and meta-ethics.[24] As human beings endowed with reason and the ability to choose, we all make moral judgments on the basis of what we believe is right, obligatory, or good. This is the realm of day-to-day moral decision-making, and is technically referred to as the realm of morality, though ethicists rely upon this realm in developing their ethical theory.

While it is the business of all rational human beings to make moral judgments in light of what a person thinks he or she 'ought to do,' 'is the right thing to do,' or 'is good to do,' it is primarily the work of philosophical ethics to critically reflect upon, analyze, and develop these moral judgments into a comprehensive, systematic, rational theory. The synopsis and synthesis of moral judgments into such a theory is the area of normative ethics and meta-ethics. Normative ethics attempts to answer questions about what is good, right, or obligatory. In order to determine the norms that will facilitate attainment of the good, one must have a *specific* definition of the good. This specific definition and the formulation of laws, rules, norms, or guidelines for the attainment of the values designated within that definition are the realm of normative ethics. Normative ethics propose norms that prohibit or prescribe certain: (1) actions; (2) intentions, dispositions, motivations or character; and (3) actions that entail both a description of the act and intention.

Modern meta-ethical inquiry emerged in the early part of this century with G.E. Moore's seminal work, *Principia Ethica*.[25] The central questions that Moore addressed were semantical—having to do with the nature and meaning of ethical terms—and the logical function of those terms. Regarding the semantic question, first, Moore addressed whether or not ethical concepts can be analyzed or defined; second, if they are definable, is it in terms of ethical or non-ethical characteristics; and finally, what are the definitions of those terms?[26] Definist meta-ethical theories, for example, claim that ethical terms do have meaning, and that meaning can be justified.[27] For example, 'good' means 'the greatest good for the greatest number.' This definition is very *general* and ambiguous and ethicists who may agree upon this definition of 'good' may have very different understandings of what norms will facilitate attainment of the good, and further, *how* both the definition of 'good' and those norms are to be *justified.* In other words, why and on what grounds is something considered valuable and therefore good, whereas something else is not?

In his definition of meta-ethics, William Frankena posits that the most important questions of meta-ethics are with the meaning of ethical terms and the justification of ethical and value judgments.[28] The meaning or use of ethical terms is considered under the auspice of semantical questions. The justification of ethical and value judgments is considered under the auspice of epistemic questions. It is the latter question that Frankena considers the primary question of meta-ethics.[29] One may legitimately ask whether or not there is any meaningful distinction between the semantic and epistemic realms when it comes to levels of ethical inquiry? Why not, as do most ethicists, address both of these realms under the auspice of 'meta-ethics'? The importance of the distinction can be seen when one looks at the relationship between meaning and the justification for that meaning, especially in Christian ethical discourse. I will investigate four possibilities of this relationship.

(1) The same *meaning or use* of ethical terms (e.g., good, right, obligation or their opposites), and *different types* or *levels* of justification;

(2) The same *meaning or use* of ethical terms, and the same *types* or *levels* of justification;

(3) A different *meaning or use* of ethical terms and the same *types* or *levels* of justification;

(4) A different meaning or use of ethical terms, and different types or levels of justification.

Before analyzing these combinations, some preliminary remarks are in order. First of all, to assert that ethical terms can be defined is to affirm a most basic meta-ethical assertion, e.g., naturalism. Second, to assert that this meaning can be justified is to make a further meta-ethical assertion on the justification or verification of meaning that frequently divides meta-ethical theories.[30] The question being addressed is not whether or not meta-ethics, and therefore meta-ethical theories, are a necessary dimension of ethical inquiry, but whether meta-ethics goes far enough in distinguishing different *types* of theories, or whether it would be helpful to parse the meta-ethical distinction between meaning on the one hand, and justification on the other? The semantic assertions would belong to meta-ethics, while the epistemic assertions would belong to method. The relationship between meta-ethics and method I will demonstrate subsequently.

Regarding the possible combinations, assertion (4) presents no inherent tension between the semantic and epistemic realms. Meta-ethical theories that define ethical terms differently and rely upon different means for justifying those definitions are clearly differentiated from one another. Assertions (1), (2), and (3), however, illustrate the need to distinguish between meaning and justification not only as distinct inquiries, but more importantly, as distinct realms of ethical inquiry. First of all, (1) claims that ethical terms can have the same meaning or use with different types of justification. For example, one can define "x is wrong" (or any ethical term represented by a variant of this statement) as "x would be disapproved by any person who knew all the relevant facts, could visualize them perfectly, and who loved all sentient beings strongly and equally."[31] Christians and atheists, for example, could both accept this definition of 'wrong,' and yet have radically different sources for justifying it. For those who espouse Christian beliefs, God's existence is their justification for the definition of wrong. To make this assertion, however, does not define 'wrong' in theological terms as does a divine-command theory. Justification itself could be divided into *proximate* and *ultimate*. The proximate justification is that this definition of 'wrong' is the same for all human beings who are able to reason and affirms that which is human.[32] The ultimate justification for Christians would be that God exists and that God affirms the goodness of every human being and, therefore, Christians are called to imitate this affirmation in their behavior.[33] The ultimate justification does not nullify the proximate justification. Rather, it affirms it on the basis of a theological principle or concept which, for Christians, affirms that which is revealed through reason and experience. In the case of the atheist, the justification for this definition of 'wrong' could be that humans deserve to be treated with respect by the very fact of their humanity. This justification does not entail any theological principles, yet adheres to the same meaning of 'wrong' that Christians would affirm. The fact that both Christians and atheists alike could agree on the definition of ethical terms and yet argue for very different types or levels of justification indicates that there is an important distinction between the meaning and justification of ethical terms that represent radically different types of ethical reasoning.

Assertion (2) highlights an important distinction between meaning and justification and their relationship to normative ethics. Consider, for example, the debate going on between revisionist and traditionalist Catholic moral theologians. Both groups could accept that 'good' is defined as that which affirms 'authentic personhood' or 'the dignity of the human person.' Further, both could accept the proximate (reason and experience) and ultimate (divine revelation) justification for this definition. It would seem, however, that if both the definition and justification of ethical terms were the same, then the norms which either frustrate or facilitate the attainment of 'authentic personhood' would be the same as well. In the normative ethical realm, however, these two groups of moral theologians differ on the normative assertions of the *what* question; namely, what fulfills 'authentic personhood'? For example, on issues such as the use of artificial birth control or masturbation for seminal analysis, they disagree on norms that fulfill 'authentic personhood.' Hence, it appears that not only is it important to distinguish between meaning and justification, but further to distinguish between the hermeneutic of the sources for justification. Both the sources for one's justification and the hermeneutic of those sources suggest an intermediate step between meta-ethics and normative ethics. I would suggest that 'method' is this intermediate realm of ethical inquiry.

Finally, assertion (3) demonstrates the need to distinguish between meaning and justification and is clearly illustrated by the difference between those who espouse a type of 'divine command theory' and those who espouse a traditional Christian (primarily Catholic) 'natural law theory.' A divine command theory defines ethical terms such as 'right' as 'that which is commanded by God,' whereas a natural law theory defines similar terms as 'that which fulfills humanity's natural end.' Though the definitions of ethical terms differ between these two meta-ethical theories, their ultimate justification relies upon divine revelation. Many philosophers, however, discount the credibility of a meta-ethic when it is based on that which is the point of departure for theologians' very discipline, i.e., faith in a personal God who has created an orderly universe in which humans can, through the use of right reason, discern that which is good or bad, right or wrong, prescribed or prohibited.

These two theories are frequently classified as 'theistic meta-ethical theories' and are then discounted on the grounds that one cannot prove God's existence.

McCloskey, for example, defines the Thomistic natural law ethic as a "theistic, teleological ethic which seeks to relate morality and the existence of God." And while natural law is not subject to the same devastating critiques as a theistic divine-command theory that defines ethical terms in theistic ones, it is still untenable as a meta-ethical theory first, and perhaps primarily, because it is based on the assertion that God exists.[34] Or again, Richard Brandt suggests that it would be difficult to rationally justify the claim that all ethical justification is derived from theological teachings.[35] Richard Garner and Bernard Rosen further suggest that it is difficult to prove the existence of the Judeo-Christian God and, therefore, that any meta-ethic which claims God as its foundation is suspect.[36] One could respond to Brandt's assertion that it is just as difficult to establish that ethical justification must be derived from personal interest (egoism) or general happiness (utilitarianism). One could also respond to Garner and Rosen's suggestion, while it is indeed difficult, if not impossible, to prove God's existence, it is also difficult, if not impossible, to disprove God's existence.[37] To respond thus, however, is to abandon the rational endeavor and take refuge too quickly behind faith assertions. While this may be an entirely acceptable, and perhaps even necessary move within certain circles (e.g., proponents of a divine-command theory), do advocates of a natural law meta-ethic want to abandon their rational argument for that theory so quickly? This question becomes all the more pressing considering the consistent teaching in Catholic Christianity regarding the reasonableness of natural law. According to that teaching, full knowledge of the natural law is attainable through human reason and experience, though for Christians, natural law and the meaning of ethical terms is ultimately justified in and through God's existence.

Thus, the divine-command and natural law theories are classified as theistic meta-ethical theories, though they differ fundamentally on their assertions regarding the definition of ethical terms and the logical dependence between theological concepts or principles and those terms. Nevertheless, on the basis of a theistic meta-ethical classification, both are equally dismissed by atheists or religious skeptics as a legitimate meta-ethic and foundation for one's normative ethic.

As a result of the aforementioned ambiguity in meta-ethical theory between the meaning of ethical terms, their justification, and the hermeneutic of the sources for justification, I propose to both narrow the definition of meta-ethics and include method, what has traditionally been considered a meta-ethical discipline,[38] as an additional realm of ethical inquiry. Essentially, this would parse the meta-ethical realm of ethical inquiry between logical and semantic considerations on the one hand, and the epistemic justification of those assertions on the other, and designate justification as the realm of method. This division between meta-ethics and method would be helpful for the following reasons. First, the traditional definition of meta-ethics is ambiguous when it comes to defining ethical terms and justifying those definitions. For example, one can define ethical terms synonymously and yet have fundamentally different, even antithetical sources for justifying those definitions. Or, one can define ethical terms antithetically and yet have recourse to the same types or sources for justification. The implication of these combinations means that one does not merely proceed from a meta-ethic and one's definition of an ethical term to a normative ethic which formulates norms that facilitate the attainment of that definition. There is an intermediary step between meta-ethical claims and normative ethical assertions. This is the realm of ethical method. According to McCloskey, "the enquiry into the logical function of moral judgments [i.e., meta-ethics] is entered into as important in its own right and as a preliminary to the normative enquiry, for it is on the basis of our conclusions in the area of meta-ethics, that we determine the appropriate *method* of reaching our normative ethic."[39] While he does not consider method a distinct realm of ethical inquiry, given the complexity of the relationship between epistemic and semantic assertions, I would posit method as a distinct realm. Not only does method allow one to reach a normative ethic, but it also provides one with the epistemic tools to justify one's meta-ethical and normative ethical assertions.

Second, whereas meta-ethics initially focused on whether or not ethical terms have meaning and, if they do have meaning, how they are to be defined, the definition of ethical terms was necessarily very general, e.g., good is defined as 'happiness' or as fulfilling 'authentic personhood.' This is so because what constitutes 'happiness' or fulfills 'authentic personhood' is dependent, in whole or in part, on culture, history, community and one's understanding of the human or anthropology. To provide a *specific* definition of 'happiness' or what fulfills 'authentic personhood' depends on the integration of these and other dimensions, their use in defining ethical terms, and the justification of these definitions. The specific definition of ethical terms and a formulation of the norms that facilitate the achievement of this definition belong to the realm of normative ethics whereas the *justification* for the general (meta-ethical) and specific (normative ethical) definition of ethical terms belongs to the realm of ethical method.

Finally, considering the radical, even opposing normative positions of those who espouse the same meta-ethic (e.g., natural law), the same definition of ethical terms (e.g., good is that which facilitates 'authentic personhood'), and even the same sources for justification, it seems evident that there is a distinct realm of ethical inquiry where these divergences are established and substantiated. Though the parameters of method are not always clearly defined, method is frequently designated as this realm among philosophers and theologians alike. Rather than classify epistemology or justification as one dimension of meta-ethics, then, I would limit meta-ethics to assertions of a general semantic and logical nature and consider the epistemic question as a distinct realm of ethical inquiry.

Ethical method, then, is the link between meta-ethics and normative ethics and has implications for both levels of ethical inquiry. Whereas it is the purpose of meta-ethics to determine whether or not ethical terms have meaning and, if so, whether or not that meaning *can* be justified, method provides the justification for meta-ethical assertions. Obviously, if ethical terms have no meaning, or that meaning cannot be justified, then a consideration of method is either non-applicable or very limited in its task. If, however, a meta-ethic claims that ethical terms do have meaning and that meaning can be justified, it is method's task to utilize all the dimensions that will justify meta-ethical assertions. These dimensions include any discipline that has implications for understanding ethics, for example, anthropology, psychology, sociology, and theology. In and through developments and insights into these dimensions, normative ethics formulates specific definitions of ethical terms. Whereas normative ethics are more dependent upon the discoveries of method, meta-ethics are also dependent upon method to the extent that methodical insights may either substantiate claims that this or that meta-ethical assertion can be justified or may disprove the plausibility of justification. For example, the divine command theory maintains that ethical terms have meaning—right is 'that which is commanded by God'—and that meaning can be justified through divine revelation. The *actual* justification of this meta-ethical claim is problematic and poses devastating challenges to divine-command theories. Normative ethics, on the other hand, is constantly being informed by method as social, historical, communal, and anthropological insights evolve and develop. These insights must, in turn, inform the specific definition of ethical terms and the norms that facilitate or frustrate the attainment of that definition.

AT WHAT LEVEL OF ETHICAL INQUIRY
IS CHRISTIAN ETHICS SPECIFIC?

Having presented the four levels of ethical inquiry, I will now consider at what level Christian ethics are specific. First, a methodical shift in Catholic natural law, especially since Vatican II, has resulted in a meta-ethical shift in the definition of ethical terms. Since Vatican II, Catholic natural law ethics has focused more on anthropology than on cosmology.[40] With this shift in method one can trace a corresponding shift in the definition of ethical terms. From a cosmological perspective one may define the 'good' as "that which directs human beings towards their natural end." In this sense, 'good' is the "perfection of being," and human beings have a natural inclination towards the good in and through their very nature.[41] From an anthropological perspective, however, one can define 'good' (or its ethical variants) as that which facilitates or fulfills "the human person integrally and adequately considered."[42] (For brevity's sake, this will be referred to as 'authentic personhood.') It is not a question of either cosmology or anthropology, but a question of degree and emphasis in the both/and. These are sources for justifying definitions of meta-ethical terms. As such, the shift itself from cosmology to anthropology reveals the impact method can have on the definition of these terms. A corresponding shift in method from essentialism to existentialism allows cultural, historical, and unique individuality—as compared to 'human nature'—flexibility in defining what fulfills 'authentic personhood.' Unlike the 'divine command theory' that defines ethical terms in theological terms natural law defines ethical terms in non-theological terms. In a natural law meta-ethic, then, ethical terms are not *logically* dependent upon theological terms or concepts.[43] Although the Christian definition of 'authentic personhood' will include a faith dimension, it is not *logically* dependent upon that dimension for its meaning. The fact that Christian ethicists posit Jesus as the paradigm of 'authentic personhood' is a specific definition of the good and the justification for that definition which belongs to the normative and methodical realms respectively. At the meta-ethical level of ethical inquiry, then, ethical terms are not defined in theological or religious terms and ethics are not specifically Christian.

If Christian ethics is not specific on the meta-ethical level, is it specific on the methodical level, the level of justification? Epistemically, Christian natural law tradition has consistently taught that knowledge of 'God's law,' 'the natural law,' or 'the natural moral law' is accessible through reason, human experience, and more recently, scientific investigation.[44] Faith in God and God's Self-communication in and through divine revelation, according to magisterial teaching on natural law, is certainly considered the *ultimate* justification for natural law assertions and provides *full* insight into the meaning, nature, and function of that law in relation to the human person,[45] this, however is a specific claim and represents a unique realm of ethical inquiry that I will address below.

Notwithstanding the difficulties in appealing to Scripture for a philosophical, let alone a theological defense of natural law,[46] it seems clear, and Roman Catholic tradition has affirmed,[47] that St. Paul recognized a moral order to which humans have access through reason and human experience. In the letter to the Romans St. Paul, though by no means arguing or developing a theory of natural law, certainly posits a vision of reality into which a concept of natural law will fit.[48] That is, human beings' access to God's law through either intuition (Rom 2:15, "the law written on their hearts") or empiricism (Rom 1:20, "Ever since the creation of the world, invisible realities, God's eternal power and divinity, have become visible, recognized through the things he has made") regardless of their faith.

Whereas it was not St. Paul's objective to develop a theory of natural law, later Christian thinkers would propose systematic conceptions of that law. These versions which were consonant with Jesus' life and teachings, borrowed extensively from pagan thinkers in the Graeco-Roman culture, especially the Stoics, who posited a rational structure and order to reality.[49] St. Augustine was one of the notable forerunners in incorporating the Stoic idea of reason and order into the whole of God's creation. Within human beings, according to Augustine, "when reason controls the movements of the soul, man is said to be ordered."[50]

It was not until Thomas Aquinas, however, that natural law theory was fully and systematically articulated.

Aquinas posits reason as human beings' source for the knowledge of natural law. Truth or rectitude is the same for all, and is equally known by all through reason.[51] The moral precepts of the law proceed from the dictate of reason.[52] This is the proximate justification for natural law. The further assertion that God is the source of that law is a faith assertion on the ultimate justification of natural law that does not have any bearing on a person's ability to know that law through reason. Therefore, the ability to know the law is the same for all, believer and non-believer alike. Aquinas' position on the knowledge of moral law through right reason has been consistently affirmed throughout Catholic tradition.[53]

Corresponding to the two levels of justification for the assertions of natural law, proximate and ultimate, are two methodical realms, philosophical ethical method (PEM) and Christian ethical method (CEM). As demonstrated above, the knowledge of natural law is accessible to all human beings through reason, human experience and scientific investigation, regardless of one's belief in divine revelation. PEM is the *proximate* justification for natural law and its definition of good as 'authentic personhood' and is both *necessary* and *sufficient* for this justification. PEM includes all those dimensions that *justify* the meta-ethical definition of ethical terms (e.g., good as 'authentic personhood') and the normative ethical claims that facilitate the achievement of that definition specifically defined. These dimensions include epistemology, anthropology, psychology, sociology, and any other discipline from which reason can extract ideas, concepts, or phenomena that have a bearing on the justification and specific definition of ethical terms.

CEM relies upon the same tools as philosophical method, that is, reason, experience, and scientific contributions, but *believes*, yet cannot prove, that the *ultimate* justification for natural law is God's creation of an orderly universe through which humans can come to know and understand the nature and contents of that law. In and through this belief, CEM has recourse to *specific* sources for its justification of the definition of ethical terms. At the level of the scientific investigation of Christian ethics, one's personal faith or commitment to the Christian tradition has no bearing on the reasonableness of ethics, Christian or other. For example, both Christian and non-Christian alike can, given the same Christian beliefs and tools of PEM, *do* Christian ethics and reach the same conclusions about ethics. That is, if one accepts the premises of

Christianity, then the conclusions logically follow from those premises, regardless of one's faith commitment. Certainly for Christian ethicists who have a living faith commitment, their participation in the Christian community will influence their perception, understanding and insight into these sources. The point is that natural law is not dependent upon Christian beliefs for its *proximate* justification, though for Christian ethicists who believe in the Christian God with all God's attributes, this God is posited as the *ultimate* justification of natural law. CEM, however, merely affirms from a specific or unique perspective what one could conclude from PEM with regard to natural law.

The sources for justification in CEM derive from divine revelation and include Scripture, tradition, ecclesiology,[54] soteriology, Christology, sacramentality, spirituality,[55] and—for Catholic Christians—the magisterium. CEM combines the tools of PEM with Christian sources to develop a specifically CEM. CEM does not change the definition of ethical terms. It merely asserts an ultimate and contextual justification for those terms that is specific to Christianity. While it is beyond the scope of this chapter to explain how these Christian ethical methodical sources impact the justification of meta-ethical and normative ethical claims, this process of justification will be illustrated in the presentation on normative ethics.

Is there a specifically Christian normative ethic with regard to actions, intentions or motivations? The answer to this question depends on the specificity of the formulation of the norm. For example, one might claim that, whereas the second part of the Decalogue entails natural law norms that can be justified through PEM and pertain to all human beings, the first part of the Decalogue is surely dependent upon CEM and is specific to monotheistic religions such as Judaism and Christianity. So the norms which state that one must "Worship the Lord your God, him only shall you serve"; or, "You must not take the Lord's name in vain"; or again, "You must Keep Holy the Sabbath" are specific to Judaism and Christianity. And further, Jesus' Sermon on the Mount in the New Testament is specific to Christianity. Certainly the *sources* and *justification* of these norms are specific to Judaism and Christianity. However, are the norms that pertain to humans and their relationship to God specific to Jews or Christians? In some sense, yes. These norms presume the existence of God and that 'authentic personhood' for a person of faith requires that we must love and respect a God that entails the characteristics of a monotheistic Judeo-Christian God. Similarly, in order to fulfill the ethical term 'good' defined as 'authentic personhood,' Muslims must love and respect Allah and atheists must love and respect benefactors. Though these norms *could* be stated specifically to address the particular communities, societies, and cultures to which an individual belongs, a natural law ethic is formulated on grounds that are inclusive not exclusive. Otherwise, one's ethic runs the risk of sectarianism where the grounds for common dialogue between and among ethicists are fragmented. While this may not be problematic for certain ethical theories (e.g., the divine command theory) it does pose serious problems for a natural law ethic that claims that all people can know that law through the use of reason. In relation to the specific ethical method of Christians, Jews, Muslims, or atheists, all could agree that the norm, 'one ought to respect and love one's benefactor' is a norm that fulfills 'authentic personhood,' though the context and communities in which one lives and faith commitments to which one adheres determines *who* or *what* is considered one's benefactor.

One might retort to this assertion that, just as 'authentic personhood' is too general a term to define good and normative ethics provides a more specific definition of 'authentic personhood,' the norm 'one ought to respect and love one's benefactor' is too general as well. Here, however, one must distinguish between the science of ethical inquiry, and the moral judgments of individuals. Natural law and the norms derived from that law that are accessible through reason are dependent upon the individual and his or her existentially lived reality for how they will be manifested concretely. This is the level of moral judgments. It is the scientific objective of ethics to define ethical terms, formulate norms that facilitate the attainment of what that definition entails, and to justify both the general and specific definition of those terms and the norms that are formulated in light of the ethical terms' specific definition. It is the *individual* in his or her existential context that lives out those norms in the form of moral judgments where the specificity of Christian natural law ethics clearly manifests itself. This, however, is the realm of morality and moral judgments rather than the scientific reflection on those moral judgments. The moral judgments of a Christian are dependent upon CEM because it provides an ultimate justification and a unique perspective for normative and meta-ethical assertions. Just as pagans in Paul's time would not worship the Christian or Jewish monotheistic God because they did not have faith in that God, many today do not have faith in the Christian God, or they have faith in other entities or realities.

Nonetheless, they may still recognize the general norm that 'one ought to respect and love one's benefactor' as fulfilling 'authentic person-hood.' On the basis of norms that are justified through reason and/or Christian sources, humans make moral judgments that reflect their understanding of 'authentic personhood' in relation to their existential social, historical, cultural, and communal context.

Along with CEM, then, moral judgments are specifically Christian as well. When one moves from the realm of meta-ethics, method and normative ethics to moral judgments, one makes a corresponding shift from ethics to morality. For a person who adopts the Christian faith and accepts divine revelation as the ultimate justification for natural law, there are specifically Christian moral judgments that are contextually situated in the history, culture, and individuality of the human person within the christian community.

SIGNIFICANCE OF THE QUADRIPARTITE DIVISION OF ETHICS AND MORALITY

Having presented a fourfold division of ethics and morality, and analyzed in what sense Christian ethics and morality are specific in relation to this division, I will now return to three questions posed at the beginning of this chapter. First, what are the implications of this division on the exchange between Rigali and Curran in particular and the specificity of Christian ethics and/or morality in general? I will address these questions in two parts. The first part will investigate the division of ethics and morality in relation to their exchange on the specificity of Christian morality; the second part will distinguish between moral judgments on the one hand, and normative material content on the other as representing two different realms of inquiry.

Recall Curran's assertion that whereas the question of universality and, by implication, specificity, belong to the realm of morality, classicism and historical consciousness belong to the realm of ethics. Curran goes on to pose the question to Rigali of whether or not he admits of any universality. Rigali, by responding to this question,[56] appears to accept Curran's assertion that the question of universality does, in fact, belong to the moral realm. It is not clear to me, however, that the question of universality belongs to this realm. Rigali bases his fourfold division of morality on the necessary balance that existentialism provides for an

essentialist view of the person and reality. Essentialism is "a philosophical approach tending to reduce reality to essences and to understand it in
terms of universals," whereas existentialism focuses "attention on the
uniqueness of the individual person in order to overcome essentialism's
concern with the universal."[57] Classicism and essentialism as well as
historical consciousness and existentialism are methodical considerations that pertain to the realm of ethics. Furthermore, it is out of a classicist, essentialist method that the question of a specifically Christian morality arises, according to Rigali. Consequently, it seems to me that the
questions of universality and specificity that develop from an essentialist
philosophical method pertain to ethics, not morality. Classicism, historical consciousness, essentialism, existentialism, universality, and specificity are *all* methodical, and therefore ethical, considerations that reflect
on moral judgments to classify those judgments into a meaningful ethical theory—meta-ethics, method and normative ethics.

If the questions of specificity and universality belong to the ethical
realm, is the question of the specificity of Christian ethics and/or morality resolved by being dissolved once one moves from classicism to historical consciousness? The methodical issues that Rigali addresses are
particularly germane to Catholic Christian ethical method and both its
history and reconstruction. And while the question of the specificity of
Christian ethics and/or morality is somewhat unique to Catholic moral
theologians demonstrated by the debates between the *Glaubensethik* and
autonomy-ethic schools, other Christian ethicists as well as philosophers
have struggled with this question. It is not necessarily the case that they
approach this question from a classicist perspective. The questions of
specificity and universality are important questions with regard to moral
pluralism and the possibility of dialogue between various ethical theories on particular ethical topics such as social justice. Therefore, it seems
that while the question of the specificity of Christian ethics and/or morality may indeed be linked to the classicism of the manualist tradition,
this does not mean that it is only a meaningful question from a classicist
worldview. This worldview is one, though the primary, methodical consideration that makes specificity an important question given the history
and the attempt to reconstruct Catholic moral theology. Other Christian
ethicists and philosophers, however, who do not embrace a classicist
worldview and do not have the same baggage as does Catholic moral
theology, consider it an important question as well.[58] Therefore, on the
level of ethics and for the sake of dialogue with other Christian and non-

Christian ethical traditions, the questions of specificity and universality remain important questions for ethicists.

The second issue to be addressed is whether or not Rigali and Curran's division between ethics and morality is sufficient to investigate the specificity of Christian morality, or if my division would perhaps facilitate further clarity in the discussion. Whereas my division posits moral judgments in the realm of morality and norms in the realm of ethics, Rigali and Curran's definition of 'morality' includes concrete decisions (moral judgments), norms, duties, normative material content, and sometimes even methodical considerations.[59] Furthermore, morality describes both what the moral agent is doing and intending, and the ethicist's reflection on what the moral agent is doing and intending. In other words, 'morality' includes both moral judgments and what could be considered various realms of ethical inquiry. Certainly Rigali is correct in positing his fourfold division of morality based on an existentialist method to compliment manualist essentialism. Rigali further notes that, far from abandoning this division, from an historically conscious methodical perspective, the division is no longer necessary because the question it addresses is a classicist question.[60] As demonstrated above, the questions of universality and specificity remain important *ethical* questions for dialogue between various ethical systems. However, a further question is, given the transformation—or process of transformation—of Catholic moral theology from a classicist method to an historically conscious method, what, if any, are the implications of that shift on the *contents* of ethics and morality? I will address this question in two parts. The first part will investigate moral judgments and the second part will investigate norms, duties, and normative material content.

Regarding moral judgments, there are two important distinctions to make between the agent who makes moral judgments and moral judgments themselves. Much of Rigali's attention correctly focuses on anthropology and understanding the moral subject from an historically conscious, existentialist method ("human-nature-in-a-culture"[61]) as compared to a classicist, essentialist method (human nature). The first comment to make is that, even in Rigali and Curran's division between ethics and morality, questions of anthropology and worldview are methodical questions that pertain to the realm of ethics. In my division, they pertain specifically to the realm of method, both Christian and philosophical. So when Rigali investigates 'The Universality of Humanness,' and states that "the universality of morality must undoubtedly have its source in the universality of humanness that joins all human beings everywhere and always,"[62] he is investigating two realms, the moral and the ethical. While it is true that one's anthropology will have an impact on how one understands the moral realm, the relationship between the ethical and moral realms is not clear because these two realms have not been recognized in this context.

Combining an historically conscious worldview with the question of the nature of the moral subject, Rigali develops an anthropological principle of "embodied spiritual self-transcendence" which, in its formal and material dimensions, constitutes a universal-particular nature.

> Formally, it is a principle, in every human being, of embodied spiritual self-transcendence in culture; and in this respect, it is universal and unchanging. Materially, however, it is a principle, in every human being, of a particular historical mode of embodied spiritual self-transcendence, possible within the limits of a particular culture; and in this respect human nature is particular, historical and variable.[63]

The universal-particular nature shared by humanity is anthropological and ethical, not moral.

Anthropology and worldview are methodical considerations and belong to the ethical realm and are distinct from the moral judgments or decisions of a moral agent. Moral judgments reflect the perceived meanings, values, purposes and goals of an acting subject. From a purely historically conscious, existentialist methodical perspective, by definition there can be no 'essentialist morality' (Christian or otherwise) in the realm of moral decisions for the authentically committed Christian. This is so because the Christian approaches reality as Christian, and makes moral judgments in light of those commitments and the influences of the history, culture and *particular* community in which he or she lives or belongs and participates. While it is true that there is a universal in the particular and a particular in the universal from an anthropological perspective, anthropology, universality and particularity are ethical reflections whereas moral judgments pertain to a specific realm of inquiry, morality. From this perspective, then, all moral judgments of a human being are personal expressions of that human being and are Christian, Buddhist, Jewish or atheist, and are personalized further in relation to the particular Christian, Buddhist, Jewish or atheistic community or historical context in which that person acts. Even if a Christian, Buddhist, Jewish, or atheistic person makes the same moral judgment as any other person, for example, to pay taxes, they make this moral judgment, if their beliefs are authentic, *as* Christian, Buddhist, Jewish, or atheist. That is, at the level of morality, one cannot distinguish the moral judgments of the individual from the beliefs, commitments and perceptions that form that individual's core identity. Granted, as members of the social community, all people may follow a general norm that prescribes paying taxes, but the *reasons* why an individual may pay taxes, or may choose not to do so, are determined by the individual's core identity.

Rigali notes that while denying the existence of a specifically Christian morality, Curran himself recognizes that "explicitly Christian consciousness does affect the judgment of the Christian and the way in which he makes his [moral] judgments."[64] Moral judgments are a unique expression of the individual human being that manifests his or her uniqueness, whereas norms function as general guidelines that direct people's behavior.

The relationship between norms and moral judgments is aptly demonstrated in Louis Janssens form of personalism, especially his eighth criterion: "All human persons are fundamentally equal, but at the same time each is an originality." Janssens goes on to explain how these two dimensions manifest themselves in norms and behavior. "Equality and originality imply that all must let their activity be guided by the universal prescriptions of morality and that at the same time each one must bring his originality to expression through his behavior."[65] The anthropological ethical assertion that every human being is a unique originality substantiates the claim that every moral judgment is a concrete expression of that unique originality with the history, culture, values, responsibilities, relationships and perceptions that an individual expresses in and through moral judgments. From an historically conscious perspective, the concrete person in history is normative.[66] This normativity, however, is manifested as concrete moral decisions or judgments, not material normative content. 'Universal prescriptions of morality'—what we would call normative ethics—are general norms which either prescribe or prohibit certain acts and/or intentions. These norms become incarnate in and through the moral judgments of a unique human person. Without the moral judgments of a human person, norms are meaningless. There is, then, an important distinction between norms or normative material content and moral judgments. The former are imposed from without and function as general guidelines for human beings, whereas the latter are a unique manifestation of the individual and his or her interpretation of the norm given the social, cultural, relational and communal dimensions in which that individual exists.

In fact, Rigali's own quadripartite division of morality *implicitly* supports the division between norms that function as general guidelines and moral judgments that are a unique expression of the individual. Essential morality is "incumbent on" a person, that is, according to the *Oxford English Dictionary*, "resting or falling upon a person as a duty or obligation," whereas existential morality originates "in the individuality of the human person"[67] and is an expression of that person as a moral decision or judgment. Within the realm of norms and normative material content, the former is imposed from without, while the latter originates from within and is manifested as a moral decision by an individual. On the level of moral decisions or judgments, then, there is no 'essential morality' (Christian or otherwise) because all moral judgments are made by a person grounded in culture and history with specific beliefs, commitments and perceptions. The question of the specificity of moral judgments, then, is resolved by being dissolved. All moral judgments are expressions of the individual in an historical, cultural, communal context out of which the individual makes those judgments.

Curran poses the question of universality to Rigali in three different areas: the social moral order, human rights or what is normative for human beings and the dignity of the human person or anthropology.[68] As explained above, anthropology belongs to the ethical realm, specifically, the methodical realm, both Christian and philosophical. The question of the nature of a social order is intimately linked to worldview, classicism and historical consciousness, and therefore pertains to the ethical realm as well. The question remains, however, of whether or not norms or normative material content belong to the ethical or moral realms?

According to Curran[69] and Rigali,[70] norms or duties belong to morality. Obviously, one can formulate a norm that is specific to a particular community, and even specific for an individual within that community, thereby claiming specificity on the normative level. Rigali lists certain norms or duties in relation to his fourfold division of ethics. An example of a "Christian essential" duty would be "to witness to Christ," whereas a "Christian existential" duty for an individual Christian is the duty "of a religious educator to instruct a particular group of children in the Christian story."[71] Curran, on the other hand, gives a more general account of norms that might apply to all people, not just Christians, e.g., "self-sacrificing love...concern for the neighbor in need, and even the realization that one finds one's life by losing it."[72] Certainly these are "essentialist" norms and are not specific to Christianity. From an historically conscious, existentialist methodical perspective, however, 'essentialist morality' is a meaningless category, i.e., it is eliminated as a category of morality by definition. One is left, then, with at least two options. One can either claim that, like moral judgments, *all* material normative content is *specifically* Christian, Buddhist, Jewish or atheist; or, one can claim that, whereas moral judgments pertain to the concrete moral decisions of the moral subject, and, therefore, morality, material normative content exists on the level of ethics. Rigali himself recognizes the existence of universal normative values such as life, friendship, society, knowledge, truth and religion.[73] Furthermore, he recognizes that in the case of essential morality there are certain norms or duties that are incumbent on a human being as a member of the human race.[74] Consequently, the first option could not be held. The second option seems the more plausible of the two.

Following my division of ethics, I would move norms from morality to the level of scientific ethical inquiry. In this way, norms are formulated as universals but take on specificity in the realm of moral judgments given the historical, cultural, communal based reality of an individual. If Catholicism continues to assert that knowledge of natural law is accessible to all human beings through the use of reason, experience, and scientific investigation as it has consistently maintained—even though the ultimate justification of that truth may depend on divine revelation—then it is imperative that ethics are, in some sense, universal. While recognizing the particularity of moral judgments and a moral agent's interpretation and application of a natural law norm, normative ethics remain universal, though not necessarily *ahistorical*.

If norms shift from the level of morality to the level of ethics in dialogue with method, then a unique question presents itself. Namely, what is the impact of CEM on the specific meaning of 'authentic personhood' and the norms that either facilitate or frustrate the attainment of 'authentic personhood'? Do the norms themselves have to be formulated to address the specific context in which they are lived out at the level of moral judgments, or can they be formulated universally? For example, while all may accept the norm 'one ought to be grateful to benefactors' the further questions of *who* is one's benefactor and *how* is one to show gratefulness to that benefactor is answered at the methodical level and lived out by the individual as a moral judgment or decision. That the Judeo-Christian God is the supreme benefactor for Christians and they show gratefulness to God in and through participation in the sacraments, for example, is a methodical consideration specific to Christianity. Living out the norm as a moral judgment by the moral agent is at the level of morality and is specifically Christian as well.

In their exchange, Curran is correct in pointing out that Rigali is mixing the moral and ethical realms by labeling Curran's universalist position classicist. Curran asserts that whereas the discussion about classicism and historical consciousness is on the level of ethics, the question of universality is on the level of morality. In fact, Rigali's major contributions to Catholic moral theological discourse have been in the realm of method and on the level of ethics. And while there is an important distinction between ethics and morality, this distinction is somewhat ambiguous and the relationship between the two is never fully developed. As a result, it is not always clear in their exchange whether they are addressing the ethical or moral realms. An advantage of my division of ethics is that both normative ethics and method belong to the scientific realm of ethics. It will be a challenge to work out that relationship, which is an ongoing project, but there is a clear distinction between the moral judgments of an agent in his or her historically, culturally, communally based reality and the norms upon which that agent is acting.

The former belongs to the moral realm whereas the latter belongs to the ethical realm.

On the basis of the foregoing, it is possible to address Curran's challenge to Rigali regarding the former's claim that one can hold "a general and an 'in principled' universality on the level of morality without necessarily embracing classicism on the level of ethics." Whereas there is no meaningful sense from an historically conscious, existentialist methodical perspective in which one can discuss *universal moral judgments*, when discussing *normative material content* it is another matter. Certainly one can formulate norms that are universal in scope, however, such formulations are on the level of ethics. I would further assert that the questions of *universality* and *specificity* belong not to the realm of morality but to the realm of ethics. Curran's above assertion could then be qualified: one can hold "a general and an 'in principled' universality on the level of *ethics* without necessarily embracing classicism." Certainly Rigali's article on universality identifies some important characteristics of such an ethic.

The second question that was raised at the beginning of this chapter was how can method, as a distinct realm of ethical inquiry, facilitate development in the reconstruction of moral theology? As indicated, much of the renewal in moral theology is taking place in the area of method. The investigation and development of, and dialogue between, philosophical and Christian (Catholic) ethical method responds to two calls made by Vatican II. First, in its address to seminarians, though this directive would certainly apply to theologians as well, the *Decree on Priestly Formation (Optatum Totius)* emphasizes the importance of seeing "the connections between philosophical argument and the mysteries of salvation...." The logical, critical and analytical tools of philosophy help to facilitate clarity in theological discourse. Theology is dependent upon philosophy for sound argumentation, though it supercedes the former through the "superior light of faith."[75] The second call is from the frequently cited statement from this same document on the renewal of moral theology:

> Special attention needs to be given to the development of moral theology. Its scientific exposition should be more thoroughly nourished by scriptural teaching. It should show the nobility of the Christian vocation of the faithful, and their obligation to bring forth fruit in charity for the life of the world.[76]

A Christian (Catholic) ethical method would include an investigation of scripture, sacramentality, ecclesiology, spirituality, and Christology among other dimensions of Catholicism, and their integration in the reconstruction of Catholic *ethical* theology. Part of the reconstruction process will entail working out the precise relationship between PEM and CEM and their implications for normative ethics.

Finally, in answering one and two, question three can be addressed: What are the implications of the distinction between the various realms of ethical inquiry on the exchange between the autonomous-ethic and *Glaubensethik* schools? Unless the latter school wants to define ethical terms in theological terms, which would both deny Catholic traditional assertions on the knowability of natural law and would face the same devastating critiques that confront 'divine-command' ethical theories, they must accept the definition of ethical terms in non-theological terms.

If this is the case, then the meta-ethical general definition of ethical terms is not the realm in which they would disagree with the faith-ethic school. Instead, it seems that the difference between these two schools resides in the methodical realm and the question of the impact of method on normative ethics. With the question of artificial birth control, for example, one could posit a different material normative content between the two schools. The question of which position is more credible entails an investigation of method, both Christian and philosophical, in arriving at one's normative content. How sound are the philosophical reasoning and argumentation and the hermeneutic of Christian sources in arriving at one's normative ethic? It is within the realm of method that the resolution of such divergences must take place.

NOTES

1. In this chapter, we will follow James Walter's distinction between 'specific' and 'distinctive.' "Whereas the term 'specific' connotes exclusivity, the term 'distinctive' only connotes a characteristic quality or set of relations which are typically associated with any given reality" ("Christian Ethics: Distinctive and Specific?" in Charles E. Curran and Richard A. McCormick, S.J., eds., *Readings in Moral Theology No. 2: The Distinctiveness of Christian Ethics* (New York: Paulist Press, 1980), 101.

2. C.E. Curran, *The Living Tradition of Catholic Moral Theology* (Notre Dame, IN: University of Notre Dame Press), 178–79.

3. Alfons Auer, *Autonome Moral und Christlicher Glaube* (Dusseldorf: Patmos-Verlag, 1971).

4. *Ibid..*, 177. See Vincent MacNamara, *Faith & Ethics: Recent Roman Catholicism* (Washington, DC: Georgetown University Press, 1985), 37–55.

5. *Grenzen der autonomen Moral* (Kösel: München, 1974).

6. *Ethik und Rationalität: Untersuchungen zum Autonomieproblem und zu seiner Bedeutung für die theologische Ethik* (Dusseldorf: Patmos, 1980).

7. See James J. Walter's article in this collection.

8. For example, see *Ibid...*; Curran and McCormick, S.J., eds., *Readings in Moral Theology No. 2*; and, Norbert Rigali, "The Uniqueness and the Distinctiveness of Christian Morality and Ethics," in Charles E. Curran, ed., *Moral Theology: Challenges for the Future* (New York: Paulist Press, 1990), 74–93.

9. Rigali, "On Christian Ethics," *Chicago Studies* 10 (1971), 236–47.

10. Curran, "Is There a Distinctively Christian Social Ethic?" in Philip D. Morris, ed., *Metropolis: Christian Presence and Responsibility* (Notre Dame, IN: University of Notre Dame Press, 1970), 114. Rigali, "Christian Morality and

Universal Morality: The One and the Many," *Louvain Studies* 19 (1994), 19, nn. 4 and 5, points out that both in Curran's article and his earlier response to it ("On Christian Ethics"), both use 'ethic' and 'ethical,' where 'moral' and 'morality' would more accurately reflect the topic being addressed.

11. Curran, *Living Tradition*, 178.

12. Rigali, "The Uniqueness and the Distinctiveness of Christian Morality and Ethics," 74–75; and *id.*, "Christian Morality and Universal Morality," 18.

13. *Id.*, "Uniqueness and Distinctiveness," 75.

14. *Id.*, "Christian Morality and Universal Morality," 19.

15. *Ibid.*.

16. *Id.*, "On Christian Ethics," 240.

17. Curran, *Living Tradition*, 177.

18. Rigali, "Uniqueness and Distinctiveness," 90.

19. See R.A. McCormick, S.J., "Notes on Moral Theology," *Theological Studies* 34 (1973), 60–61; *id.*, *The Critical Calling: Reflections on Moral Dilemmas since Vatican II* (Washington, DC: Georgetown University Press, 1989), 67 and 194–96; and James Walter, "The Dependence of Christian Morality on Faith: A Critical Assessment," *Église et Théologie* 12 (1981), 261–62; and Curran, *Living Tradition*, 177–78.

20. Rigali, "Uniqueness and Distinctiveness," 88.

21. Curran, *Living Tradition*, 178.

22. Rigali, "Christian Morality and Universal Morality."

23. Other articles on Rigali's treatment of method include: "The Unity of the Moral Order," *Chicago Studies* 8 (1969), 125–43; "New Epistemology and the Moralist," *Chicago Studies* 11 (1972), 237–44; "Human Experience and Moral Meaning," *Chicago Studies* 13 (1974), 88–104; "Morality and Historical Consciousness," *Chicago Studies* 18 (1979), 161–68; "The Moral Act," *Horizons* 10 (1983), 252–66; "The Unity of Moral and Pastoral Truth," *Chicago Studies* 25 (1986), 224–32; "Models of the Person in Moral Theology," *Chicago Studies* 32 (1993), 177–85; and "Reimaging Morality: A Matter of Metaphors," *The Heythrop Journal* 35 (1994), 1–14.

24. Henry J. McCloskey, *Meta-ethics and Normative Ethics* (The Hague: Martinus Nijhoff, 1969), 7.

25. George E. Moore, *Principia Ethica* (Cambridge: Cambridge University Press, 1903, repr. 1968).

26. *Ibid.*, 5–6.

27. William K. Frankena, *Ethics* (Englewood Cliffs, NJ: Prentice Hall,1973, 2nd ed.), 97–102.

28. *Ibid.*, 96.

29. *Ibid.*.

30. Kai Nielsen, "Ethics, Problems of," in Paul Edwards ed., *The Encyclopedia of Philosophy* (New York: MacMillan, 1967), III, 127.

31. Richard B. Brandt, *Ethical Theory: The Problems of Normative and Critical Ethics* (Englewood Cliffs, NJ: Prentice Hall, 1959), 73 and 173–76. For the development of this proposition as the foundation for a naturalist meta-ethic, see Roderick Firth, "Ethical Absolutism and the Ideal Observer," *Philosophy and Phenomenological Research* 12 (1952), 317–45.

32. See Thomas Aquinas, *S.T.*, I–II, q. 94, aa. 2 and 4.

33. *Id., S.T.*, II–II, q. 17, a. 1; q. 23, aa. 3 and 6; q. 27, a. 6.

34. McCloskey, *Meta-Ethics and Normative Ethics*, 17.

35. Brandt, *Ethical Theory*, 61–82.

36. Richard T. Garner and Bernard Rosen, *Moral Philosophy: A Systematic Introduction to Normative Ethics and Meta-Ethics* (New York: Macmillan, 1967), 235–37.

37. John W. Carlson, "Meta-Ethics and the Context of Faith," *The Modern Schoolman* 60 (1982), 29.

38. Abraham Edel, *Method in Ethical Theory* (New Brunswick, NJ: Transaction Publishers, repr., 1994), 216.

39. McCloskey, *Meta-Ethics and Normative Ethics*, v (emphasis added). See also, Richard B. Brandt, *Ethical Theory*, 9–10, who concurs with McCloskey when he writes, "Obviously it is necessary to answer the main questions of critical ethics [i.e., meta-ethics] before we have firm grounds for constructing a system of normative ethics."

40. This shift from cosmology to anthropology can be seen in the corresponding terminological shift from 'human nature' to 'human person' or 'human dignity.' See John Mahoney, *The Making of Moral Theology: A Study of the Roman Catholic Tradition* (Oxford: Clarendon Press, 1987), 113–15.

41. Aquinas, *S.T.*, I–II, q. 94, a. 2.

42. *Schema constitutionis pastoralis de ecclesia in mundo huius temporis: Expensio modorum partis secundae* (Vatican City: Vatican Press, 1965), 37–38. See Louis Janssens, "Artificial Insemination: Ethical Considerations," *Louvain Studies* 8 (1980), 3–29, for his development of "the human person adequately considered" into a 'personalist method.'

43. W.K. Frankena, "Is Morality Logically Dependent on Religion?" in Gene Outka and John P. Reeder, Jr., eds., *Religion and Morality: A Collection of Essays* (Garden City, NY: Anchor Press/Doubleday, 1973), 295–317; and Walter, "Dependence of Christian Morality on Faith," 251–62.

44. See, for example, "Letter to Bishops on the Pastoral Care of Homosexual Persons," *Pope Speaks* 32 (1987), 62.

45. See Pope John Paul II, *Veritatis Splendor* (Vatican City: Libreria Editrice Vaticana, 1993), § 36.

46. Gerard J. Hughes, "The Authority of Christian Tradition and of Natural Law," in Charles E. Curran and Richard A. McCormick, S.J., *Readings in Moral Theology No. 7: Natural Law and Theology* (Mahwah, NJ: Paulist Press, 1991),

27–35.

47. Heinrich Denzinger, *Enchiridion symbolorum* (Fribourg: Herder, 1947, 26th ed.), § 1785. See Josef Fuchs, *Natural Law: A Theological Investigation*, Helmut Reckter, S.J., and John A. Dowling, trans. (New York: Sheed and Ward, 1965), 147–50.

48. Timothy O'Connell, *Principles for a Catholic Morality* (San Francisco: HarperSanFrancisco, 1990, rev. ed.), 147.

49. Mahoney, *The Making of Moral Theology*, 72.

50. *PL* 32, 1231: "Hisce igitur motibus animae cum ratio dominatur, ordinatus homo dicendus est." Cited in Mahoney, *The Making of Moral Theology*, 75 and n. 16.

51. Aquinas, *S.T.*, I–II, q. 94, a. 4; q. 91, a. 3, ad 3.

52. *Id.*, *S.T.*, I–II, q. 108, a. 2, ad 1: "Matters of faith are above human reason, and so we cannot attain to them except through grace. Consequently, when grace came to be bestowed more abundantly, the result was an increase in the number of explicit points of faith. On the other hand, it is through human reason that we are directed to works of virtue, for it is the rule of human action, as stated above. Wherefore in such matters as these there was no need for any precepts to be given besides the moral precepts of the Law, which proceed from the dictate of reason."

53. See Fuchs, *Natural Law*, 144–62.

54. See Curran's article in this collection.

55. See O'Keefe, Keenan and Vacek's articles in this collection.

56. Rigali, "Christian Morality and Universal Morality," 18–33.

57. *Ibid.*, 19–20.

58. See, for example, the collection of essays in Outka and Reeder, eds., *Religion and Morality*; and *id.*, *Prospects for a Common Morality* (Princeton, NJ: Princeton University Press, 1993).

59. Curran, *Toward an American Catholic Moral Theology*, 54, defines Christian ethics as "a thematic, systematic, and *methodological* approach to the understanding of Christian morality" (emphasis added). At different points, however, methodological considerations permeate Rigali and Curran's discussions of morality and obscure the lines of where method resides, in morality or ethics. See *id.*, *The Living Tradition of Catholic Moral Theology*, 178.

60. Rigali, "Christian Morality and Universal Morality," 19–20.

61. *Ibid.*, 29.

62. *Ibid.*, 28.

63. *Ibid.*, 29.

64. Curran, "Is There a Distinctively Christian Social Ethic?" in Philip D. Morris, ed., *Metropolis*, 114. Cited in Rigali, "On Christian Ethics," 235.

65. Louis Janssens, "Artificial Insemination: Ethical Considerations," 12.

66. Rigali, "The Uniqueness and the Distinctiveness of Christian Morality

208 METHOD AND CATHOLIC MORAL THEOLOGY

and Ethics," 87.

67. *Id.*, "Christian Morality and Universal Morality," 19.

68. Curran, *The Living Tradition of Catholic Moral Theology*, 178–79.

69. *Id.*, *Toward an American Catholic Moral Theology*, 58.

70. Rigali, "The Uniqueness and the Distinctiveness of Christian Morality and Ethics," 87.

71. *Ibid.*.

72. Curran, *Toward an American Catholic Moral Theology*, 60.

73. Rigali, "Christian Morality and Universal Morality," 32.

74. *Ibid.*, 19.

75. "Decree on Priestly Formation (*Optatum Totius*)," in Walter M. Abbot (ed.), *The Documents of Vatican II* (New York: America Press, 1966), § 15.

76. *Ibid.*, § 16.

The Natural Law and the Specificity of Christian Morality: A Survey of Recent Work and an Agenda for Future Research

Jean Porter

Is there a specifically Christian morality, which is substantially different in normative content from the moral codes of other religious and cultural groups? Or is there only one human morality, derived from human nature or from some fundamental characteristic of human existence, to which Christianity adds new motivation and perhaps new duties, without substantially altering its normative content?

Throughout the modern period, the Catholic answer to these questions would have favored the latter alternative. More specifically, Catholic theologians have usually held that there is a universal human morality, knowable to and binding on all persons, namely the natural law, which comprises those moral norms which are derived from human nature as such. Christian morality was accordingly seen as being substantially equivalent to the natural law, even though many theologians held that Christianity adds new duties to the norms of the natural law.

After the Second Vatican Council, and even more after the negative reaction to *Humanae vitae*, the doctrine of the natural law, as it developed in the modern period and was expressed in official Catholic teachings, was subject to widespread criticism. Increasingly, this doctrine was seen as an expression of a classical worldview, which fails to take account of the historicity of human experience. Yet in spite of this rejection of the "classical" doctrine of the natural law, a number of Catholic theologians, including most notably Joseph Fuchs and Charles Curran, continued to argue that there is no specifically Christian morality, but only a morality of genuine humanness, to which Christianity adds new depth and motivation but no new moral laws.

In an influential series of essays extending over more than twenty years, Norbert Rigali argues that the position set forth by Fuchs and Curran, among others, still reflects a mindset which is inadequately informed by historical consciousness.[1] The very question, "Is there a specifically Christian morality?" presupposes that we have one essence, namely human morality, to which another (possibly existing) essence, Christian morality, must be somehow related. This is a fundamental misunderstanding, in Rigali's view. There is no human morality as such, nor is there one fixed Christian morality; what we have, rather, are historically and culturally specific ways of living out the moral life, including a plurality of Christian moralities. Hence, the task of the Christian is not to identify the specific contours of an abstract Christian morality, but to discern what it means for the individual to follow Christ in a particular time and place. Thus, he concludes, "For historical consciousness, therefore, the debate question [whether there is a specifically Christian morality] is resolved by being dissolved."[2]

Rigali's articles on the specificity of Christian morality represent an important contribution to the debate on this topic. He is quite right, in my view, to maintain that Fuchs and Curran presuppose the classicism that they have repudiated in other contexts. Furthermore, he has performed an important service by calling attention to the vagueness of terms such as "the truly human," and by insisting that the meaning and content of Christian morality be understood in concrete and historically situated terms.

Yet Rigali's contribution leaves important questions unresolved. Perhaps the most serious of these pertains to the possibility of establishing a basis for moral dialogue in today's pluralistic society. If we cannot speak of a universal or properly human morality at all, what basis can there be for dialogue with representatives of moral traditions other than our own? Is there not a danger here of falling into a sectarian posture through an over-emphasis on the historical specificity of Christian morality?[3]

These questions suggest that Rigali spoke prematurely when he claimed that the debate over the specificity of Christian morality has been resolved. This debate reflects a chronic tension within the Christian community, which is once again becoming acute, between defending the integrity of the Christian moral tradition and maintaining a stance of openness towards those who speak from different perspectives.

Within the Catholic tradition, these tensions have traditionally been addressed by means of a theory of the natural law. Yet Rigali speaks for many when he insists that the modern doctrine of the natural law is no

longer viable, given the contemporary awareness of the historical character of human existence. Given the widespread acceptance of this critique, is the natural law tradition still a viable source for theological reflection?

The answer to this question is yes, but a qualified yes. The fact is,
almost no Catholic moral theologian has been prepared to give up on the
idea of a natural law altogether, and some have proposed theories of the
natural law which supposedly avoid the difficulties of earlier accounts.
Rigali's critique, taken together with the questions raised above, suggests a criterion for evaluating these theories. That is, a satisfactory
doctrine of the natural law must allow for a "both/and": *both* an affirmation that there is a common basis for moral dialogue within a pluralistic
society, *and* an acknowledgement of the historically and culturally con-
ditioned character of human existence, and therefore of all actual moral
traditions.

In this essay, I will examine two approaches to the natural law
which have emerged since Vatican II, namely, the "new natural law"
theory proposed by Germain Grisez and John Finnis, and the return to
the natural as a basis for moral norms, as advocated by a number of
theologians including James Gustafson, Stephen Pope and Martin Cook.
I will argue that, from the perspective of the criterion set forth above, the
latter approach to the natural law is the more promising, although it is
still in the process of being developed.

In order to appreciate the significance of these approaches to the
natural law, it is necessary to have some sense of what their proponents
are reacting against. Accordingly, I will begin by examining the modern
Catholic doctrine of the natural law, seen in the context of the issues
raised by Rigali and others.

THE NATURAL LAW IN MODERN CATHOLIC THOUGHT

Probably the most familiar version of the natural law is the account
which has been endorsed by the Catholic magisterium throughout the
modern period, continuing with some qualifications to the present day.[4]
On this view, moral norms are grounded in the processes and inclinations of the human person, including sensual, rational, and spiritual inclinations (as these were traditionally understood), seen as being intrinsically purposive and thus normatively binding. The fundamental princi-

ple of the natural law, so understood, is that the human person should act in accordance with the normative functions of human nature, as those are discerned through intelligent observation of human life.

To some degree, this conception of the natural law allows for the contingency and social variability of human mores and laws, precisely because the exigencies of human life do not generally dictate any one particular means of fulfillment. Thus, for example, the human inclination to live in community can be fulfilled in any one of many specific forms of community, even though some may be better than others. Moreover, the concrete laws and customs which sustain a community may be considered to be legitimate expressions of the natural law (providing they are not morally problematic), even though they are not specifically required by anything in reason or nature.

Because the natural law, so understood, is most open to interpretation at the level of social structures, it has received its most interesting developments in the areas of political philosophy and Christian social ethics. As David Hollenbach observes, the modern Catholic doctrine of the natural law was one important foundation for the affirmation of natural human rights in official Catholic social teachings, beginning with the encyclical *Rerum novarum*.[5] Some theologians have gone still farther in the direction of incorporating modern notions of rights into a traditional natural law framework. Jacques Maritain argued that the human person's innate capacities for knowledge and responsible action give rise to natural rights. Similarly, John Courtney Murray defended the consistency of the political structure of the United States with the modern Catholic conception of the natural law, arguing further that the natural law provides a more secure foundation for the American commitment to human rights than the philosophical systems of John Locke and others.[6]

Of course, the natural law understood in this way does require the observance of specific moral laws, and so its flexibility is not limitless. The traditional moral rules (such as prohibitions against murder, theft, or lying) are considered to be expressions of the natural law which are universal and exceptionless, and therefore are not open to cultural reinterpretation. Nonetheless, in this respect the modern Catholic conception of the natural law is essentially in accordance with the common morality of Western societies.

However, on some issues the traditional Catholic interpretation of the natural law is strikingly at odds with common morality. The best known point of divergence is the official Catholic teaching that no form of artificial contraception is morally licit:

> Nonetheless, the Church, calling men back to the observance of the norms of the natural law, as interpreted by her constant doctrine, teaches that each and every marriage act must remain open to the transmission of life.
>
> That teaching, often set forth by the Magisterium, is founded upon the inseparable connection, willed by God and unable to be broken by man on his own initiative, between the two meanings of the conjugal act: the unitive meaning and the procreative meaning. Indeed, by its intimate structure, the conjugal act, while most closely uniting husband and wife, capacitates them for the generation of new lives, according to laws inscribed in the very being of man and woman. By safeguarding both these essential aspects, the unitive and the procreative, the conjugal act preserves in its fullness the sense of true mutual love and its ordination towards man's most high calling to parenthood. We believe that the men of our day are particularly capable of seizing the deeply reasonable and human character of this fundamental principle.[7]

Subsequently, this teaching has been extended to cover artificial forms of reproduction outside the sex act. In addition, as is well known, the natural law so understood also rules out homosexuality and other "deviant" forms of sexuality as violations of the intrinsic principles of human sexuality.

The hopeful prediction of *Humanae vitae*, that its reasonableness would be widely appreciated, proved not to be the case. To the contrary, the promulgation of this document set off a wave of protest within Catholic circles which has still not exhausted itself. It is true, of course, that the modern Catholic conception of the natural law had been widely criticized from outside the Catholic community for some time, both by philosophers and by theologians from other traditions. However, the promulgation of *Humanae vitae* served to focus criticisms of the natural law from within the Catholic community as well. Most radically, a number of theologians questioned the assumption that there is such a thing as an essential human nature, which is unchangeable and which serves as a basis for specific and yet universal moral laws. Although this line of argument was not new—it had been put forth by both Karl Rahner and Bernard Lonergan—it gained new force and widespread acceptance as a result of reactions to the encyclical.[8]

Perhaps because these criticisms came from within the Catholic community, they proved to be more corrosive of the modern Catholic conception of the natural law than did the formidable criticisms of David Hume and other philosophers. At any rate, in the years since the promulgation of *Humanae vitae*, there have been very few theologians prepared to defend this version of the natural law in anything like its modern form. As we will see in the next section, even Grisez and Finnis, who staunchly defend the prohibition against the use of contraceptives, do so on the basis of a very different understanding of the natural law.

From our vantage point almost thirty years later, it is easy to see why the modern Catholic version of the natural law as set forth in *Humanae vitae* is so difficult to defend. For one thing, social forces have conspired to make some of the practical consequences of this version of the natural law, particularly those pertaining to sexual morality, almost incredible to most men and women in Western societies today. This was not the case until fairly recently; at the turn of the century, the Catholic attitude towards sexual matters generally, and towards contraceptives in particular, was widely held, although not necessarily on the grounds offered by the Catholic magisterium. But for a variety of reasons, these attitudes were undermined and transformed, until today it is difficult for most people even to consider the official Catholic position on the use of contraceptives.[9]

Of course, it might be the case that the modern Catholic interpretation of the natural law is right, even though it is counter-cultural. But as the critique summarized above indicates, there are intrinsic difficulties with this position, not only philosophical but also theological in character. Most significantly, seen from the standpoint of the issues that concern us here, the modern Catholic version of the natural law presents a paradox. It is understood by its proponents as a rational theory of morality, yielding precepts which are "deeply reasonable and human," and which can therefore be affirmed by all men and women of good will. Yet at this point, it is difficult to deny the extent to which this version of the natural law reflects a specific tradition, namely Catholicism, and generates norms, which are only plausible within the framework of a specific community. As Rigali observes in a provocative article, the teachings of *Humanae vitae* make far more sense considered as expressions of a specifically Christian affirmation of the value of sexual restraint, than as expressions of a universally valid rationality.[10]

At the same time, the official Catholic version of the natural law has appeared rationally compelling to many intelligent people, and it would be a mistake to dismiss it out of hand. Part of the attractiveness of this position undoubtedly lies in the fact that it offered moral certainty and clear, unambiguous guidelines for individual and social life. In addition, and more distinctively, this version of the natural law offers a way to think morally about the bodily dimensions of human existence. It calls on men and women to take cognizance of the limitations imposed upon us by our physical and animal nature, and it suggests that no lasting individual happiness or social peace can be attained unless those limits are acknowledged. In this way, it stands in sharp contrast to the regnant versions of classical liberalism, which identified the reality of the human person in terms of his or her rationality alone, and sometimes seemed to assume that there are no limits to human freedom or social possibilities. It is true that this version of the natural law developed its own contrasting position in a way that was too simplistic and seemed sometimes to leave the specifically rational and spiritual out of consideration. Nonetheless, this tradition provided an important alternative voice on these matters. As we will see, there are still a number of theologians, not all of them Catholics, who are still attracted by what they consider to be the central insights of this version of the natural law.

Before turning to more recent attempts to retrieve some idea of the normativity of nature, however, we must first consider an alternative, and very different, version of the natural law.

THE NATURAL LAW WITHOUT NATURE: THE "NEW NATURAL LAW"

We have already had occasion to mention David Hume's argument that it is logically impossible to derive moral conclusions from factual premises, an argument which subsequently came to be known by the slogan, "no ought from is."[11] Many proponents of the natural law have attempted to respond to Hume's argument, and a number of philosophers who have no stake in natural law theories of ethics now consider it to be fallacious or unconvincing. However, the "new natural law" theory developed by Grisez and Finnis and their collaborators is developed on the assumption that Hume is right to claim that facts of nature cannot serve as a basis for moral conclusions. Instead, they develop their theory of moral judgement out of a general account of practical reason, which is then narrowed down into a theory of moral action, interpreted as action that is rational in the fullest possible sense.[12]

In developing this theory, they begin with the observation that all rational agents act in order to obtain or to preserve something that at least seems to be good. But even the most reasonable person can be mistaken as to whether this concrete desideratum is *truly* good, and in such a case, an action is likely to be self-frustrating or even harmful to the agent (to say nothing of its consequences for others). Hence, the exigencies of practical reason itself, prior to the introduction of any properly moral consideration, force us to ask whether the seeming goods for which we act are true goods, and therefore desirable, not only for this or that individual or in these special circumstances, but desirable *per se*, for every individual and in all situations.

How do we know what counts as a *true* human good, that is, how do we determine which among the possible objects of human desire is intrinsically desirable for any rational agent? Grisez and Finnis respond that the true human goods are self-evidently such to us, even though our knowledge of these goods is not innate, in the sense of being present prior to all experience.[13] Hence, our knowledge of these goods is not derived from our knowledge of the natural world, nor does it depend on any particular philosophical or theological worldview. Specifically, there are eight such basic human goods, of which the first three are substantive (they exist prior to our choices) and the rest are reflexive (they depend on our choices): human life (including health and procreation), knowledge and aesthetic appreciation, skilled performances of all kinds, self-integration, authenticity/practical reasonableness, justice and friendship, religion/holiness, and (a recent addition), marriage.[14]

The first principle of practical reasoning, "The good is to be done and pursued; the bad is to be avoided," is also self-evident.[15] Moreover, it is prior to all other deliverances of practical reasoning, since it is the foundation for them all. Unless someone's behavior expresses this principle, it does not count as an action at all, because a putative action must be intelligible in terms of the agent's intentions in order to count as a true action.

Yet it is possible for an action to be rational, to a degree sufficient to count as a true human action, and yet to fall short of the standard of full reasonableness. A putative action is truly such only if it is aimed (directly or indirectly) at securing one (or more) of the eight basic human goods. But because each of these basic goods is immediately self-evident, they are incommensurable and stand in no intrinsic order to one another. Hence, an action that aims at one basic good while arbitrarily slighting others is unreasonable to the extent that it turns from a basic good without adequate reason, even though it retains sufficient rational intelligibility to count as an action. Of course, we cannot aim at all the basic goods all the time; yet we can always act in such a way as to remain open to those basic goods which we are not actively pursuing. And this is what we must do if our action is to be fully reasonable, and therefore, morally good. Thus, the first principle of morality is, "In voluntarily acting for human goods and avoiding what is opposed to them, one ought to choose and otherwise will those and only those possibilities whose willing is compatible with a will toward integral human fulfillment."[16]

The first principle of morality is further explicated by means of what Grisez refers to as eight modes of responsibility, which are simply specifications of this principle: "Each mode of responsibility simply excludes a particular way in which a person can limit himself or herself to a quite partial and inadequate fulfillment."[17] While all of these modes are morally significant, the last two are the most stringent: "One should not be moved by hostility to freely accept or choose the destruction, damage, or impeding of any intelligible good.... One should not be moved by a stronger desire for one instance of an intelligible good to act for it by choosing to destroy, damage, or impede some other instance of an intelligible good...."[18]

Although Grisez and Finnis later refine the way in which they express it, the general idea conveyed by these prohibitions is summed up in their early statements that we are never morally justified in acting against a basic good.[19] Hence, they reaffirm the traditional view that there are some kinds of actions that can never be morally justified, but are intrinsically morally evil—namely, they add, those kinds of actions that involve direct attacks on some basic good, for example, direct homicide, deliberate contraception, lying, or adultery.

What are we to make of this reinterpretation of the natural law? While this "new natural law" theory departs from the older Catholic version in one important way, in that it denies that the physical nature of the human person has intrinsic moral significance, it is in continuity with the older view with respect to its emphasis on the universality and rationality of the precepts of the natural law. Indeed, Grisez and Finnis go beyond the official Catholic view by asserting that not only the first principles, but the intermediate modes of responsibility are self-evident. On the face of it, what we have here is a moral theory which is meant to be universal in its scope, and not an account of what is proper to the Christian moral life. If this theory were sound, it would offer a rational basis for moral discernment for any community whatever.

At the same time, even a cursory acquaintance with their writings makes it very clear that Grisez and Finnis are committed to articulating and defending the teachings of the Catholic magisterium in terms of their theory of morality.[20] There is nothing wrong with defending an institutional agenda, but what Grisez and Finnis attempt to do is to show that the agenda of the institution to which they are committed is not only cogent and praiseworthy, but rationally necessary. This proves to be a difficult argument to sustain. The official teachings of the Catholic Church clearly reflect the specific history and institutional arrangements of that community, as we would expect, and it proves to be difficult to reconcile the logic of Grisez and Finnis' highly abstract moral analysis with the particularities of this rich and complex history.

This difficulty is especially apparent with respect to the Catholic teachings on the moral issues that arise at the beginning and the end of life. Clearly, Grisez and Finnis have a special concern with these issues. Although they insist on eight equally basic goods, most of the actual cases discussed by Grisez and Finnis have to do with the good of life. They are adamantly opposed to abortion, euthanasia, or suicide, which to them, represent direct attacks on human life. They are equally insistent that any use of contraceptives can never be morally justified. But significantly, their argument for this view does not depend on an appeal to the moral significance of the natural process of reproduction, since on their view such an appeal would represent an illegitimate inference from a matter of fact to a moral norm. Rather, they argue that someone who uses contraceptives is acting against the good of life, since he wills that a person who might otherwise be conceived not come into existence; hence, they claim that someone who uses contraceptives reveals a will which is formally equivalent to the will of someone who murders.[21]

It is at this point, however, that the difficulty emerges. Since at least the Middle Ages, the Catholic Church has taught that killing is morally permissible under certain circumstances, specifically, in pursuit of a justifiable military engagement and for the punishment of some kinds of criminals. How can these views be reconciled with the claim that it is never morally permissible directly to act against the basic good of life?

The answer, as summarized by Grisez, is that "human life can never rightly be directly attacked, but that indirect killing covers more cases than has generally been supposed."[22] That is, Grisez and Finnis appeal to the distinction between direct and indirect action, in order to distinguish between direct killing, which, being an attack on the basic good of human life, is never justifiable, and indirect killing, which involves tolerating but not willing someone's death.[23]

However, it is critical to note that for Grisez and Finnis, unlike the earlier tradition, the distinction between willing an effect, and allowing it to come about, is not interpreted in terms of causality. That is, on this view, unlike the earlier view, it is possible to bring about an effect in the realm of physical causality, and yet not to will it directly. What does it mean, then, directly to will an attack on a basic good? As Grisez explains, an act involves an evil will in the moral sense if either of two conditions is met: If the bad effect is the very point of the act, or if the good sought can only be attained through some further action, either by the agent, or by someone else.[24]

Yet this reformulation of the direct/indirect distinction raises a still more serious problem for the "new natural law" proposed by Grisez and Finnis. In traditional moral theology, the analysis of the causal structure of the act was morally significant, because it provided an objective basis for assessing the intention of the agent. Without some such basis, the agent's intention could be described in terms of whatever could be said to be the agent's purpose or motive in acting. Grisez and Finnis reject this appeal to the causal structure of an act as a basis for an objective determination of the agent's will. But they do not seem to have anything comparable to put in its place.

Consider the first criterion which Grisez offers for determining whether a given act should count as direct or indirect killing (for example). He says that an action with both good and bad effects is not to be described from the moral point of view in terms of the bad effect unless the latter is necessarily included in the agent's intention. But since the kind of necessity in question is not causal, and Grisez does not offer any other interpretation, we can only conclude that it must be logical. In other words, if the agent's aim in acting can be logically described with reference to the good that she seeks, without mentioning the harm that she brings about, her act is morally licit; otherwise, not. Thus, for example, a woman who defends herself from a rapist by killing her assailant may be said to will her defense, and merely to tolerate the death which she brings about, since if she could save herself without killing her assailant, she would do so.[25]

The difficulty with this line of argument is that almost any action can logically be described in terms of the good which the agent seeks, and not the harm which she brings about. The intention of a physician who kills her patient in order to relieve his intractable suffering may be described as "relieving suffering," without mentioning the means by which the suffering is ended; in this case, too, if the agent could bring about the good end without killing, she would do so. (I am presuming that the physician means well, and is not taking advantage of a difficult situation as a pretext for a killing which is desired on other grounds; but the same presumption must be extended to the woman who kills in self-defense if her action is to be justified.) There is no sort of purely logical necessity which would allow for killing in some cases of self-defense, and rule it out in every instance of euthanasia. More generally, there is no logical basis for the claim that some instances of attacking basic goods, but not others, are necessarily included in the agent's intention in acting.

Grisez's second criterion, that the different components of the agent's act must be indivisible, is likewise difficult to defend. The problem here lies in determining what counts as one unitary action, in distinction from components of a complex action. It would be natural to say that discrete bodily movements are discrete acts, and in some cases that is indeed what we do assume. Yet we do not understand every action in this way; many activities which we think of as unitary actions involve many discrete bodily movements, all of which are united by one intention, for example, baking a cake or writing a book. So also, in the case of a craniotomy to save the mother's life, which Grisez considers to be indirect killing, and therefore morally licit, the physician performs a number of discreet bodily motions in order to carry out the procedure: he crushes the head of the infant, he pulls it out of the birth canal, he administers drugs to the mother, and so forth, all of them discrete bodily movements which are comprised under one intention.[26] Here again,

Grisez cannot appeal to the logical distinctions that he needs in order to make his case.

What, then, is the basis for distinguishing between direct and indirect actions? There does not seem to be any logical criterion on the basis of which this distinction can be drawn, prior to a moral evaluation on the kind of act in question. In other words, Grisez and Finnis seem to distinguish between direct and indirect forms of killing (and, where relevant, other forms of attacks on basic goods) on the basis of prior judgements on the moral licitness of these kinds of actions. If that is so, then their logical analysis of goods and actions is not doing the normative work; it serves, rather, to justify moral judgements which have been arrived at on other grounds.

Yet perhaps that is their intent. So far, we have considered the "new natural law" as if it were solely a philosophical analysis of morality. Yet Grisez and Finnis do believe that there is a specifically Christian morality, which presupposes and builds upon, but goes beyond, the natural law as generated by reason. In his synthetic development of this theory, Grisez remarks that, "The teachings of faith neither conflict with any of the general principles of morality nor add any new principles to them. Yet faith does generate specific norms proper to the Christian life."[27] He goes on to explain that Christian faith both completes and corrects our knowledge of the moral law, and adds new duties by proposing new possibilities for action, which bring new material norms with them. Yet the new norms added to the moral law in this way are not external impositions; rather, they clarify and build upon the norms of the natural law as knowable through reason alone. Thus, non-believers can grasp the rational character of these specifically Christian norms, even though human reason unilluminated by faith cannot in every case discern these norms.

Perhaps the distinctions discussed above are meant to be understood as clarifications and extensions of the rational natural law, seen in the light of Christian faith. In that case, we should take the specific applications of the direct/indirect distinction, in accordance with which, for example, killing in self-defense is indirect but euthanasia is direct, to be examples of material norms which, although they are intrinsically reasonable, cannot be generated by human reason operating outside the context of faith.

Yet if this is so—and I am not aware of anything in the writings of Grisez or Finnis which directly supports such an interpretation—then the deliverances of moral reason are much more exiguous than the terms of their analysis would have led us to suppose. After all, moral norms having to do with killing are a fundamental component of any moral code, not just Christian morality. If men and women operating outside the parameters of revelation cannot get these norms right, then we should expect to find very little genuine moral goodness outside the church.

This may well be Grisez and Finnis's final view. Nor is it intrinsically illogical, taken on its own terms. However, if we are to conclude that moral reasoning is so vitiated that it cannot generate even the most basic moral norms without the help of revelation, then the "new natural law" proposed by Grisez and Finnis does not, in the end, offer much in the way of a basis for moral dialogue within a pluralistic society. What seems at first to be a moral theory which makes strong claims for universality turns out to be, in effect, a reformulation of one specific moral tradition.

THE RETURN TO THE NATURAL AS A BASIS FOR ETHICS

Although the theory of Grisez and Finnis is frequently referred to as *the* "new" theory of the natural law, in fact there have recently been a number of attempts to retrieve the insights of older natural law theories, while correcting their errors. These efforts have not been limited to Catholic scholars; indeed, to a considerable degree, they have been inspired by the work of the Protestant theologian James Gustafson, who remarks that "I do not think that my *basic* move in drawing from the sciences . . . is essentially different from that of Thomas Aquinas or Schleiermacher or others."[28] Unlike the work of Grisez and Finnis, many of these attempts have been characterized by an openness to the natural as a source for normative guidance. This is not surprising, when we consider that many of these attempts are motivated by a desire for moral guidance in light of our growing ability to alter the fundamental biological parameters of human existence. Faced with such possibilities, the claim that morality consists solely in respect for autonomy begins to seem a little thin. In the words of Martin Cook:

> . . . we may well be advised to reflect on the degree to which aspects of human biology and of the traditional socially sanctioned uses of our bodies—things which

have traditionally been "givens"—are properly subject to indefinite alteration, manipulation, and technological control. Cumulatively, these technologies bring us back to questions once dismissed as irrelevant to proper ethical reflection: Are there naturally preferred forms of human conduct and social organization which we tamper with at our peril? Can we look to naturally based considerations as a guide, if not a determiner, of morally correct action and judgement? If we believe that richer concepts than individual rights, choice, autonomy, and harms to others are needed to guide our choices and moral judgements, can we develop sufficiently coherent alternative concepts to govern adequately our assessments of the courses of action opened by these technologies?[29]

At the same time, new developments in the natural sciences, particularly biology, have led a number of scientists and scholars to attempt to analyze morality itself as a natural phenomenon. The most significant such effort is the discipline of sociobiology or evolutionary psychology which has developed in the wake of the pioneering work of E. O. Wilson and attempts to understand social life in general, and moral norms in particular, as adaptive behaviors generated by natural selection.[30] In turn, a number of theologians, led by Stephen Pope, have attempted to respond to the challenges posed by this work to traditional morality, by appropriating and reinterpreting it in the light of theological perspectives.[31]

Unlike the official Catholic version of the natural law or the theory developed by Grisez, Finnis and their collaborators, these attempts to develop alternative accounts of the moral force of nature cannot be described as one theory. Rather, what we find here are congeries of theories and proposals which reflect a variety of perspectives and concerns. While some of these scholars are prepared to offer fairly specific proposals, most of them focus on exploring the questions and challenges presented by contemporary science and philosophy.

Nonetheless, it is fair to say that these authors do share certain convictions. Negatively, most of them would agree, in Cook's words, that the concepts which have dominated moral discourse until recently, such as autonomy, rights, and freedom, are too impoverished to provide all the resources that we need for moral reflection. Positively, they share a sense that there is something of moral significance in natural processes and boundaries, however nature is to be understood, and however its value is to be articulated and defended. Those who come to this discussion from within the Christian tradition are also united by a commitment to take serious account of the findings of modern science in theological reflection, and often they express a sense that modern theology has not yet done so.

Because these writings cannot be brought under the rubric of a single theory, and because they tend to be tentative and exploratory, it is more difficult to assess the strengths and weaknesses of the approach to the natural law which they represent. Clearly, like the official Catholic approach, but unlike the theory developed by Grisez and Finnis, this approach is characterized by an openness to the moral significance of nature. Moreover, seen in comparison to both of the other two approaches, this third approach is more open to ambiguity, and its proponents do not generally rush to closure on the questions which they raise. While these authors do not accept the absolutism of the traditional Catholic approach, they also do not offer any detailed positive account of the ways in which moral reflection draws on our observations of a natural order.[32] As a result, their writings can give the impression of normative thinness or vagueness.

Yet seen from the standpoint of the issues raised at the beginning of this essay, this seeming deficiency is potentially one of the great advantages of this approach. That is, precisely because this approach to the natural law does not offer well-defined moral norms, it leaves space to develop a Christian morality which does justice both to the specificity of Christian morality and the commonalities between Christianity and other moral traditions.

AN AGENDA FOR FUTURE WORK

What might such an account look like? Without attempting to develop such an account of the natural law in detail here, it is possible to suggest the main lines that such a development might take.

The starting point for such an account, I would suggest, should be the re-affirmation of one of the most ancient tenets of Christian belief, namely, the goodness of creation and its status as an expression of God's wisdom and beneficent kindness. The God who speaks to us in Scripture is one and the same God who speaks to us through the regularities and the goodness of the natural world. For this reason, any genuine Christian morality will necessarily reflect those needs and inclinations which are natural to us as human persons.

It does not follow that a Christian morality will be simply equivalent to a human morality; rather, as Rigali might say, it will be one expression, a specifically Christian expression, of a natural morality. Hence, we should not expect to find that Christian morality is simply equivalent to the moral views of all persons of good will. Human nature, as understood by the theologians just considered, shapes morality but does not generate one determinate set of moral laws, either normatively or as a matter of social fact. For this reason, we should not be surprised to discover that the moralities of different societies are strikingly different in the specific codes they prescribe and in the overall orientation which they help to foster.

At the same time, if Christian morality, like other moral systems, is in part an expression of human nature, then we can also expect to find commonalities between Christians and representatives of other moral traditions, and therefore some basis for moral dialogue, whether the arena is provided by our own secular society or by the world community. There is no theory of the natural which can reliably provide us with a map for locating these commonalities in advance, although the burgeoning research on sociobiology offers many helpful pointers. The only fully satisfactory way to identify these commonalities is through the process of dialogue itself. In and through our search for common ground, we will learn together what our natural commonalities are, and this in turn will teach us something about the meaning of "the truly human" that we could learn in no other way.

It may seem that this approach threatens the specificity of Christian morality, or at least could lead to a weakening of our particular commitments and witness. There are always dangers whenever we attempt to enter into conversation with those in other communities. Yet the approach to the natural law being suggested here does not require us to elide the differences between a Christian morality and other forms of morality. It is entirely possible to take the central commitments of Christianity as the fundamental criteria for the adequacy of any Christian morality, without denying that any such morality will also contain some elements in common with other moral systems, as expressions of a shared humanity.

At the same time, there is room within such an approach to develop a critique of a particular form of Christian morality on the grounds that it is insufficiently open to, or distorts, some element of human nature. This is in fact the line that many Catholic theologians have taken in their critique of official church teachings on sexuality.[33] While most Catholic theologians would affirm the overall spirit of this teaching, they question whether the detailed prescriptions which it offers are either necessary, or even appropriate expressions of human nature.

The difference between these theologians and their forbearers is not, by and large, that our contemporaries deny the importance of grounding sexual ethics in nature; the difference is rather that contemporary theologians have a different sense of what human sexual nature is, and therefore of what it means for sexual behavior to be in accordance with nature. Our contemporaries have a sense of the complex dimensions of human sexuality, its diverse purposes and its place in a network of human relationships which our forbearers lacked. It is no wonder, therefore, that many contemporary theologians have offered reformulations of a Catholic sexual ethic, precisely in order to do justice to our fuller sense of what human nature involves.

This work in sexual ethics can serve as a model for a more general reformulation of the modern Catholic conception of the natural law, a reformulation which will leave room for both the specificity and the naturalness of Christian morality. This work is well underway, and we have good reason to be hopeful for its future development.[34]

NOTES

1. In this essay, I rely on the following: Norbert Rigali, S.J., "Christian Ethics and Perfection," *Chicago Studies* 14 (1975), 227–40; "Christ et Morale," *Concilium: Revue Internationale de Théologie* 130 (1977), reprinted as "Christ and Morality," in Charles E. Curran and Richard A. McCormick, S.J., eds., *Readings in Moral Theology No. 2: The Distinctiveness of Christian Ethics* (New York: Paulist Press, 1980), 111–20; "Moral Pluralism and Christian Ethics," *Louvain Studies* 13 (1988), 305–21; "The Uniqueness and Distinctiveness of Christian Morality and Ethics," in Charles E. Curran, ed., *Moral Theology: Challenges for the Future* (New York: Paulist Press, 1990), 74–93; and "Chris-

tian Morality and Universal Morality: The One and the Many," *Louvain Studies* 19 (1994), 18–33.

2.   "The Uniqueness and the Distinctiveness of Christian Morality and Ethics," 90.

3.   This objection is frequently raised. For a recent example, see Lisa Sowle Cahill, *Sex, Gender and Christian Ethics* (Cambridge: Cambridge University Press, 1996), 68–69.

4.   Although the "classical" doctrine of the natural law is generally thought to date from medieval times, Michael Crowe argues convincingly that this version of the natural law is in fact a product of the early modern period; see *The Changing Profile of the Natural Law* (The Hague: Martinus Nijhoff, 1977), 223–45.

5.   David Hollenbach, *Claims in Conflict: Retrieving and Renewing the Catholic Human Rights Tradition* (New York: Paulist, 1979), 108–18.

6.   See Jacques Maritain, *Man and the State* (Chicago: University of Chicago Press, 1951), 76–107; and John Courtney Murray, S. J., *We Hold These Truths: Catholic Reflections on the American Proposition* (New York: Sheed and Ward, 1960), 280–317.

7.   Paul VI, "On the Regulation of Birth *(Humanae vitae)*," *AAS* 60 (1968), §§ 11, 12.

8.   For a helpful discussion of Rahner's reformulation of the natural law, with an extensive bibliographic note, see James F. Bresnahan, "An Ethics of Faith," in Leo J. O'Donovan, ed., *A World of Grace: An Introduction to the Themes and Foundations of Karl Rahner's Theology* (New York: Crossroad, 1981), 169–184. Michael J. Himes offers a good overview and assessment of Lonergan's work on the natural law in "The Human Person in Contemporary Theology: From Human Nature to Authentic Subjectivity," in Ronald R. Hamel and Kenneth R. Himes, O.F.M., eds., *Introduction to Christian Ethics: A Reader* (New York: Paulist Press), 49–62. Charles Curran offers a critique of "classical" natural law theory which incorporates the insights of both authors in his "Natural Law in Moral Theology," in Charles E. Curran and Richard A. McCormick, eds., *Readings in Moral Theology No. 7: Natural Law and Theology* (New York: Paulist Press, 1991), 247–95.

9.   For an illuminating account of changes in sexual ethics in the United States see Peter Gardella, *Innocent Ecstasy: How Christianity Gave America an Ethic of Sexual Pleasure* (Oxford: Oxford University Press, 1985); with reference to changing attitudes about contraceptive use, see 130–40 in particular.

10.   In "Christian Ethics and Perfection," see in particular 236–38.

11.   The original passage is found in David Hume, *A Treatise of Human Nature*, L.A. Selby-Bigge, ed. (Oxford: Oxford University Press, 1888), 469.

12.   In my summary of the theory of morality put forth by Grisez and Finnis, I have relied primarily on the following works: John Finnis, *Natural Law*

and Natural Rights (Oxford: Clarendon Press, 1980) and *Fundamentals of Ethics* (Washington, DC: Georgetown University Press, 1983); Germain Grisez, *The Way of the Lord Jesus, Volume One: Christian Moral Principles* (Chicago: Franciscan Herald Press, 1983) and *The Way of The Lord Jesus, Volume Two: Living a Christian Life* (Quincy, IL: Franciscan Herald Press, 1993); and Germain Grisez, Joseph Boyle, and John Finnis, "Practical Principles, Moral Truth, and Ultimate Ends," *The American Journal of Jurisprudence* 32 (1987), 99–151.

13. See, for example, *Natural Law and Natural Rights*, 33–34.

14. The list of basic goods is taken from *Christian Moral Principles*, 124, and "Practical Principles, Moral Truth, and Ultimate Ends," 107–8. Finnis' earlier list is somewhat different, but not, in my opinion, fundamentally so; see *Natural Law and Natural Rights*, 86–90. More recently, Grisez has added an eighth good, marriage, to the list; see *Living a Christian Life*, 568.

15. *Christian Moral Principles*, 178.

16. *Ibid.*, 184; emphasis in the original has been deleted.

17. *Ibid.*, 191; emphasis in the original has been deleted.

18. *Ibid.*, 225–26; emphasis in the original has been deleted.

19. See *ibid.*, 227, n. 2, for a later comment on these statements.

20. However, Grisez does note that on some specific points, he departs from traditional Catholic moral teachings. He repeatedly insists that capital punishment is never morally justified, while acknowledging that this is not traditional Catholic moral teaching; see, for example, *Christian Moral Principles*, 219–22 and *Living a Christian Life*, 891–94. He also considers some forms of abortion to be forms of indirect killing, and therefore permissible, but he is careful to add that he submits his judgement to the final judgement of the magisterium on this point (and all others); for example, see *Christian Moral Principles*, 309; see also, "Toward a Consistent Natural-Law Ethics of Killing," *American Journal of Jurisprudence* 15 (1970), 96.

21. Germain Grisez, Joseph Boyle, John Finnis, and William May, "Every Marital Act Ought to Be Open to New Life: Towards a Clearer Understanding," *The Thomist* 52 (1988), 385.

22. "Towards a Consistent Natural Law Ethics of Killing," 66.

23. In what follows, I am summarizing a critique I have developed in more detail in "Direct/Indirect Action in Grisez's Theory of Morality," *Theological Studies* 57 (1996), 611–32.

24. This is explained most fully in "Toward a Consistent Natural Law Ethic of Killing." As far as I can determine, Finnis accepts the main lines of Grisez's analysis; however, he disagrees with him with respect to its application, specifically with respect to capital punishment. See *Fundamentals of Ethics*, 128–30.

25. This is a case which Grisez discusses several times; see, for example, *Living a Christian Life*, 473.

26. Grisez discusses the case of a life-saving craniotomy several times; see most recently *Living a Christian Life*, 502. It would be interesting to see him apply his analysis of this procedure to the recent controversy over "partial birth" abortions, but to my knowledge, he has not done so.

27. *Christian Moral Principles*, 607; emphasis in the original has been deleted. The whole chapter, 599–626, should be consulted on this question. In addition, Grisez's remarks on the necessity for interpretation of the norms of the natural law should be consulted in this context; see *ibid.* 175–78.

28. James M. Gustafson, "A Response to Critics," *Journal of Religious Ethics* 13 (1985), 193.

29. Martin L. Cook, "Ways of Thinking Naturally," *The Annual of the Society of Christian Ethics* (1988), 163–64.

30. Edward O. Wilson, *Sociobiology: The New Synthesis* (Cambridge, MA: Harvard University Press, 1978). Galen Strawson provides a useful survey of the development of this discipline since Wilson's seminal work in his, "In Deepest Sympathy," a Review Essay on Matt Ridley's *The Origins of Virtue* (New York: Viking Press, 1996), *The Times Literary Supplement* (November 29, 1996), 3–4. In addition, some philosophers have recently argued for a renewed consideration of the significance of human nature for morality; see especially Mary Midgley, *Beast and Man: The Roots of Human Nature* (Ithaca, NY: Cornell University Press, 1978), and Leon R. Kass, *Toward a More Natural Science: Biology and Human Affairs* (New York: Macmillan, 1985).

31. See in particular Stephen J. Pope, *The Evolution of Altruism and the Ordering of Love* (Washington, DC: Georgetown University Press, 1994).

32. However, Pope's analysis of preferential relations seen in the light of sociobiological research is a promising first move in this direction; see *ibid.*, 128–51.

33. Lisa Sowle Cahill makes this point in her survey and analysis of recent Catholic sexual ethics, "Human Sexuality," in Charles E. Curran, ed., *Moral Theology: Challenges for the Future*, 193–212.

34. I am grateful to Joseph Blenkinsopp for his helpful comments on an earlier draft of this essay.

METHOD, CATHOLIC TRADITION, AND BIOETHICS

Euthanasia: The Practical and Social Significance of Double Effect

Lisa Sowle Cahill

As a means of examining recent developments in Catholic moral theology, this essay will take up the issue of physician-assisted suicide. Specifically, it will address twentieth century evolution of use of the principle of double effect, especially its key provision, that any evil effect caused in the pursuit of a human good be only indirectly intended, even if the evil is balanced by a proportionate good. The reexamination of the principle under the impact of historical consciousness has also affected other categories on which it depends, such as intrinsic evil and proportionality.

The thesis of this essay is that recent controversies over the continued viability of this standard principle of moral theology have resulted from increased awareness that the application of the principle is highly context-dependent, and that to contextualize an act means to place it within the scope of many overlapping moral relationships. Double effect cannot be used as a scientific first principle, from which applications to cases can be simply deduced. It cannot provide clear and certain answers that obviate the need for prudence or remove any trace of moral risk.

However, the contingency and social referentiality of double effect are not, after all, new realizations. Traditional formulations did incorporate references to context and to prudential reasoning. If the contextual nature of the principle is put into proper perspective, then some of the apparent incoherencies in its provisions and application are reduced. It will become evident that the principle cannot serve as an indispensable and incontrovertible method of removing moral ambiguity. Still, the moral considerations represented by double effect have continuing importance for the analysis of killing in the medical context. Perhaps one of the most valuable of these is the link between individual freedom and communal membership. To speak of the contextualization of moral agency, moral acts, and even moral principles need not imply that moral judgment is entirely relative to context. The point is, rather, that what is usually termed the "objectivity" of moral truth is now understood to be integrally dependent on the contingent circumstances and diachronic human relationships that converge in a particular occasion of agency.[1] To understand the full scope of the principle of double effect is to realize the "objective" yet fully social, historical, and particular nature of moral knowledge about concrete actions. It is to realize, as Norbert Rigali has shown, that morality refers not only to universal laws, but to the moral subject; and not only to the moral subject, but to the social reality in which the life of the subject originates.[2]

TODAY'S DEBATE ABOUT EUTHANASIA

The idea that the physician's calling to relieve suffering could include the administration of death-inducing drugs is not a new one. Hippocrates instructed the physician to swear, "I will neither give a deadly drug to anybody if asked for it, nor will I make a suggestion to this effect."[3] As today, the fact that the ancient Greeks needed instruction on the matter is an indication that the practice was not unknown. But the shape of euthanasia is different in the modern West. Our great concerns with personal autonomy, and our dislike for medical paternalism, lead us to accept suicide more readily than death-dealing acts of "mercy" at the initiative of medical professionals. Moreover, the highly developed varieties of life-prolonging technology available in modern medical facilities lead us to fear an indefinite period of entrapment in a state of quasi-life, almost as much as we fear a painful "natural" death. Thus, rather than mercy-killing by doctors, many would prefer access to means of suicide that can be used before our own powers of independent action have been devastated.

The "right to die" movement has been gathering momentum in the United States since the 1970's. The Hemlock Society's *Final Exit* gives the terminally ill patient instructions for a painless suicide. Jack Kevorkian, M.D., provides "suicide machines" that have administered barbiturates to dozens of patients, not all of them terminally ill. Kevorkian has never been convicted, despite legislation enacted in Michigan, his home state, to discourage physician-assisted suicide. Other physicians have admitted acceding to patient requests for aid in dying. When such decisions are left up to individual patients and physicians, moral deliberation about their justifiability is not only limited, but understandably biased. In a now famous essay in the *Journal of the American Medical Association*, Timothy E. Quill, M.D., recounted how, as an overstressed resident, he was summoned in the night to the bedside of a young woman with ovarian cancer, suffering grievously from deprivation of sleep, food, and oxygen. She says, "Let's get this over with." Without investigating measures to improve her palliative care, or engaging her in further conversation about her suffering or needs, he responds with an injection of morphine that ends her life within minutes.[4]

The Netherlands provides a case study in social acceptance of such measures that has been of great interest to participants in the North American debate. In the Netherlands, euthanasia remains a criminal offense under the Dutch penal code, but a court decision in 1981 established that physicians providing voluntary euthanasia would not be prosecuted for murder, if certain conditions are observed. The patient must make a free, informed, and repeated request; the patient must be in a state of severe, unrelievable suffering; the appropriateness of physician-assisted suicide or euthanasia must be confirmed by a second physician; and the performing physician must report the facts of the case to the coroner, allowing supervision of cases. However, reports on actual practice suggest that, in addition to the approximately 3600 cases of physician-assisted suicide and euthanasia reported annually, there are also about 1000 cases of nonvoluntary euthanasia. In most of the latter, the patients killed were no longer competent, and thus were not able to request or to give informed consent to the action. In some cases, these patients were newborns.[5]

This gradual extension of the euthanasia policy should give pause to U. S. advocates of physician-assisted suicide. On June 26, 1997, the United States Supreme Court rejected circuit court opinions in New York and Washington that had overturned state laws against physician-assisted suicide. The Court's unanimous decision rejected constitutional status for a right to commit suicide, even in cases of terminal illness. The majority opinion upheld a more limited right to refuse unwanted treatment, but said that a decision in favor of a right to die would undercut longstanding U.S. legal traditions rejecting suicide and euthanasia, represented in the policies of almost all states. The justices did not foreclose the possibility of successful future challenges to the law. But for the time being, they deferred to state legislatures' decisions about whether a ban on suicide and euthanasia is necessary. Thus they encouraged public debate about the matter at the state level. Oregon is the only state at present that has passed legislation permitting euthanasia.[6]

Polls show that about two-thirds of Americans support assisted suicide, but half of those who accept it would narrow conditions to just a few circumstances. Most Americans do not support killing patients who fear being a burden, or when they fail to find meaning in a prolonged, terminal illness. Furthermore, many formulations of the question do not distinguish between direct killing, and refusal or removal of life-prolonging treatment.[7] More disturbingly, those who are likely to favor physician-assisted suicide are those who are better off financially and better educated. Those who are most opposed are blacks and people over 70; women are more likely to be opposed than men.[8] In other words, people who are most accustomed to being in control of their personal and social circumstances are most likely to advocate individual control of death. Those who are most likely to have experienced social marginalization and lack of social and material resources seem most distrustful of laws permitting a "right to die" by active means.

THE CATHOLIC ANALYSIS

Roman Catholic moral theologians and official church teaching have traditionally opposed active causation of death, even for suffering, terminally ill patients. All direct killing of innocent persons has been defined to be evil in itself, not permitted for any individual or contextual reasons. This is not to say, however, that life is seen as an absolute good, nor death as an absolute evil. The death of a terminally ill person, or one undergoing extreme suffering, may certainly be accepted, even to the extent of refusing or withdrawing treatments that could prolong life. While suffering may have a redemptive meaning when intentionally united with the Cross of Christ, the mission of caregivers—indeed, of all Christians—is to serve the neighbor by alleviating suffering. Hence, from the time of Pius XII onward, the Church has explicitly permitted the refusal of life-extending measures that do not significantly improve the individual patient's physical condition, or that are excessively burdensome for him or her to use; as well as the use of methods of pain relief that will ultimately shorten life (e.g., doses of morphine that depress breathing and heartbeat).[9]

The decisive distinction in Catholic moral theology is between direct means of causing death, and indirect means. A patient may never be killed directly, even when good reasons seem to be present not to avoid death, and even to welcome it. In 1958, Gerald Kelly, S.J., wrote a commentary on the then current *Ethical and Religious Directives for Catholic Hospitals*, in which he provided a succinct formulation of the difference between permissible and prohibited ways to bring about the death of a seriously ill patient. All "positive means to end life" are forbidden, e.g., an overdose of drugs. Writing so shortly after the atrocities of Nazi medicine, the social setting of euthanasia that Kelly most has in mind is the direct termination of individuals who are evaluated to be of no use to society. However, in considering whether indefinite prolongation of life is always necessary, he focuses on the good of the individual as a reason to cause death indirectly. By the indirect causation of death is meant the withdrawal or refusal of means to prolong life, if they offer no reasonable hope of benefit to the patient, or if they involve excessive "expense, pain, or other hardship to oneself or others." Such optional means are called "extraordinary," a term that has come to mean "not morally mandatory."[10]

The various available means do not carry an intrinsic moral character apart from the consideration of context. For one thing, a means that is virtually useless or very dangerous in one era of medical practice may greatly improve in efficacy as time goes on. Similarly, what may not be tolerable or efficacious for one patient may be reasonable and useful for another. Yet the patient considering the acceptance of death must sometimes take into account the "common good," for which he or she may still have an important role, and not only his or her own individual welfare.[11]

A couple of decades later, the Vatican's *Declaration on Euthanasia* expressed more appreciation of the fact that mercy-killing can be motivated by concern for the suffering of the patient, but restated the same point.

> By euthanasia is understood an action or an omission which of itself or by intention causes death, in order that all suffering may in this way be eliminated. Euthanasia's terms of reference, therefore, are to be found in the intention of the will and in the methods used.[12]

Means to prolong life may be declined or removed if they are "dispro-portionate." In making a judgment, the agents involved must take into account, not only the risk and benefits of the treatment, but also its availability and cost, as well as the "physical and moral resources" of the sick person, his or her "reasonable wishes," and those of the family. "Excessive expense" is also a consideration, not only in relation to the finances of the patient, but also in view of the resources of the commu-nity.[13]

In 1995, the *Committee on Doctrine of the National Conference of Catholic Bishops* (U.S.) developed a revised *Ethical and Religious Di-rectives for Catholic Health Care Services*.[14] Important changes in pres-entation include much greater attention to the social responsibilities of health caregivers and to the gospel values motivating health care, and especially the mission of Catholic institutions to care for the poor. The prerogative of the patient to freely refuse burdensome, useless, or exces-sively costly treatment is reaffirmed.[15] Effective pain management is stressed as part of appropriate care.[16] However, the *intention* of causing death is rejected, even when measures are taken that ensure that death will follow. The intention must always be focused on relief of suffering, with death as a foreseen but unintended secondary effect.[17] In this con-text the new *Directives* address a recent controversy among some Catholic bishops and theologians about when and why artificial nutrition and hydration must be provided to permanently comatose patients. The Vatican has taken no position on this issue. However, some have argued that a comatose patient cannot suffer, and that therefore no treatment can be considered too burdensome, as long as it preserves biological life (a benefit). Moreover, the notion of "burden" must be referred to the unde-sirable effects of the given treatment being proposed, and not to the gen-eral quality of life it is expected to sustain for the patient. Others have argued, to the contrary, that the preservation of biological life in and of itself is not a worthwhile benefit to a patient who is unconscious; to be maintained indefinitely in a comatose condition is an assault on the dig-nity of the person; "burden" may indeed be referred holistically to the total state of life, and not to the isolated treatment only; and considera-tions of benefit to the patient in relation to the expenditure of medical resources should also be taken into account.[18] We will return to the sig-nificance of this debate later.

DOUBLE EFFECT

Behind all of these analyses of euthanasia and physician-assisted suicide
lies the principle of double effect. We may turn once again to Kelly for
the operative modern formulation. "The principle of double effect, as the
name itself implies, supposes that an action produces two effects. One of
these effects is something good which may be legitimately intended; the
other is an evil that may not be intended."[19] He lays out the four standard
conditions of the principle in the following terms. "1) *The action, considered by itself and independently of its effects, must not be morally evil*
["intrinsically evil"].... 2) *The Evil effect must not be the means of producing the good effect....* 3) *The evil effect is sincerely not intended, but
merely tolerated....* 4) *There must be a proportionate reason for performing the action, in spite of its evil consequences.*" Kelly then adds,
"In some cases the difficulty of estimating the proportionate reason is so
great that even the most eminent theologians may disagree in their solutions," and states that proportionality must be assessed in view of "the
total picture." He allows that double effect is not only a "complicated
principle," but is perhaps best understood as "a practical formula" that
requires common sense and experience for its application.[20]

   In the 1970s, this principle came under sustained attack by moral
theologians who perceived that, despite Kelly's caveats, double effect
had been applied to cases like a mathematical formula. It had been employed in an aura of certainty about results that is undermined when
those results are more thoughtfully and critically considered in relation
to circumstances. Moreover, the provisions of the principle, when sub-
jected to sustained scrutiny in the light of the ambiguity of real moral
situations, seemed arbitrary and disjointed, even incoherent. The key
precipitating event in this debate was the 1968 publication of an encyclical[21] forbidding the use of contraception as "intrinsically evil" (in violation of double effect's first provision), and hence intolerable in any
situation, even before the gravest threat to the life of a woman who
might become pregnant. Proportion of good results could never trump
the forbidden character of a type of act defined as "intrinsically (morally) evil" in and of itself. Contraception was such an act. In such a case,
circumstances and proportion did not count. Only if the evil effect of
sterility were indirectly intended and caused could it be tolerated, and in
such a case would not be defined morally as "contraception." An example would be sterility (temporary or permanent) caused as a side effect

by a medical treatment directed to some other improvement of health. In the case of euthanasia, directly killing any innocent person would be considered an intrinsically evil act. So only the indirect causation of death could be permitted, e.g., when a large dose of morphine or the removal of a respirator is directed to relief of suffering, acknowledging that death will shortly follow too.

Criticisms of double effect focused on two questions. First, does the category "intrinsic evil" make sufficient sense? How can a physical act, abstractly defined, be known in advance to be *morally* evil? Doesn't morality imply circumstances in which a conflict among goods is resolved by choosing one over another? In that case, moral evaluation would depend on knowing whether the right choice was made and the higher or more urgent good chosen. Second, is it so easy to distinguish and separate an outcome that is intended from one that is merely "foreseen" and "tolerated"? And even if there is a legitimate distinction to be made between direct and indirect intention, can this distinction bear such heavy and decisive moral weight in making a moral judgment in complicated circumstances? Critics of double effect tended to place more importance on the total balance of good effects over harmful ones, and to argue that a proper intention was implied by the very fact that the criterion of proportionality was satisfied in the outcome of the act. Acts could not be judged "intrinsically evil" apart from an assessment of proportionality in concrete situations; and if an "evil" effect or aspect of an act or choice was counterbalanced by the overall good, then it was relatively unimportant whether the harm caused was prior to the good, subsequent to it, or even part of the means of accomplishing it.[22]

Because of their emphasis on proportion of good and bad aspects and outcomes of a decision or action, these critics of double effect have been termed "proportionalists," mostly by their adversaries. However, the objections to the standard principle of double effect by these critics do not in reality amount to a unified school of thought. Instead, they constitute a fairly diverse series of concerns about whether the moral theology of the early decades of this century was excessively abstract and restrictive in what it considered relevant to moral judgment. The underlining of the criterion of proportion is just one way to highlight the contextual and relational nature of moral responsibility and moral discernment. The principle of double effect, in fact, only makes sense as a *practical* generalization about relational factors that impinge in complex ways on any particular occasion of choice.

I will develop this point by situating the function of double effect within some new perspectives on the nature of moral knowledge. First, though, I will further exemplify the problem of understanding double effect in traditional terms by presenting a couple of specific objections to the way the principle has been used to judge the morality of physician-assisted suicide and euthanasia. Both objections focus on the problem of intentionality, and essentially call attention to the fact that the agent's responsibility within an occasion of moral choice cannot be fully appreciated without seeing such an occasion as complex, diachronic, and multivalent.

In a recent lecture on "The Choice of Death in a Medical Context," Margaret Farley has argued that, although there is a "profound difference" between the "moral experience" of accepting death by removing barriers and the experience of actively, directly taking life, this difference is not enough to decide the issue of morality. First of all, "indirect" causation and intention are still causation and intention. The agent still provides an occasion of death, and hastens death by a particular action. Moral responsibility for death cannot be avoided, even if the means is omission and the choice is evaluated to be morally good.[23] Going further, it is still a question whether "direct and active intervention with the intention to kill can ever be justified."[24] In particular, Farley considers a situation in which great suffering threatens the very integrity of the self by "ravaging the spirit."

> Without erasing the difference between...letting go and a more active taking of...life, is it nonetheless possible that all the elements of religious acceptance could have been incorporated into one or the other?.... Is it possible that, when death becomes inevitable and surrender to God is made in the face of it, then communal bonds can be preserved and not violated in an active as well as a passive dying-into-life?[25]

Although Farley is willing to contemplate the possibility of exceptions to the general moral and social barrier against direct euthanasia, she believes that policy must ensure that such cases not become the rule. She does not finally decide whether they should receive strictly limited approval under the law, or whether keeping them beyond the boundary of the legally approved is the only way to maintain their genuinely border-line character.

Timothy Quill, as a physician who has felt morally compelled to assist suicide, believes that the law should define and accept the assistance of suicide that morality and physician accountability require. He joins two colleagues in making a critique of double effect as setting limits on public policy.[26] Of their five objections, one is simply that the principle originates in a religious tradition; I shall return to this below. Two other objections concern intentionality; and two center on the primacy of patient autonomy. The best counter-argument to double effect they offer is, in my view, their observation that the difference between intended and merely foreseen effects cannot be unambiguously ascertained in many problematic cases. The purposes behind acts like "providing terminal sedation," or withdrawing life support systems, are not always clear and unidirectional. Rather, in light of modern psychology, one must admit that "human intention is multilayered, ambiguous, subjective, and often contradictory."[27] And far from diminishing responsibility for our actions, this realization works to hold us accountable for *foreseen* consequences of our actions, and not only those we centrally desire to occur. Therefore, proportionality—not intention—is central in evaluating the causation of bad effects. Because Quill and his co-authors see autonomy as central to moral legitimacy, they place informed consent foremost among the goods that legalization of physician-assisted suicide and euthanasia would promote. Although the rule of double effect may be useful in encouraging better palliative care, "the rule's absolute prohibitions, unrealistic characterizations of physicians' intention, and failure to account for patients' wishes," are enough to render it largely useless.[28]

In sum, then, both Quill and Farley raise the possibility that killing can express an intention of respect for God and care for the patient. Equally important is that indirect action to cause death is still responsible causation, and that with *in*direct killing, the attitude toward the death caused may be ambivalent. Certainly, one would choose a more healthy, meaningful *life* for the patient, if possible. But in cases of terminal suffering, is it wrong to *want* death, even when one refrains from direct killing?

MORAL KNOWLEDGE: NEW PERSPECTIVES

Norbert Rigali has accurately diagnosed the fact that moral epistemology today cannot avoid morality's thoroughly social and historical nature. Moral subjects, moral agency, and moral acts extenuate indefinitely into their contexts, and, in fact, are qualified in their innermost reality by their contingent settings.

> Through historical consciousness there comes into view the fact that morality originates, not in the individual of whose life it is a dimension, but in the social reality of a culture. More than a dimension of a person's life, morality is a dimension of a culture and a society. Fundamentally, it is a sociocultural reality; secondarily, it is, through the individual's participation in the sociocultural reality, an individual reality, a reality in a moral subject.[29]

When the field of bioethics came into full force in the early 1970s, the model of moral knowledge that was dominant in the U.S. was a liberal, quasi-scientific one, in which clearly distinguished, universal, rational principles were applied to practical dilemmas. Childress and Beauchamp's influential introductory text enunciated four such principles: justice, autonomy, beneficence, and nonmaleficence.[30] However, in the fourth edition of this work, the authors make clear at the outset that "it is unreasonable to expect any theory to overcome all limitations of time and place and reach a universally acceptable perspective."[31] Instead, more universally oriented "principles, rules, theories" should be linked dialectically with more particular "feelings, perceptions, case judgments, practices, parables."[32] James Childress is now persuaded that principles exist in a symbiotic relationship with casuistry, and that he and Beauchamp "have clearly taken an historicist turn" in their understanding of the derivation and function of principles.[33] Ethical reflection occurs within communities and traditions, and is always embedded in ongoing practices. Childress rejects the idea that principles must be ahistorical norms from which judgments are simply deduced. A more historical view of principles converges with moralities that reserve a central place for virtue, relationship, and practical casuistry.

Along similar lines, Barbara Andolsen distinguishes a feminist approach to bioethics from an abstract form of moral reasoning in which the autonomous agent is seen as an impartial deliberator. In the latter model of ethics, "the most skillful moral agent is able to engage in clear, abstract reasoning about a theoretical scale of values and to persuade others of the soundness of his or her reasoning." In contrast, feminist thought presupposes relationality, is more aware of complexity, attends to the particularities and ambiguities of moral questions, and takes into account the needs, perspectives, and actions of a variety of persons who may be involved in a "moral predicament."[34] Feminist ethicists are not only practically committed to women's equality with men, and hence attuned to the bias that exists in actual social relationships, they are "seeking new understandings of women (and men) as embodied moral subjects who exercise autonomy as a moral power in relationships."[35] Relationality is key to the feminist understanding of moral agency, moral knowledge, and moral judgment; and relationality is historical and diachronic, not limited to the social network that constitutes "horizontally" a particular moral moment.

Examples of recent historical and social interpretations of ethics could be multiplied almost without end. For the limited purposes of this essay, I will simply allude to a few more instances in Catholic fundamental ethics, then move to consider their relevance to death and dying issues. A major reference point for the entry of a more historical approach in Catholic moral theology has been the reinterpretation of casuistry, i.e., the analysis of concrete cases, traditionally in light of more general principles. Several authors have pointed out[36] that it is a mistake to assume that cases can be—or ever were—settled by applying principles or norms to them in a deductive manner. Instead, cases are resolved analogically, with principles expressing similarities and differences among moral situations, and showing the way to understanding similar but different experiences. Moral reasoning about cases is more inductive than it is deductive. Principles simply help us discern, on the basis of past experience, what in a new situation is like or unlike a prior situation in which an understanding of moral obligation has already been accomplished. Principles (like double effect) may be *presented* as if they are the first-order base of moral reasoning, self-evident *a priori* to the moral subject; but principles are in fact themselves derived from and reflective of an ongoing, historical and cultural process of negotiation among conflicting goods, relationships, and obligations. The moral casuistry of the neoscholastic manuals, modeled on a modern scientific ideal of truth and rationality, may have been perceived by their authors as "moving deductively from self-evident and unchanging principles to particular and unchanging situations," so that "solutions could be presented with a great deal of certainty and were universally applicable."[37] But this was not in reality the case. The casuists themselves always worked within an historical location that provided their principles, provoked their identification of the morally relevant aspects of cases, and guided their solutions in accord with their social interests and the values affirmed in the context within which they thought.

According to Albert Jonsen, the analysis of representative cases is one way in which ethics unbraids individual experiences of understanding and will, separating out the multitude of strands that influence "acts of conscience." These must be stated at some level of generality in order to be intelligible. "This is the place of the 'the case,' the confluence of persons, places, times and things about which arguments must be made and decisions taken. It is the peculiar skill of casuistry to identify these elements and to construct and examine arguments about them."[38] Yet, as Charles Curran points out, the casuistic approach to morals is not always "rational" in the modern, scientific sense. Sometimes the grasp of a resolution eludes immediate explication by logical argument. Instead, the agent or analyst pondering a case comes to an intuitive, almost affective, recognition of its moral import, without having first proceeded through a "logical" examination of its aspects.[39] This fact reveals, not the irrationality or ultimate subjectivism of casuistry, but its reliance on a more complex form of moral cognition than that delivered by abstract, principled analysis. Or, from another perspective, casuistry reveals that principled analysis also proceeds out of a highly dynamic and interactive "sociocultural reality" (Rigali). James Keenan notes that successful casuistry requires some sort of overarching or guiding vision of the common good and of a variety of particular goods, as well as the cultivation of prudence in the discernment of how goods are realized in the concrete and particular—though not discontinuous—choices represented by cases.[40]

The historicity of casuistry, and hence of the formulation of principles in light of a common vision of the good, calls into question the sense in which moral discernment can still be understood to be "objective," "true," or "nonrelative." All such terms need, no doubt, to be reinterpreted in light of historical consciousness. However, the question is whether the resulting moral epistemology is historicist in the strong sense; that is, whether it goes beyond noting the historical mediation of moral ideas to assert that their truth value is completely relative to their context. For instance, Thomas Kopfensteiner rightly points out that, in casuistry, theory and praxis are mutually dependent. Casuistic reasoning may be understood as a metaphoric process in which an equilibrium between norms and praxis is sought against an "epistemic horizon" that sets moral phenomena within a field of meaning. Kopfensteiner then goes on to conclude that the base of analysis of moral acts has shifted from "an objectivist and essentialist metaphysics" to "a personalist and historical metaphysics." Casuistry becomes a metaphoric and hermeneutical process of defining the limits and possibilities of human freedom within a given moral tradition. In Catholic tradition, casuistry represents the active role of moral reasoning in establishing normativity in metaphorical, and hence open-ended, terms. Within that tradition, an avenue toward multiple interpretations of human actions is opened. The even more radical possibility is left open that other traditions may establish the "epistemic horizon" of meaning quite differently.[41]

In a review essay concerning European trends, focused particularly on the work of Klaus Demmer,[42] Keenan and Kopfensteiner argue for the importance of a moral theology that sees context as the ultimate constituent of moral truth, that defines moral reasoning as a "creative, imaginative and inventive competency," and that sees this competency as always "enlightened and informed by faith."[43] If moral theology concedes that context alone constitutes truth, that reasoning invents it, and that knowledge of it is dependent on faith, this has serious implications for consistency and communication across religious and cultural boundaries, along with the public intelligibility of tradition-based moral discourse (e.g., about valid and spurious rationales for killing people). If the manualists were all too often guilty of what Keenan and Kopfensteiner term a "naive realist epistemology," the challenge before Catholic moral theologians today may be to take the historical turn without veering off into a thick underbrush of relativity impenetrable to the moral compass that casuistic thinking has always aimed to provide. Are naive realism and radical historicism the only options left?

BACK TO THE CASE AT HAND

Some of the above general observations about the profoundly historical and creative nature of morality, along with its basis in faith, are fleshed out in a recent article by Thomas Kopfensteiner on "Death with Dignity."[44] This article deals not with physician-assisted suicide or euthanasia, but with permitting to die. Specifically, Kopfensteiner argues that the refusal of some forms of disproportionate treatment by the dying patient is consistent with human dignity, and can and should still be accompanied by compassionate care in a spirit of solidarity. Treatments that may be refused include artificial nutrition and hydration. He identifies the base of his argument as "Christian morality," which establishes a "horizon" or "cognitive matrix" against which moral norms indicate a distinctive "vision" of "human flourishing," "human dignity," "equality," and the integration of death into human life. Kopfensteiner argues primarily that this position is consistent with Catholic tradition; however, he also makes repeated references to "human dignity," "human solidarity," "humanization," etc.[45]

Kopfensteiner rejects the notion of human identity proffered within the "modern project," insofar as it sees dependency and dignity as antithetical. His main target seems to be a truncated view of the person in which freedom and autonomy become the only satisfying answers to excessive or futile technology. But his alternate view, while clearly consistent with and inspired by Christian ideals, is not necessarily contingent on Christian identity. Rather, it is essentially a proposal about a more adequate appreciation of the meaning of *human* life, approached from within the particular horizon of Christian experience.

In this spirit, Kopfensteiner reviews three metaphors for removal of nutrition and hydration in a "persistent vegetative state" (like the other three, this metaphor should not be taken for granted, in my view). The removal can be portrayed as "starvation," the condition can be seen as a "mental impairment," or the state can be equated with "dying." While the first two metaphors militate against removal of artificial means of sustenance, the third invites a broader context for the weighing of benefits and burdens of continued treatment. In the broader setting, the means is measured not just in relation to the prospect it offers of physical nutrition; the inevitability of death upon the removal of nutrition is not determinative. The inability of the patient to communicate with his or her surroundings is also relevant in assessing benefits and burdens.

Thus, "the criterion judging the proportionality of any treatment is the total well-being of the patient which cannot be divorced from one's convictions about a meaningful life and a dignified death." Removal, understood and enacted in proper perspective, can signify "acceptance of the human condition," not "abandonment" of the patient.[46]

As noted, although Kopfensteiner presents his arguments in terms of a grounding in faith and tradition, their actual content furthers a view of the human person that presumably is intended to represent a more adequate anthropology as such. Certainly the repeated use of the qualifier "human" (not only "Christian") creates the impression that Kopfensteiner does not intend a sectarian ethic. Moreover, although the three metaphors for the patient in PVS are presented simply as alternates with different practical implications, it would be inaccurate to suggest that the author's tone is merely comparative and descriptive, as though choice among the three were simply relative to three incommensurable and equally viable "horizons." I understand Kopfensteiner to forward the third metaphor as most adequate to the *reality* of the PVS patient's situation, a reality that is illumined (but not invented) by the Christian horizon or vision. The third metaphor allows the concrete reality and relationships ("total wellbeing") of the permanently comatose patient to come fully into play in discerning his or her moral situation and that of caregivers and loved ones. Christian conviction assists the insight that the comparison of the PVS patient to the dying patient captures the situational factors most relevant to service of the patient's total wellbeing.

In a somewhat similar study, Kevin W. Wildes, S.J., also argues that Catholic tradition hardly demands the strict position on the provision of artificial nutrition that some have claimed. Like Kopfensteiner, Wildes is addressing a primarily Catholic audience regarding a point about which he already has the agreement of most participants in the public debate. Hence, a specifically religious framing of the argument will not endanger the public viability of his conclusions. Like Kopfensteiner, Wildes rejects a pseudo-scientific approach, in which it is pretended that benefits and burdens can be calculated in a mathematical and "objectivized" fashion, in clear and simple relation to the isolated goal of preserving biological life. Instead, a quality-of-life judgment is required, demanding the same kind of situation-specific prudence that determination of "extraordinary means" also implied.[47] According to Wildes, no absolute distinction can be drawn between the quality of ongoing life as a whole, and the burdensomeness of means used to preserve it. Like amputation, artificial feeding becomes part of a patient's life; in neither case can the morality of means be separated out from the life situation, evaluated in a patient-centered manner.[48] Thus, although Wildes represents "secular" bioethical models as misguided, his position seems ultimately to amount to a generally applicable, and not only a specifically Christian, assessment of the situation of patients in PVS. This is not to say, of course, that the terms of his assessment are somehow religiously "neutral," but only that a Christian orientation has inspired insight into the fullness of human life as finite, mortal, social, and historical.

Both Kopfensteiner's three metaphors, and Wildes's criterion of quality-of-life integrally considered, are means of placing the individual patient and particular interventions within their social context, and of viewing diachronic sociality and contingency as aspects of the human condition that also constitute indispensable aspects of "intrinsic" morality. For both authors, the problem with arguments about the moral necessity of supplying artificial nutrients to virtually all PVS patients is that such arguments first break apart the person and his or her body, then scientifically calculate the results of actions upon the body, taken in supposed abstraction from the relationships within which the person lives or dies.

In the cases of euthanasia and physician-assisted suicide, direct killing is involved, and with it the thorny issue of intentionality and the difference it makes. Yet, as with withdrawal of artificial nutrition, an historical methodology, epistemology and "ontology" (view of the nature of reality) must be engaged for an adequate grasp of the problem in its full contextuality. Intention and causation cannot realistically be sliced away from context as segregated parts of an "act in itself," whose morality is always already given. This, to be sure, was never the import of double effect, understood in its more nuanced formulations. The most evident way in which past interpreters of double effect invoked social context was to define acts from the outset as having multiple effects, and then to explicate their moral importance by means of the criterion of proportionality. At least partly for this reason, it is proportionality that recent, more historically-minded critics lift up as critical to the principle's meaning. The so-called "proportionalists" are, at a minimum, trying to grasp considerations of sociality as key to morality and key to interpreting double effect.

For instance, Richard McCormick attempts to explain the immorality of killing the innocent by making social outcomes part of the very determination of what would otherwise be termed "intrinsic evil."

> Why is only 'direct killing of an innocent person' regarded as wrong at all times?... The only answer seems to be that in some instances of conflict (self-defense, warfare), killing can represent...the lesser evil when compared to the only other available alternative. Obviously such a conclusion roots in the weighing of the effects of two alternatives.... So when one says that 'direct killing of the innocent' is forbidden, he need not and should not imply that such killing is morally wrong 'independently of whatever reasons the agent may have had.' He may and ought to imply that the conceivable reasons for killing in such circumstances are, under careful analysis, not proportionate to the harm done....[49]

Now it was just such attempts to relate intrinsic morality to judgments of social consequence that earned the "proportionalist" critics of double effect the label "utilitarian" or "consequentialist." Their critics, in turn, perceived them to be capitulating to a pragmatism that made short shrift of justice and equality. If, for example, it could be demonstrated that directly killing innocent persons was not, on the whole, more harmful, then, so it was counterargued, the moral barriers to murder would come quickly down.[50] The barriers to direct intention and causation of innocent death, presumably held in place by double effect's conditions, also protected against a utilitarian estimate of "the greater good" that might justify unconscionable violations of personal dignity and human rights.

Traditional readings of double effect have seen social consequences as important, but secondary. The proportionalists were trying to grasp the significance of context, including consequences, as integral, not subsequent to, the essential moral status of an act. Their liability was, perhaps, that they tried to build a social dimension into action without sufficiently bringing to the fore the paradigm of social relationships upon which they intended to rely, showing at once how it differed from that of classical utilitarianism and from the more abstract forms of principled, manualist casuistry.

For example, the utilitarianism of Jeremy Bentham and John Stuart Mill partook of the reigning eighteenth- and nineteenth-century "scientific" methodology. It operated on a conception of utility that presumed the self-evidence of certain intrinsic goods that every person values, no matter what their personal circumstances, as well as the ability to commensurate their value, predict their production, and distribute their effects. Many proportionalist thinkers found it difficult to clearly distance themselves from this approach, or to suggest a more persuasive option that still kept casuistry contextually grounded.

More recent interpreters of casuistry and double effect have had the advantage of a more highly developed philosophical movement ("postmodernism") favoring the blurring if not dissolution of boundaries among acts, subjects, intentions and social networks of other similar points of moral experience. Now our challenge is twofold. It is, first, to *avoid* the kind of *historicism* that is fundamentally inimical to moral realism and to policy engagement, both of which have always been strong suits of Catholic moral theology. And it is, second, to *reclaim contextuality* in a new voice, keeping the role of *Christian identity* strong in the way human experiences like illness, suffering and death are reappropriated by Catholic contributors to bioethics.

Current examples of Catholic teaching about death and dying denounce euthanasia while keeping the focus, positively, on social supports for the dying person; and, negatively, on social practices that would lead to a general erosion of respect for life, of dedicated care for those who suffer, or to fewer available resources for the ill and dying.[51] For instance, *The Gospel of Life* states in no uncertain terms that "'You shall not kill' has absolute force when it refers to the *innocent person*." But the next sentence contextualizes this norm with themes that have been sounded at length throughout the encyclical: "And all the more so in the case of weak and defenseless human beings, who find their ultimate defense against the arrogance and caprice of others only in the absolute binding force of God's commandment."[52] Of euthanasia specifically, the pope says that it is a "*grave violation*" of the divine and natural law, and "the deliberate and morally unacceptable killing of a human person."[53] But he devotes most of his explanatory remarks to "advanced" and technology-obsessed cultures that emphasize autonomy to the point that control of death becomes an overriding objective. The pope laments the "culture of death" and its "excessive preoccupation with efficiency," one which "sees the growing number of elderly and disabled people as intolerable and too burdensome," causing isolation and despair.[54]

Similarly, in the week before his death from cancer in November, 1996, Joseph Cardinal Bernardin wrote a letter to the Supreme Court, urging it not to accept physician-assisted suicide. The last several months of Bernardin's life were a witness to Christian meaning-making in the face of death, as he refused any treatments that would end his ministry to the Catholics of Chicago, or his attempt to bring understanding and unity to an American church often polarized between tradition and change. His defining theological and episcopal contribution was the "consistent ethic of life," in which he broadened Catholic opposition to abortion and euthanasia to include positive "quality of life" ventures in support of society's marginalized, including care of the dying, and access to health care for the presently uninsured.[55]

Bernardin, John Paul II and many other Catholic authors set the question of euthanasia in a different sort of *social* paradigm than that assumed by most current North American advocates of physician-assisted suicide. The paradigm of Catholic social ethics is the interdependent participation of all in the common good, a social view of the person in which the common good is truly served only when all members of society enjoy the opportunity, not only to receive, but also to contribute. The person's value does not diminish, however, with diminishment of capacity; dependency is a given for all lives at all times in some degree, and in varying degrees according to circumstances that vary over time. This paradigm, in differing cultural and historical expressions, has undergirded the tradition of papal social encyclicals since 1891. In this heritage, autonomy is neither the only nor the most important category with which to understand morality. Autonomy, free choice, and informed consent are not taken for granted as the criteria to guide morality; nor can the unquestioned premise of autonomous decision-making be the final determinant of whether the principle of double effect makes sense.

Central, instead, are the gospel and example of Jesus; the traditions and teachings of the Christian church, especially the Catholic magisterium; and formation within Christian community. These all enable, augment, and improve appreciation of the value of the individual person, of the inherent sociality of persons, and especially of the moral obligation to take a "preferential option for the poor." This is an historically generated and particular moral knowledge, without being either entirely relativistic or limited in scope to the Christian faithful. Norbert Rigali expresses well this integration of historicity and commonality when he calls Christian morality a "particularization-of-universality." He does not mean by this phrase that some preexistent moral essence takes shape in some limited but repeatable historical form; rather, particularity belongs to the very "reality" of morality as such. The Christian individual is always also a human being, and thus always a member in some sense of a "human community," entailing stronger and weaker lines of interdependence and thus of moral responsibility. All human beings, as constituted by "embodied spiritual self-transcendence," are oriented toward goods "such as life, friendship, society, knowledge, truth, and religion." But these values exist and are known only within particular cultural experiences and their moral expressions. Christian morality represents "a particular system of moral values which in turn is rooted in a particular world view, all of which is part of a particular culture created through the particular story of a particular people."[56]

This worldview is marked by the value and interrelatedness of life, the solidarity with the poor that characterizes the good society, the compassionate friendship everyone needs to face death courageously, the humility of human knowledge in the face of the expansive mystery of truth, and openness to the transcendent, experienced in particularity as God revealed in Christ. The stories and symbols of this particular experience of God and of humanity in relation to God (e.g., creation, sin, incarnation, cross, forgiveness, resurrection, Eucharist) may sometimes evoke an imaginative response in non-Christians, leading to points of intersection in moral vision. To this extent, Christian symbols may be appropriate and potent stimulants to public conversation. Their moral force in such a context owes to their resonance with dimensions of the human reality that are given expression in all cultures: finitude, bodiliness, suffering, sacrificial caregiving, and the possibility of transformation.

CONCLUSION

To return to the principle of double effect, with its criteria of intentionality and proportionality, we find that the scientific objectivization of moral judgment that it may have represented in some of the moral manuals is neither most consistent with its core meaning, nor viable today. The provisions of double effect have always had a social reference via the proportionality of multiple effects, and the complex intentionality with which agents relate to contexts. These provisions have actually never made much sense as an internally coherent formula, ensuring certitude and obviating the need for prudence, creativity, and risk. The principle becomes "incoherent" at just the point when its mutually illuminating and suggestive conditions are submerged within the ideology of a "scientific morality." Double effect's provisions are better understood together as a collective hermeneutic, a constellation of insights in shifting balance, a shorthand reference to experience that may link present moral realities with the wisdom of the past.

The most significant shift in moral epistemology with which historical consciousness and postmodernism present us is not so much historicity in the sense of duration, continuity, and variability in time. It is the realization that "our historical situation" entails the indefinite *horizontal* reciprocity of every reality and experience, *as well as* chronicity or timeliness.[57] This shift can be seen in the evolution of double effect, or, to put it another way, the devaluation of its "manualist" form as a means of resolving moral difficulties. What older interpretations perceived to be *secondary* in the analysis—social effects—now enter into an act's primary moral determination, its "intrinsic morality." To some, this seems a dilution of moral rigor and a slackening of moral accountability. However, this reaction may be due to the fact that sociality is still assumed to be relatively unimportant in defining where moral obligation lies. Instead, as the above references to current papal teaching illustrate, social and relational considerations can be (or should be) just as effective in establishing a sense of "absoluteness" or compellingness in morality, as categorizations of intrinsically evil individual acts once seemed to be.

Resistance to physician-assisted suicide, even among moral theologians who might not accept the type of definition of "intrinsic evil" assumed by the first condition of double effect, derives from the conviction that *social* reasoning is *integral* to a firm negative evaluation of euthanasia. The moral exclusion of physician-assisted suicide is necessary in order to protect society from an expansive death-dealing practice within the institution of medical caregiving (as in Holland). Just as importantly, exclusion of physician-assisted suicide is essential in view of the social nature of the suffering or dying patient. Not even such a patient can be a "reality in herself." Her value, dignity, and very selfhood as suffering, dying, despairing or hoping, are socially constituted, not in a relativist sense, but in the sense that reality as such is extenuating, interrelational, fluid, chronic, receptive, and influential. The morality of social practices surrounding such a person are in no way "secondary" to the morality of the singular acts that give them expression.

The distinction of intentionality in double effect has illuminative power insofar as it corresponds to the human (and Christian) reality of *ordered* moral responsibility. We are sometimes more accountable for the neighbor near at hand than for persons of equal value whom we do not stand so immediately to affect. To use the distinction between direct and indirect as a way of avoiding moral responsibility for "merely foreseen" effects is another variety of the individualist, "scientific," and objectivist mentality that wants to dissect and thereby control the complex realities of action. It is better and more true to those realities to see the distinction as a means of differentiating among the agent's multiple *responsibilities*. (This is where Quill's objections to double effect take force.)

To forbid the *direct* taking of innocent life is to keep the moral attention focused on the need of the one with whose physical survival we are immediately confronted, especially in circumstances that give us "power over" the vulnerable other. To argue persuasively that the immediate need of that other *requires* killing would mean demonstrating that the web of reciprocity sustaining that person (and being sustained by her) is incapable of endowing her suffering presence with transformed and transformative meaning. Such a conclusion would in virtually all cases represent a human and Christian failure of community and connection; to institutionalize death-dealing compensations for such failures would surely be to diminish the courage, compassion, and resources necessary to overcome them for others.

It is true that, once the fully social nature of morality is taken into account, specific moral absolutes become less numerous and clear. This does not mean that moral truth is less real. But it is discovered in the way that the casuistry of double effect has long suggested: by a sensitive probing of moral scenarios that may be analogous to moments of our past, but are never merely repetitions.

NOTES

1. For an early statement of this insight, see Josef Fuchs, S.J., "The Absolutenes of Moral Terms," in Charles E. Curran and Richard A. McCormick, S.J., eds., *Readings in Moral Theology No. 1: Moral Norms and Catholic Tradition* (New York/Ramsey, Toronto: Paulist Press, 1979), 94–137; originally published in *Gregorianum* 52 (1971).

2. Norbert J. Rigali, S.J., "Christian Morality and Universal Morality: The One and the Many," *Louvain Studies* 19 (1994), 21–22.

3. "The Hippocratic Oath," in John Arras and Robert Hunt, eds., *Ethical Issues in Modern Medicine* (Palo Alto, CA: Mayfield Publishing Company, 1983, 2nd ed.), 46.

4. Anonymous, "It's Over, Debbie," *Journal of the American Medical Association* 259 (1988), 272.

5. See P.J. Van der Maas, G. Van der Wal, I. Haverkate, *et al.*, "Euthanasia, Physician-Assisted Suicide, and Other Medical Practices Involving the End of Life in the Netherlands, 1990–95," *New England Journal of Medicine* 335 (1996), 1699–1711; and Ezekiel Emanuel, "Whose Right to Die?" *The Atlantic Monthly* 279 (March 1997), 73–79.

6. See NCCB Secretariat for Pro-Life Activities, "High Court Upholds Assisted Suicide Bans," *Life at Risk: A Chronicle of Euthanasia Trends in America* 7 (June 1997), 1–4; Richard A. McCormick, "*Vive la Différence!* Killing and Allowing to Die," *America* 177 (December 6, 1997), 6–12; and James F. Bresnahan, "Palliative Care or Assisted Suicide?" *America* 178 (March 14, 1998), 16–21.

7. Ezekiel, "Whose Right to Die?" 74.

8. David E. Rosenbaum, "Americans Want a Right to Die. Or So They Think," *The New York Times* (June 8, 1997), E3.

9. Pius XII, "Address to the Italian Anesthesiological Society," *Acta Apostolicae Sedis* 49 (1957), 146.

10. Gerald Kelly, S.J., *Medico-Moral Problems* (St. Louis, MO: Catholic Hospital Association, 1958), 128–35.

11. *Ibid.*, 135.

12. Sacred Congregation for the Doctrine of the Faith, *Declaration on Euthanasia* (Boston: St. Paul Editions, 1980), 8.

13. *Ibid.*, 11–12.

14. National Conference of Catholic Bishops, *Ethical and Religious Directives for Catholic Health Care Services* (Washington, DC: United States Catholic Conference, 1995).

15. *Ibid.*, § 32.

16. *Ibid.*, 21 ("Introduction" to Part V).

17. *Ibid.*, 21, and § 61.
18. For references, see *ibid.*, 22; Richard A. McCormick, S.J., "Technology, the Consistent Ethic and Assisted Suicide," *Origins* 25 (December 21, 1995), 461–62; and Kevin W. Wildes, S.J., "Ordinary and Extraordinary Means and the Quality of Life," *Theological Studies* 57 (1996), 500–12.
19. Kelly, *Medico-Moral Problems*, 12.
20. *Ibid.*, 13–15.
21. Paul VI, *On the Regulation of Birth (Humanae vitae)* (New York: Paulist Press, 1968).
22. Many contributions to this debate are included in Curran and McCormick, eds., *Readings in Moral Theology No. 1.* Some of the key names are Peter Knauer, Josef Fuchs, Louis Janssens, Bruno Schüller, and Richard McCormick.
23. Margaret A. Farley, "Issues in Contemporary Christian Ethics: The Choice of Death in a Medical Context," in *The Santa Clara Lectures* (Santa Clara, CA: Department of Religious Studies, Santa Clara University, 95053, 1995), I, 7–10.
24. *Ibid.*, 11.
25. *Ibid.*, 14.
26. Timothy E. Quill, M.D., Rebecca Dresser, J.D., and Dan W. Brock, Ph.D., "The Rule of Double Effect—A Critique of Its Role in End-of-Life Decision Making," *The New England Journal of Medicine* 337 (December 11, 1997), 1768–71.
27. *Ibid.*, 1170.
28. *Ibid.*, 1771.
29. Rigali, "Christian Morality and Universal Morality," 21–22.
30. Thomas L. Beauchamp and James F. Childress, *Principles of Biomedical Ethics* (New York: Oxford University Press, 1979, 1st ed.).
31. Thomas L. Beauchamp and James F. Childress, *Principles of Biomedical Ethics* (New York: Oxford University Press, 1994, 4th ed.), 3.
32. *Ibid.*, 111.
33. James F. Childress, "Ethical Theories, Principles, and Casuistry in Bioethics: An Interpretation and Defense of Principlism," in Paul F. Camenisch, ed., *Religious Methods and Resources in Bioethics* (Dordrecht/Boston/London: Kluwer Academic Publishers, 1994), 196.
34. Barbara Hilkert Andolsen, "Elements of a Feminist Approach to Bioethics," in Camenisch, ed., *Religious Methods*, 240–41.
35. *Ibid.*, 242.
36. The landmark work is Albert R. Jonsen and Stephen Toulmin, *The Abuse of Casuistry* (Berkeley, CA: University of California Press, 1988).
37. Thomas F. Kopfensteiner, "Science, Metaphor, and Moral Casuistry," in James F. Keenan, S.J., and Thomas A. Shannon, eds., *The Context of Casu-*

istry (Washington, DC: Georgetown University Press, 1995), 207.

38. Albert R. Jonsen, "Foreword," in Keenan and Shannon, eds., *Context of Casuistry*, xii–xiii.

39. Charles E. Curran, "The Manual and Casuistry of Aloysius Sabetti," in Keenan and Shannon, eds., *Context of Casuistry*, 183.

40. James F. Keenan, S.J., "The Casuistry of John Mair, Nominalist Professor of Paris," in Keenan and Shannon, eds., *Context of Casuistry*, 98.

41. Kopfensteiner, "Science, Metaphor, and Moral Casuistry," in Keenan and Shannon, eds., *The Context of Casuistry*, 218.

42. For example, see Klaus Demmer, *Die Wahrheit leben, Theorie des Handelns* (Freiburg: Herder, 1991); and "Die sittliche Personlichkeit," in Wilhelm Ernst and Konrad Feiereis, eds., *Moraltheologie im Dienst der Kirche* (Leipzig: Benno, 1992).

43. James F. Keenan, S.J., and Thomas R. Kopfensteiner, "Moral Theology out of Western Europe," *Theological Studies* 59 (1998), 107–35.

44. Thomas R. Kopfensteiner, "Death with Dignity: A Roman Catholic Perspective," *Linacre Quarterly* 63 (1996), 64–75.

45. *Ibid.*, 67.

46. *Ibid.*, 73–74.

47. Wildes, "Ordinary and Extraordinary Means," 508.

48. *Ibid.*, 510.

49. Richard A. McCormick. S.J., "Reflections on the Literature," in Curran and McCormick, eds., *Readings in Moral Theology No. 1*, 307; originally published in *Theological Studies* 38 (1975).

50. See John R. Connery, S.J., "Morality of Consequences: A Critical Appraisal," and Paul M. Quay, S.J., "Morality by Calculation of Values," both in Curran and McCormick, eds., *Readings in Moral Theology No. 1*, 244–66 and 267–93, respectively.

51. Michael Manning, M.D., provides a good overview of the current context of the physician-assisted suicide debate in the United States, as well as of the relevance of Catholic tradition to it, in *Euthanasia and Physician-Assisted Suicide: Killing or Caring?* (New York/Mahwah: Paulist Press, 1998). See also Jon Fuller, S.J., M.D., "Physician-Assisted Suicide: An Unnecessary Crisis," *America* 177 (1997), 9–26; McCormick, "Technology, the Consistent Ethic and Assisted Suicide," and *id.*, "*Vive la Différrence!*".

52. John Paul II, *The Gospel of Life* (Boston: St. Paul Books, 1995), § 57.

53. *Ibid.*, § 65.

54. *Ibid.*, § 64.

55. See Cardinal Joseph Bernardin, *The Consistent Ethic of Life* (Kansas City: Sheed and Ward, 1988).

56. Rigali, "Christian Morality and Universal Morality," 31–32.

57. Charles Curran makes a similar point in saying that a historical view "sees reality more in terms of relations than of substances and natures," and that reality "can be understood only in terms of the relations that exist among individual beings" ("Natural Law and Moral Theology," in Curran and McCormick, eds., *Readings in Moral Theology No. 1*, 276; originally published in *Contemporary Problems in Moral Theology* (Notre Dame, IN: University of Notre Dame Press, 1970).

Ethics and Genetic Research

Richard A. McCormick, S.J.

A brief return to the writings of Norbert Rigali, S.J., which span several decades, tempts one to conclude that Rigali has been primarily concerned with how issues are framed. He often comes up with an unexpected and fruitful suggestion about a different approach.

In honoring him, then, it would be fitting to see how Catholic theology might approach genetic research and the problems it casts up.

First, I will say a few words about the state of the art. Then I will discuss some problems associated with the Genome Project.

Jeff Lyon, a Pulitzer Prize-winning columnist for the *Chicago Tribune*, begins an article on genetics in the Winter issue of *Notre Dame Magazine* with the following cases.

> For nearly 40 years, he has worked in the acrid confines of a chemical factory. Now, a few months short of retirement, he's been told by his physician that he has early stage lung cancer.
>
> Like most of us, he assumes that the news means almost certain doom, that soon he will become one of the 146,000 Americans who each year die of a pitiless disease that spares only a small fraction of the people it strikes.
>
> But his doctor appears not to know these simple truths. Within hours, the doctor has scheduled an awesome new treatment, which to the patient sounds like science fiction. A Genetic analysis of the young tumor has told the medical team that deep in the patient's cancer cells, a key pair of watchdog genes have been damaged beyond repair by a lifetime of inhaling toxic fumes. When the genes, known as p53 genes, went bad, one of the myriad cells in the man's lungs lost a crucial

fail-safe ability; the runaway cell division that is cancer began.

In the days that follow, the patient undergoes a near-painless procedure to restore healthy p53 genes to his malignant cells, halting the errant signal to divide and stopping the cancer's growth. The treatment will have to be repeated at periodic intervals to arrest any new spread, but the cancer is effectively defeated. The man can look forward to years of enjoyable retirement.

In another hospital hundreds of miles away, a middle-aged woman undergoes an equally stunning therapy for her advanced heart disease. While a heart transplant would provide the ultimate cure, finding a donor organ for her is problematic. Three out of four patients die before a transplant can be carried out because there are not enough donor hearts to go around.

But the woman's doctors have added a powerful new weapon to their arsenal: Growth factors that promote development of new blood vessels within the heart to provide fresh circulation and revive the dying organ. With great care, the genes for these growth factors are infused in the woman's myocardial tissue using immature muscle cells as the cargo vessels. Soon the genes are cranking out growth factors in sufficient quantities to keep her alive until a new heart can be found even if it takes years.[1]

Lyon goes on to paint a fairly rhapsodic picture of what is going on in genetic medicine. He says that a host of ingenious methodologies are in the pipeline to combat diseases like sickle-cell anemia and cystic fibrosis all the way to cancer, cardiovascular disease and AIDS. He states that "researchers are well into unlocking the genetic basis of such tragic maladies as Alzheimer's disease, diabetes, multiple sclerosis, Lou Gehrig's disease, and mental illness. Treatments are sure to follow."

It is true that more than 200 human trials have been approved involving 1500 patients. It is also true that the "logic behind gene therapy is so compelling, the science is so deep, there is no question it is going to work" (Dr. Ronald Crystal of Cornell University Medical College).[2] And Dr. French Anderson of University of Southern California says: "I don't think there's anybody out there now who doubts that gene therapy will revolutionize medicine. It won't happen next year. It will take 10, perhaps 20 years. But it's going to happen."[3]

That seems to be the hunch of just about everyone. To date several hundred human trials have been approved, with more than 200 underway. Some 1500 people have been injected with altered genetic material. Hundreds more are waiting.

But thus far the results are sobering. Not a single person has been cured of anything. But that may change soon. In the April 1 issue of *Nature Genetics*,[4] scientists reported the synthesis of artificial human chromosomes. These will, they predict, act as vectors or taxi cabs for therapeutic human genes. So far, many attempts to introduce curative genes into patients have fizzled—the major reason being the unstable character of the viruses used as vectors.

It all started on September 14, 1990. French Anderson, Michael Blaese, and colleagues got approval from RAC (Recombinant DNA Advisory Committee) to treat Ashanthi De Silva and another young girl by injecting healthy genes to replace her defective ones. She was born with adenosine deaminase deficiency (ADA deficiency), a lethal condition of the immune system. Due to a faulty gene, her body made no ADA, a substance required for the survival of healthy T cells, the heart of the immune system. The Anderson-Blaese team used genetically altered viruses as their delivery vehicle to put healthy copies of the ADA gene into Ashanthi.

As Jeff Lyon reports, she now can make antibodies to fight a variety of infectious agents. She goes to school, plays with friends, etc. But she is not cured. Ashanthi must take weekly doses of an ADA supplement.

Because the doctors refuse to take her off this supplement, the results remain a bit ambiguous. Did the genes do it? Or is the supplement doing it? As the *New York Times* reported (October 20, 1995): "All agree that something happened when researchers added the genes. All agree that the cells took up the genes and started using them."[5] But the supplement gets in the way of saying that the treatment *fully* worked, though Dr. Anderson says he is 99% sure.[6]

Other attempts at gene therapy have not been nearly so successful. In September 1995, two articles in *The New England Journal of Medicine* reported that the most commonly used genetic treatments for cystic fibrosis and muscular dystrophy had hit dead ends.[7] In both cases scientists inserting normal genes were unable to elicit corrective changes in patients' bodies.

Before going on, let me give a quick biological review of the human body:

- 100 trillion cells
- Nucleus in each (except red)
- 46 chromosomes in nucleus (pairs of 23)
- 1 chromosome of each pair from each parent
- Chromosomes filled with DNA (Dioxy-Ribo-Nucleic)
- Genes are segments of DNA. Contain instructions to make proteins.

2. There are 100,000 human genes. Already over 6000 have been isolated, many of them, when defective (mutated) are responsible for disease.

3. Already discovered: genes for
   - Huntington's disease
   - Lou Gehrig's disease
   - "Bubble boy" disease
   - Major form of ataxia
   - Common kind of colon cancer
   - Breast and ovarian cancer (BRCA I, BRCA II)

4. Locating a gene from scratch is very difficult. Francis Collins, director of the National Center for Genome Research, admits: it is like "trying to find a burned-out light bulb in a house located somewhere between the East and West coasts without knowing the state, much less the town or street the house is on."[8]

DNA tests are already available for many diseases.

- Down's syndrome
- Amyotrophic Lateral Sclerosis (ALS)
- ADA deficiency
- Familial hypercholesterolemia

- Amyloidosis
- Hemophilia
- Muscular Dystrophy
- Gaucher's disease
- Retinitis Pigmentosa
- Cystic Fibrosis
- Sickle Cell Anemia and others

POSSIBLE USES IN HUMANS

The *Hearings Before the Subcommittee on Investigations and Oversight of the House Committee on Science and Technology* distinguished four distinct possible uses of DNA technology.

1. *Somatic-cell therapy* refers to the attempt to treat a discrete population of the patient's bodily cells other than germ (reproductive) cells in order to alter the functioning of a defective gene (or eventually replace it) and thus cure the disease at its root. It involves *changes limited to the person being treated.* Four steps are involved in this technology: 1) cloning the normal gene; 2) introducing the cloned gene in a stable fashion into appropriate target cells by means of a vector; 3) regulating the production of the gene product; 4) and ensuring that no harm occurs to the host cells.[9]

French Anderson has argued that before gene therapies are attempted in human beings, three requirements should be verified in animal studies. It should be shown that 1) the new gene can be put into the correct target cells and will remain there long enough to be effective; 2) the new gene will be expressed in the cell at an appropriate level; and 3) the new gene will not harm the cell, or by extension, the animal.[10] *Some regard extensive prior animal runs as too conservative* where devastating and lethal diseases are concerned. Whatever the case, all seem to agree that somatic-cell gene therapy, when technologically feasible, *is nothing more than an extension of medical practice* in an attempt to aid victims of currently intractable diseases. It is essentially a transplant. Given effectiveness and safety, there should be no insuperable ethical obstacles.

2. *Germ-line cell (reproductive cells) therapy* is a remarkably different thing. The altered gene would affect not only the individual, but *that individual would pass the altered gene to his or her offspring.* Such

intervention, since it would affect the genetic inheritance of future generations, would involve "a significant departure from standard medical therapy."[11] Obviously, this kind of therapy involves ethical issues of much greater complexity and magnitude than somatic-cell intervention. For instance, what will be the effect of modifying a gene for future generations? Is the gene that is responsible for the present disease also responsible for beneficial effects, as is true of the gene that is responsible for sickle-cell anemia but seems also to resist malaria? In other words, do we know enough to take steps that will affect future generations?

3. Third, there is *enhancement genetic engineering*. This refers to the insertion of a gene or several genes to produce a characteristic desired by the individual, e.g., black hair, larger muscles, and sharper memory. This is not therapy in any traditional sense; nor is it scientifically feasible at present. Furthermore, it raises two serious ethical concerns. First, the concept involves gene-insertion into a healthy human being with the possibility, even likelihood, that many non-targeted functions would be adversely affected. Second, such programming involves a subtle but very real change in our attitudes toward human persons. We can easily begin to evaluate them not for the *whole* that they are—unique refractions of the Creator, images of God—but for the *part* that we select. Such attitudes can powerfully nourish actions and practices that ought to be abhorrent to civilized people. Furthermore, the line between enhancement genetic engineering and eugenic engineering is fuzzy at best.

4. Finally, *there is eugenic genetic engineering*. This refers to the systematic preferential breeding of superior individuals (genotypes). It involves the attempt to intervene genetically to select for character traits, intelligence, various talents and mental and emotional characteristics. Scientifically, such proposals are sheer fancy because the traits in question are probably influenced by many unknown genetic factors. Furthermore, such genetic backgrounds interact with the environment in as yet very mysterious ways. Ethically, the matter is quite straightforward; most scientists and theologians believe eugenic genetic engineering is presently unethical. What characteristics are to be maximized to get a "better" human being? Is brighter necessarily better? Or, more pointedly, is white skin preferable to yellow or black? And who decides all of this? Questions like this point inevitably to the wisdom of C.S. Lewis's assertion: "The power of man to make himself what he pleases

means, as we have seen, the power of some men to make other men what they please."[12] For these and other reasons contemporary scientists rightly run from positive eugenics as if it were the plague.

Before turning to the Genome Project and the moral problems it poses, let me propose the criterion we should use in judging what actions and policies are right or wrong.

When dealing with the methods of responsible parenthood, Vatican II stated: "The moral aspect of any procedure...must be determined by objective standards which are based on the nature of the person and the person's acts."[13] The official commentary on this sentence underlined two points.[14] First, the criterion represents a general principle that applies to all human actions, not just to those in the sexual sphere. Second, the human person must be understood as "the human person integrally and adequately considered," that is, taking account of all the characteristics of human persons both as individuals and in their various relationships—familial, social, political, and religious. No dimension of the human person may be omitted in understanding and applying the criterion; nor may any single dimension be so isolated and highlighted that distortion results.

The proposal of such a criterion may seem a modest gain. Actually, it is enormously important. Negatively, it moves away from a more narrow focus on mere physical givenness, or facticity, as a moral criterion of our actions—a focus that assumes we can judge actions by looking at the external act alone. But, more positively, the criterion we propose suggests the questions we ought to be asking and the method necessary for discovering the answers. The central question always is: Will this or that intervention (or omission, exception, policy, law) *promote or undermine human persons* "integrally and adequately considered"? For instance, is the use of *in vitro* fertilization with embryo transfer in cases of sterility likely to support and promote human persons in their essential dimensions, or is it likely to undermine them? Pope John Paul II seemed to have this criterion in mind when, in speaking of genetic experiments, he referred to the fact that "they will contribute to the integral well-being of man."[15] The answer to such a question—if we take the criterion seriously—cannot be deduced from a metaphysical blueprint of the human person. It is necessarily inductive, involving experience and reflection upon it. Of course, there remain things that we have already learned from past experience (e.g., violence begets violence, adultery is harmful to those who engage in it); and there are things that so assault our sense of the sacred and the proper that no experience is necessary to expose their moral character (e.g., the Nazi medical experiments). Nonetheless, the principle remains: To judge the moral character of many human actions, experience of its impact on persons is essential. This reflects St. Thomas's assertion that "we do not wrong God unless we wrong our own good."[16]

It should be noted here that there may well be disagreements about whether an action or policy supports or is detrimental to persons. For instance, official Church teaching rejects artificial insemination by husband and *in vitro* fertilization even when using the gametes of husband and wife. Many theologians (I myself included) disagree with the official position. This should surprise no one (yet it does). The American bishops in *The Challenge of Peace* distinguish general principles from their applications and admit that there can be differences of opinion where applications are concerned. This reflects Vatican II's statement that "often enough the Christian view of things will itself suggest some specific solution in certain circumstances. Yet it happens rather frequently, and legitimately so, that with equal sincerity some of the faithful will disagree with others on a given matter."[17]

I want to conclude this first section on therapy with a word about cloning, and specifically cloning of humans. It's going to be done, I have no doubt. Scotland's Ian Wilmut made this a safe bet by giving us Dolly.

I can think of no morally defensible reasons for cloning a human being. It is not therapy in any sense of the word. 1) If you do it to get a compatible organ donor, you have brought a human being in the world *as a means*, not for herself. 2) If you do it to replace a dying youngster, you have brought a human being into the world *as a replacement*, not for herself. You have instrumentalized her. 3) If you do it as an act of genetic self-continuation, you also instrumentalize the clone. Furthermore, you betray colossal narcissism.

THE GENOME PROJECT

The explicit purpose of the Genome Project is to sequence all the DNA in the human genome. At a cost of 3 billion dollars, it is scheduled for completion by 2005, but will probably beat that date considerably. We are on a gene-a-day pace. When it is completed, we will have an enormously powerful information base.

Let me list some potential benefits and harms of this database.[18]

> *Benefits*
> 1. *Better patient information* (enhancing patient choice)
>   - About carrier status (expanding reproductive choice)
>   - About fetal disabilities
>   - About metabolic abnormalities (that can lead to changes in diet and lifestyle to prevent onset of symptomatology)
>   - About enhanced risk for certain diseases (e.g., cancer) that can help people avoid stresses and environmental toxins.
>
> 2. *Improved research.* Genetic research holds the potential for better detection, prevention and treatment of genetic disease.
>   - Frequency and distribution of genetic traits in various populations
>   - The interconnections between genotypes and phenotypes
>   - Safety and efficacy of various interventions
>
> 3. *Protection of public health.* Genomic information can help track incidence, patterns and trends of genetic carrier states.
>
>
> *Harms.* Breach of privacy can lead to:
> 1. *Economic harms.* Loss of insurance, employment, housing.
> 2. *Social or psychological harms.* Loss of self-esteem; social isolation ("genetic wall-flowers"). This is especially true when revelation involves drug and/or alcohol dependency, mental illness, retardation, obesity, etc.

I will present a case that embodies many of the ethical concerns that genomic information involves.[19] The patient is a patient of Dr. Barbara Weber of the University of Pennsylvania. The woman had been tested at Dr. Weber's clinic for the mutated genes (BRCA I and II) that predispose for ovarian and breast cancer. Dr. Weber told her the results. Since some studies indicate that women with the mutated gene have a 90 percent chance of developing breast cancer, the woman wanted both of her breasts removed right away. Before she had the operation, she submitted a claim to her insurance company, Dr. Weber said, not disclosing that she had the genetic test but reporting a strong family history of breast cancer.

The company turned her down, according to Dr. Weber, on the grounds that it did not pay for preventive medicine. So, at the woman's request, Dr. Weber submitted the woman's genetic test results. At that point, Dr. Weber said, the company told the woman that it would not pay for the surgery because she had a preexisting condition—a genetic defect—when she took out her health policy.

The woman had the surgery anyway.

Afterward, Dr. Weber recalls, when pathologists examined the woman's breast tissue, they found a cancerous tumor that had been missed by mammograms.

It is cases like this and fears of similar treatment that are convincing some women and researchers that it might be too dangerous to put genetic testing results on medical charts and in clinical records, where privacy cannot be assured.

Women worry that insurers will raise their rates, or refuse to insure them, that employers will not hire them or promote them, and even that friends and family members might treat them differently if they knew that they were tainted with a deadly gene.

The two major ethical dimensions that now confront us in genetic technology are *genetic privacy* and *fairness*. They are closely connected but not identical.

PRIVACY

This is a huge umbrella. George Annas, *et al.* have concluded that legislation, to be effective, must govern activities at four levels: collection of DNA, analysis of DNA, storage of DNA and information derived from it, and distribution of DNA samples and information derived from it.[20] That is a pretty good listing of how privacy can be violated and the person harmed thereby.

Under the category of "collection" I would include the tough little dilemma of whether to get tested or not. For instance, take Huntington's disease. It is almost always fatal by middle age. The burden of knowledge from a positive test may be so enormous and unmanageable that one's lifestyle becomes one long depression and affliction. The same can be said for tests for BRCA I and II, though in this case preventive intervention is possible.

For what should be obvious reasons, experts advise anyone considering testing to meet with a genetics counselor first. Benefits and drawbacks can be thoroughly discussed.

Nearly everyone admits that present laws are inadequate for the protection of genetic privacy. Because of the very intimate and predictive character of genomic information, protective policies remain an urgent moral imperative.

FAIRNESS

Genetic information can be used to deny or terminate employment, to deny insurance, and to stigmatize individuals or families. These are all forms of discrimination that harm individuals. Some 20 states have laws preventing HMOs and insurance companies from charging more because of a gene mutation.

Even fear of such abuses is itself a problem. Dr. E. Virginia Lapham of Georgetown University School of Medicine conducted a study of 332 people who belonged to support groups for families with a variety of genetic disorders.[21] Twenty-five percent believed they were denied life insurance because of their disorder; 22 percent thought they were denied health insurance; and 13 percent believed they were terminated or not hired for genetic reasons.

These fears have led to a cloak-and-dagger atmosphere about genetic testing. Some researchers test for breast cancer genes under research protocols so they don't have to reveal anything. Some women do not tell their private doctor of test results if the doctor is going to enter the results in the medical record. Some use aliases at treatment centers to protect their privacy. As Dr. Francis Collins, director for the

National Center for Human Genome Research, put it: "The system forces people to take drastic steps to protect themselves."[22]

We have in modern genetics an enormously powerful tool. It can be used for great good—and great harm.

So what does theology, specifically Catholic theology, have to say to this problem? Vatican II states: "Faith throws a new light on everything, manifests God's design for the person's total vocation, and thus directs the mind to solutions which are fully human."[23]

The Catholic tradition has encapsulated the way faith "directs the mind to solutions" in the phrase "reason informed by faith." Reason informed by faith is neither reason *replaced* by faith, nor reason *without* faith. It is reason shaped by faith.

In relating moral theology to the Genome Project, I would avoid what I consider extreme positions: the sources of faith have nothing to say, the sources of faith give concrete answers. I would propose that theology provides the essential context for moral reasoning and therefore affects genetics deeply. Love of and loyalty to Jesus Christ, the perfect human, sensitizes us to the meaning of persons. The Christian tradition is anchored in faith in the meaning and decisive significance of God's covenant with humanity, especially as manifested in the saving incarnation of Jesus Christ, his eschatological kingdom which is here aborning but will finally only be given. Faith in these events, love of and loyalty to this central figure, yields a decisive way of viewing and intending the world, of interpreting its meaning, and of hierarchizing its values. In this sense the Christian tradition only illumines human values, supports them, and provides a context for their reading at given points in history. It aids us in staying human by underlining the truly human against all cultural attempts to distort the human. It is by steadying our gaze on the basic human values that are the parents of more concrete norms and rules that faith influences moral judgment and decision-making. That is how I understand "reason informed or shaped by faith."

This shaping takes the form of general perspectives that lead believers to see things in a particular way because they are particular sorts of people. What is this *particular* way? From a Catholic point of view, I believe that Cardinal Joseph Bernardin's notion of a "consistent ethic of life" should play a dominant role in shaping Catholic consciousness. Bernardin describes this idea as "primarily a theological concept, derived from biblical and ecclesial tradition about the sacredness of human life, about our responsibilities to protect, defend, nurture, and enhance God's gift of life."[24] The key word is "consistent." What this means is that we bring to a whole spectrum of very different life issues (war, capital punishment, abortion, care of the dying, genetics, sexuality) the same basic attitude: respect. To the extent that this respect is weakened or absent in one area, the entire life-ethic is weakened, and other areas of the protection and enhancement of life are threatened. Bernardin makes it very clear that the consistent ethic of life applies to life-*enhancing* issues as well as life-*protecting* ones, to the *quality of life* as well as to the *right to life*.

I believe that John Paul II's *Evangelium Vitae* (March 25, 1995) lends powerful support to the moral vision Bernardin proposed. The encyclical states:

> Where life is involved, the service of charity must be profoundly consistent. It cannot tolerate bias and discrimination, for human life is sacred and inviolable at every stage and in every situation; it is an indivisible good.[25]

The commanding attitude in the consistent ethic of life is *respect*. It is engendered by the co-relative objective *dignity* of life. John Paul II's *Evangelium Vitae* weaves together a wealth of biblical texts to highlight this dignity. Basically, such dignity is linked to life's beginning from God and its ultimate destiny with God. The sacredness of life as God's gift gives rise to its inviolability.

I believe it is accurate to say that Catholic consciousness, as it confronts the Genome Project, will be dominantly shaped by this dignity-respect duo.

Where genetics is concerned, moral theology will be rooted in the equal dignity of all persons, a dignity that will demand appropriate *privacy* and sensitive *fairness*. After that, it is our responsibility to work out together what moral and legal policies are required to be true to "the person integrally and adequately considered."

To expect more from moral theology will be, I believe, disappointing. To settle for less will be impoverishing.

NOTES

1. Jeff Lyon, "It's in the Genes," *Notre Dame Magazine* 25 (1996–97), 24–28.

2. Cited in *Newsweek* (October 9, 1995), 62.

3. Cited in Jeff Lyon, "It's in the Genes," 24.

4. Cited in *New York Times* (April 1, 1997), B13.

5. *New York Times* (October 20, 1995), A13.

6. *Ibid.*

7. M. R. Knowles, *et al.*, "A Controlled Study of Adenoviral-Vector-Mediated Gene Transfer in the Nasal Epithelium of Patients with Cystic Fibrosis," *New England Journal of Medicine* 333 (September 28, 1995), 823–31; and J.R. Mendell, *et al.*, "Myoblast Transfer in the Treatment of Duchenne's Muscular Dystrophy," *New England Journal of Medicine* 333 (September 28, 1995), 832–38.

8. *Time* (January 17, 1994), 48.

9. *Splicing Life* (Washington, DC: U.S. Government Printing Office, 1982), 42. This is a report on genetic engineering by the *President's Commission for the Study of Ethical Problems in Medicine and Biomedical and Behavioral Research.*

10. In *Human Genetic Engineering: Hearings Before the Subcommittee on Investigations and Oversight of the Committee on Science and Technology, U.S. House of Representatives* (Washington, DC: Government Printing Office, 1982), 286.

11. *Splicing Life,* 46.

12. C.S. Lewis, *The Abolition of Man* (New York: Macmillan, 1947), 72.

13. "Pastoral Constitution on the Church in the Modern World," in Austin Flannery, O.P., ed., *Vatican Council II: Constitutions, Decrees, Declarations* (Northport, NY: Costello Publishing Co., 1996), § 51.

14. *Schema constitutionis pastoralis de ecclesia in mundo huius temporis: Expensio modorum partis secundae* (Vatican City: Vatican Press, 1965), 37–38.

15. *L'Osservatore Romano* (October 24, 1982).

16. *Contra Gentiles*, b. III, c. 122.

17. "Pastoral Constitution on the Church in the Modern World," § 43.

18. I draw these from Lawrence O. Gostin, "Genetic Privacy," *The Journal of Law, Medicine and Ethics* 23 (1995), 320–30.

19. I take this from *New York Times* (February 4, 1997), B9.

20. George J. Annas, Leonard H. Glantz, Patricia A. Roche, "Drafting the Genetic Privacy Act: Science, Policy and Practical Considerations," *Journal of Law, Medicine and Ethics* 23 (1995),360–66.

21. *New York Times* (February 4, 1997), B9.

22. *Ibid.*, B13.

23. "Pastoral Constitution on the Church in the Modern World," § 11.

24. Joseph Bernardin, *The Consistent Ethic of Life* (Kansas City: Sheed and Ward, 1988), 58.

25. John Paul II, *Evangelium Vitae, Origins* 24 (April 6, 1995), § 87.

Bibliography

1968
Die Selbstkonstitution der Geschichte im Denken von Karl Jaspers. Monographien zur philosophischen Forschung 49 (Meisenheim/Glan: Verlag Anton Hain, 1968).

1969
"The Community in Relation to the Apostolate." *Woodstock Letters* 98/2 (Winter 1969) 33–52.
"Right, Duty and Dissent." *The Catholic World* 208, No. 1,247 (February 1969) 214–218.
"Moral Theology: Old and New." *Chicago Studies* 8/1 (Spring 1969) 41–57.
"Karl Jaspers: The Inward Path." *Commonweal* 90/2 (28 March 1969) 38–39.
"Theology of the Walkout." *The Catholic World* 209, No. 1,254 (September 1969) 251–255.
"The Unity of the Moral Order." *Chicago Studies* 8/2 (Summer 1969) 125–143.

1970
"Is Theology Thinking about God?" *The Catholic World* 210, No. 1,259 (February 1970) 204–207.
"The Appearance of War." *The National Catholic Reporter* 6/14 (4 February 1970) 6.
"A New Axis: Karl Jaspers' Philosophy of History." *International Philosophical Quarterly* 10/3 (September 1970) 441–457.

1971
"Catholics and Liberalized Abortion Laws." *Catholic World* 213, No. 1,278 (September 1971) 283–285.
"On Christian Ethics." *Chicago Studies* 10/3 (Fall 1971) 227–247.
"Anthropology from Above," review article (Wolfhart Pannenberg, *What Is Man? Contemporary Anthropology in Theological Perspective). Interpretation* 25/4 (October 1971) 502–505.

1972
"New Epistemology and the Moralist." *Chicago Studies* 11/3 (Fall 1972) 237–244.

1973
"Theology and Euthanasia." *Pastoral Life* 22/8 (September 1973) 32–34.

1974

"The Meaning of Freedom: Dialogue with John Giles Milhaven." *Homiletic and Pastoral Review* 74/4 (January 1974) 61–68.

"New Theology and Infant Baptism." *The Priest* 30/2 (February 1974) 13–17.

"What's Christian about Morality?" (a seven-part series). *Focus on Hope* 8/1–7 (1974):

"What Influence Do Conscience and God Have on Morality?" No. 1 (22 February) 12–14.

"What Do Christ and the Church Have To Do with Morality?" No. 2 (1 March) 11–13.

"Whatever Happened to Natural Law?" No. 3 (8 March) 11–12.

"Let's Look at Moral Decisions in Light of Original Sin!" No. 4 (15 March) 10–13.

"Does Christian Faith Change Morality?" No. 5 (22 March) 11–13.

"Love Your Neighbor!" No. 6 (29 March) 11–13.

"Is there Any Future for Christian Morality?" No. 7 (5 April) 10–13.

"Theologians and Abortion." *The Priest* 30/6 (June 1974) 22–25.

"Human Experience and Moral Meaning." *Chicago Studies* 13/1 (Spring 1974) 88–104.

"Morality As an Encounter with God." *Cross and Crown: A Spiritual Quarterly* 26/3 (September 1974) 262–268.

"Faith, Hope and Love." *Chicago Studies* 13/3 (Fall 1974. Special issue: *An American Catechism, Part II: Moral*) 253–264. Reprinted in *An American Catholic Catechism,* ed. George J. Dyer (New York: Seabury Press, 1975); German edition: *Ein katholischer Katechismus* (Munich: Kosel, 1976); Italian edition: *Esposizione della Dottrina Cattolica: Un Catechismo Cattolico Americano* (Brescia: Queriniana, 1977).

1975

"The New Legalism." *Homiletic and Pastoral Review* 75/11–12 (August–September 1975) 68–73. Reproduced as a cassette recording (New London, Conn.: Cardinal Communications, 1975).

"Notes on Conscience Formation." *The Priest* 31/10 (October 1975) 37–38.

"The Fragmented Christian Life." *Cross and Crown: A Spiritual Quarterly* 27/4 (December 1975) 352–359.

"Christian Ethics and Perfection." *Chicago Studies* 14/3 (Fall 1975) 227–240.

1976

"Love and Christian Morality." *Homiletic and Pastoral Review* 76/4 (Janu-

ary 1976) 60–64.
"The Historical Meaning of the *Humanae Vitae* Controversy." *Chicago Studies* 15/2 (Summer 1976) 127–138.

1977
"Contemporary Theology of Sin." *Homiletic and Pastoral Review* 77/4 (January 1977) 31–32, 48–51.
"You Can't Live by the Commandments." *Sign* 56/7 (April 1977) 14–16.
"Moral Theology in Transition." In *Theology Confronts a Changing World*, ed. Thomas M. McFadden (West Mystic, Conn.: Twenty-Third Publications, 1977).
"Dialogue with Richard McCormick." *Chicago Studies* 16/3 (Fall 1977) 299–308.
"Toward a Moral Theology of Social Consciousness." *Horizons* 4/2 (Fall 1977) 169–181.
"Christ et Morale." *Concilium: Revue Internationale de Theologie* 130 (1977) 25–34. Published also in German, Spanish, Italian, Dutch, French and English. English edition: *Concilium* 110 (1978) 12–20.

1978
"Faith and the Theologian." *The Priest* 34/4 (April 1978) 10–14.

1979
"Morality and Historical Consciousness." *Chicago Studies* 18/2 (Summer 1979) 161–168.
"Love (Theology)." *New Catholic Encyclopedia* 17 (Supplement: *Change in the Church)* (New York: Publishers Guild, 1979) 379–380.

1981
"Evil and Models of Christian Ethics." *Horizons* 8/1 (Spring 1981) 7–22.
"After the Moral Catechism." *Chicago Studies* 20/2 (Summer 1981) 151–162.
"The Future of Christian Morality." *Chicago Studies* 20/3 (Fall 1981) 281–289.

1983
"Charles Curran's Understanding of Christian Ethics." *Chicago Studies* 22/2 (August 1983) 123–132.
"The Moral Act." *Horizons* 10/2 (Fall 1983) 252–266.

1984
"Just War and Pacifism." *America* 150/12 (31 March 1984) 233–236.
"Sin in a Relational World." *Chicago Studies* 23/3 (November 1984) 321–

332.
"Human Solidarity and Sin in the Apostolic Exhortation, 'Reconciliation and Penance'." *The Living Light* 21/4 (June 1985) 337–344.

1986
"The Unity of Moral and Pastoral Truth." *Chicago Studies* 25/2 (August 1986) 224–232.
"Artificial Birth Control: An Impasse Revisited." *Theological Studies* 47/4 (September 1986) 681–690.

1988
"Moral Theology and the Magisterium." *Horizons* 15/1 (Spring 1988) 116–124.
"The Story of Christian Morality." *Chicago Studies* 27/2 (August 1988) 173–180.
"Moral Pluralism and Christian Ethics." *Louvain Studies* 13/4 (Winter 1988) 305–321.

1989
"Moral Theology (Contemporary Trends)." *New Catholic Encyclopedia* 18 (Palatine, Ill.: Jack Heraty & Associates, 1989) 306–310.

1990
"The Uniqueness and the Distinctiveness of Christian Morality and Ethics." In *Moral Theology: Challenges for the Future: Essays in Honor of Richard A. McCormick, S.J.*, ed. Charles E. Curran (New York: Paulist Press, 1990) 74–93.

1993
"Models of the Person in Moral Theology." *Chicago Studies* 32/2 (August 1993) 177–185.

1994
"Reimaging Morality: A Matter of Metaphors." *The Heythrop Journal* 35/1 (January 1994) 1–14.
"Christian Morality and Universal Morality: The One and the Many." *Louvain Studies* 19/1 (Spring 1994) 18–33.
"Church Responses to Pedophilia." *Theological Studies* 55/1 (March 1994) 124–139.
"Magisterium"; "Pluralism." In *The New Dictionary of Catholic Thought*, ed. Judith A. Dwyer (Collegeville, Minn.: Liturgical Press, 1994) 556–559; 744.

98
    "On the *Humanae Vitae* Process: Ethics of Teaching Morality." *Louvain
udies* 23/1 (Spring 1998) 3–21.